NGOs, Civil Society,

M000031732

Nongovernmental organizations act on behalf of citizens in politics and society. Yet many question their legitimacy and ask for whom they speak. This book investigates how NGOs can become stronger advocates for citizens and better representatives of their interests. Sabine Lang analyzes the choices that NGOs face in their work for policy change between working in institutional settings and practicing public advocacy that incorporates constituents' voices. Whereas most books on NGOs focus on policy effectiveness, using approaches that treat accountability largely as a matter of internal performance measurements, Lang instead argues that it is ultimately *public* accountability that informs NGO legitimacy. The case studies in this book use empirical research from the European Union, the United States, and Germany to point to governments' role in redefining the conditions for NGOs' public advocacy.

Sabine Lang is Associate Professor of International Studies in the Henry M. Jackson School of International Studies at the University of Washington.

NGOs, Civil Society, and the Public Sphere

SABINE LANG

University of Washington

 **CAMBRIDGE**
UNIVERSITY PRESS

CAMBRIDGE
UNIVERSITY PRESS

32 Avenue of the Americas, New York NY 10013-2473, USA

Cambridge University Press is part of the University of Cambridge.

It furthers the University's mission by disseminating knowledge in the pursuit of
education, learning and research at the highest international levels of excellence.

www.cambridge.org
Information on this title: www.cambridge.org/9781107417557

© Sabine Lang 2013

First published 2013
First paperback edition 2014

A catalogue record for this publication is available from the British Library

Library of Congress Cataloguing in Publication data
Lang, Sabine, 1959–
NGOs, civil society, and the public sphere / Sabine Lang.
pages cm
Includes bibliographical references and index.
ISBN 978-1-107-02499-1
1. Non-governmental organizations. 2. Civil society. I. Title.
JZ4841.L36 2013
300–DC23 2012019845

ISBN 978-1-107-02499-1 Hardback
ISBN 978-1-107-41755-7 Paperback

Contents

Tables

Figures

Preface

The idea for this book started fermenting during some of the lengthy Thursday afternoons in the 1990s when the State Parliament in Berlin, Germany, was in session. My job as Chief of Staff of the State Secretary of Labor and Women's Affairs included organizing and participating in meetings between NGOs and the Secretary. The parliamentary Thursdays presented opportunities to do just that, with NGO representatives lingering in the halls and politicians floating in and out of the plenary. What I observed was a strangely patterned dance between politicians and NGO representatives. At its center seemed to be unacknowledged power dynamics, and in particular a tacit co-dependency among unequals.

The core task at the time was to prevent the complete collapse of the Eastern labor market. In 1991 in Berlin alone, 300,000 jobs had vanished. Former East German industrial plants closed, cultural institutions disappeared, kindergartens shut down, and poverty grew. Neither state nor market offered solutions up front. Instead, state–civil society cooperation became the economic lifeline. In 1991, the Berlin Senate introduced what came to be the largest postwar NGO sector creation program. Already-operating civic groups were called upon to apply for project funds that would generate jobs. New NGOs were founded with encouragement, logistical help, and funding from government agencies. Government nudged civic activists whose loose network coalitions had advanced the revolutionary processes in Eastern Germany into forming NGOs. Formerly state-employed East Germans became civic entrepreneurs. At the same time, movement actors from the West contemplated strategies on how to transform their commitments to civic causes into paying jobs with benefits while keeping radical agendas alive. NGO–state agency cooperation became a daily routine. Seemingly out of nowhere, hundreds of new NGOs were established in Berlin alone that got federal and state funding for their project tasks, infrastructure, and labor costs. They restored decrepit churches and in the process trained unemployed youths in crafts and construction. They founded satirical comedy nonprofits that provided a haven for unemployed musicians and actors. They created women's shelters, alternative media cooperatives, and East-West cultural centers. NGO expertise fueled innovative projects while offering an exciting laboratory for civic engagement.

Yet while I was partaking in a government-centered revitalization of civil society, I also started to wonder about some broader implications. Most notably, the Berlin government had turned into a huge donor agency that set the terms of engagement of civil society with the state. These terms of engagement were more often based on ad hoc decisions and utilitarian reasoning than on long-term strategizing and institutional deliberation. NGO expertise was valued as spearheading a combined job, civic, and East-West integration drive, but it was much less valued in the policy-making arena. Neither the executive and its bureaucracy nor parliament sought regular NGO input on what kinds of programs and projects should be funded. Those closest to the actual dynamics of economic and social transformations were routinely sidelined in the formal institutional contexts in which their voice might have added substance to the policy-making process.

A second pattern that emerged involved NGOs that organized to advocate *publicly* on behalf of a particular policy: They were typically perceived as unruly and were tacitly sanctioned. Most NGOs learned quickly that publicly mobilizing and organizing citizens was not as successful an advocacy strategy as institutional lobbying. In order to secure government access and resources, NGOs were restricted in their public voice by the very terms of engagement that had brought many of them into existence or made them flourish.

A third observation I made was that despite this fairly restrictive contact pattern between government and NGOs, when an official claimed he or she was speaking for large segments of the population, input from the NGO sector was often cited as evidence for having consulted the public. The nongovernmental sector was constructed by officials to represent the public. The irony here of course was that the NGOs most likely to be cast in the role of publics were precisely those that had been conditioned politically away from engaging or mobilizing citizens in their advocacy work.

That time in the Berlin government jumpstarted my interest in the ties that bind the civic sector and the state. When I left, the experience of the tensions built into civic engagement and advocacy in late modern societies guided my research. I was interested in whether what I had witnessed during exceptional postunification times also was at work in other places and at other times. This book tries to uncover, articulate, and explain some of these tensions. It investigates structural and institutional impediments to NGOs' role as public advocates in late modern public spheres, and it explores conditions under which NGOs can help activate public voice.

Many colleagues and friends over the years helped me think and rethink the argument. Joan W. Scott was the first to encourage me to continue the work on NGOization. Michael Edwards, Myra Marx Ferree, and Alex Warleigh provided helpful comments at the early stages of the research. Inderpal Grewal and Victoria Bernal brought together an inspiring group of scholars in Bellagio's Rockefeller Center for a week of intense discussions that helped center the argument. I am grateful to Margit Mayer for sharing her knowledge of urban politics and movements, to Wolf-Dieter Narr for insisting that social science writing can be simple and graceful, and to Aaron Cicourel for reminding me to cut out the "white noise" from my interviews. Many more friends and scholars over the years have given me feedback on parts of the argument and have provided support whenever needed, in particular Birgit Sauer, Petra Ahrens, Troy Duster, Petra Meier, Celeste Montoya, Joyce Mushaben, Elisabeth Pruegl, and Alison Woodward.

Qualitative work means being on the road, and I am grateful for the many people who opened their homes, offices, or meetings to me over the years for interviews, participant observation, background talks, follow-up conversations, or simply for a bed, breakfast, and nightly "debriefing sessions." They are far too many to name, but some have accompanied me and this research for a long time: Jochen (Barlo) Barloschky, who some call the pope of German urban development mobilization, Sabine Offe, and Ursula Staudinger in Bremen; the late Christian Fenner in Leipzig; Bev Crawford, James MacBean, and Troy Duster in Berkeley, where in particular Troy's knowledge of and connections in Oakland helped open more doors than I could have found myself; Conny Reuter in Brussels; Norma Damashek, Michael Schudson, and Nico Calavita in San Diego; and John Fox, Brent Crook, and Charlie McAteer in Seattle. Financial support for the fieldwork was provided by the German Fulbright Commission and the German Academic Exchange Office, as well as the Center for West

European Studies, the European Union Center, and the Nancy M. Bell Center at the University of Washington.

Various colleagues heard parts of the argument at conferences of the International Studies Association, the ECPR yearly meetings and Joint Sessions, the European Sociological Association, and the American Political Science Association. I cannot do justice to all the ideas I got from these audiences. I am also indebted to my fellow colleagues at the University of Washington's Jackson School Faculty Research Group for providing feedback on parts of the book, in particular Joel Migdal, Gad Barzilai, Matt Sparke, Robert Pekkanen, Sunila Kale, and Scott Radnitz, and to the many students who allowed me to debate ideas in my readings course on "Civil Society and the Public Sphere" and in other contexts, in particular Garrett Strain, Gillian Frackelton, Elizabeth Lyons, and Matt Reed. Tim Hannon was always one phone call away when my technology skills proved insufficient. Elizabeth Zherka deserves special praise for not only sticking with me as my research assistant throughout this project, but also for her close reading and copyediting of the manuscript.

Thanks finally to my editor, Eric Crahan, whose belief in the manuscript carried me over many hurdles; to the anonymous reviewers of Cambridge University Press, whose ideas have shaped this book in more than one way; and to the production crew, first and foremost Rebecca McCary, Chris Miller, and Gail Chalew, who improved not only my Germanic writing style but also the imagery on the pages. Fred Goykhman took the clues from our conversations to distill the ideas into an amazing cover.

Without friends and family on both sides of the Atlantic, the many travels to Europe and back would have been much less pleasurable. My father, Wolfgang Lang, from whom I caught the bug for politics, and all the other Langs, Bucks, Rohweders, and Obermaiers helped to keep my life in perspective whenever work threatened to take over. In Berlin, Roscha and Angelika fed me more often than I ever can repay; Helga, Peter, Bettina, and Terry shared their Berlin stories; and Astrid offered escape routes into the arts. Gertrud and Eckhart helped me feel at home in Berlin. In Seattle, Alice, Annie, Axel, Daphne, Eric, Peter, and Heidi were there to listen and to relax with during Sunday soccer. Irene, Stephen, and John helped me dance.

I am indebted in more than one way to my husband, colleague, and friend Lance Bennett. He not only carried the brunt of long hours, anxieties, and debates at home with his usual grace but also read and commented on many chapters at several stages. Finally, I want to thank Oliver for helping me balance life and work and for making me smile so often. Sometimes, while looking over my shoulder onto the computer screen at age eleven or twelve, he started a little rap song and dance that went something like "formalistic, isomorphic, public NGOization." I truly hope that the book does not have as many "big words" as Oliver professed to see on any given page, and I dedicate this book to him.

David or Goliath? Situating NGOs in Politics

The 21st century is the "era of NGOs."

Kofi Annan

When the former Secretary-General of the United Nations Kofi Annan proclaimed the 21st century to be the era of NGOs,[1] he probably did not foresee just how controversial a proposition this would turn out to be. Some see the NGO explosion of recent decades as an indicator of revitalized democracies across the globe. For others, the increasing number and influence of NGOs undermine the very foundations of representative democracy. Glorifying portrayals of NGOs as the savior of citizen involvement in public affairs compete with dismissive accounts of self-proclaimed and nonrepresentative groups bolstered by an unelected activist elite. The question at the core of these strikingly different perceptions is: What makes NGOs legitimate players in late modern public affairs? Is it their reputation of getting things done better, faster, and less bureaucratically than established institutions? Is it that NGOs have acquired substantial field expertise and policy know-how that are invaluable for governance? Is NGO legitimacy based on measurable management criteria of accountability and fiscal transparency? Or does legitimacy increase with representing a certain number of members? The argument of this book is that these four most frequently cited answers provide all reasonable, but ultimately not sufficient, criteria for assessing NGO legitimacy. Instead, the most salient source of legitimacy of the nongovernmental sector is public engagement. Yet it is this very quality, as

---

[1] See http://www.unece.org/indust/sme/ngo.htm (accessed November 18, 2007).

organizers of publics, that NGOs frequently set aside in favor of providing effective programs and policy expertise. This book explores why many NGOs neglect or avoid public engagement and thus underutilize this particular source of legitimacy.

The "effectiveness" yardstick suggests that NGOs are legitimate because they tend to accomplish results more effectively than government. As a former director of Transparency International for Central and Eastern Europe stated, "We need civil society organizations not because they 'represent the people'; we need them because through them we can get things done better" (Marschall 2002: 3). Numerous studies provide evidence that NGOs have stepped in where governments are unwilling to act, have withdrawn, or have failed (e.g., Hudock 1999; Hopgood 2006). Yet even in cases where results are strong and welcomed by majorities of citizens, such as when European environmental NGOs fought successfully for an EU-wide ban on animal testing in the cosmetics industry, the legitimacy of NGO activists to speak for citizens is routinely put into question. Moreover, getting the job done effectively can mean different things in different contexts and is often difficult to measure (e.g., Vedder 2007). Thus, if NGOs are indeed to be game changers of 21st-century democracy, then assessing their performance solely through the lens of functional mission success is not sufficient to legitimize their work.

An alternative mode of awarding legitimacy is based on the argument that NGOs contribute invaluable expertise in policy arenas where governments or business lack resources or specific "on the ground" knowledge. This is a legitimacy source that NGOs increasingly draw on, claiming that without their specialized knowledge entering decision-making processes, political choices in democratic polities would be seriously limited. When assessing NGO legitimacy in its expertise mode, it is crucial to reflect on the kind of expertise that is being called upon. Inclusion based on technical expertise alone would award the environmental NGO that fights greenhouse emissions the same legitimacy as a scientist working for a coal mining company. Yet NGOs tend not to be seen as special interests; they are perceived as speaking for underrepresented issues *as well as* for affected constituents. If NGO legitimacy is based on technical issue expertise alone, it de-emphasizes NGOs' role in providing grounded knowledge and in giving voice to underrepresented interests.

A third legitimacy mode focuses on transparency and procedural accountability in NGO operations. In this perspective, NGOs gain legitimacy if they adhere to standards of professional conduct that are generally drawn from management practices. In recent years, the accountability debate has expanded from concerns about internal transparency and professional conduct to a new public management focus on outcome measures (e.g., Thomson 2010). In addition to demanding formalized inner-organizational procedures, funders increasingly request quantifiable data to measure program implementation and outcomes (Alexander et al. 2010). The criteria and effectiveness of performance measurements are at this point much debated in NGO, philanthropy, and public policy circles from local to transnational levels (i.e., Brown and Moore 2001; Morrison and Salipante 2007; Knutsen and Brower 2010). In fact, many NGOs find the expansive requests made in the name of accountability to be increasingly burdensome, and research has started to question the flurry of indicators and data that often are "generated for symbolic purposes" alone (Alexander et al. 2010: 566). A related legitimacy mode that relies on so-called stakeholder accountability seems to be mired in similar problems: Organizations tend to identify, or rather construct, stakeholders ex ante while not using adequate communication strategies that would organize outreach and allow stakeholder publics to form in connection with, but still somewhat independent from, preconceived organizational goals (i.e., Rasche and Esser 2006: 11). Accountability is thus often used to document NGO effects instead of actual public engagement practices. We discuss later these specific accountability modes of legitimacy; at this point it is important to note that achieving accountability, either in its "internal" professional or in its output-oriented new public management or stakeholder version, does not place demands on NGOs to pursue active public engagement.

The distinctly *public* dimension of nongovernmental work is epitomized in a fourth mode of legitimacy, captured by this question: Whom do NGOs speak for; whom do they represent? As straightforward as accounting for this fourth mode of awarding legitimacy may seem, it also harbors ambiguities. After all, an NGO constituency is rarely defined clearly, and its spokespersons are most often not elected. From a state-centered institutional perspective, it has become common to use the lack of formalized representation to dismiss the sector's overall legitimacy.[2]

---

[2] A different angle of the debate within the representational paradigm focuses on this question: Do NGOs represent special or public interests? This is a challenging and at times politically charged attempt to distinguish between a common good claim and a group enrichment claim. However, I am not convinced that we can only ascribe public status to those who seek "a collective good, the advancement of which will not selectively or materially benefit the membership or activists of an organization" (Berry 1977: 7; for a critical assessment see Edwards 2004: 63 and Jenkins 2006: 308). As Michael Edwards

I submit that awarding legitimacy on the grounds of formal representativeness is just as misguided a yardstick for NGOs as tying legitimacy exclusively to policy effectiveness, expertise, and accountability. The formal
representational claim seems to draw on a party analogy. Yet NGOs do
not stand for election. Their broader public interest claims must depend
on a different kind of validation. It is a validation based on engaging with
or, in the first place, helping generate the publics that an organization
claims to represent.

If we assume that NGOs speak for broader public interests, then they
must draw legitimacy from communicating in the public sphere. Thus,
according to the argument put forward in the following chapters, NGO
legitimacy rests on the sector's capacity to generate and sustain publics. As
opposed to fostering mere instrumental or stakeholder accountabilities,
NGOs need to develop *public* accountability, understood here to mean
accountability to broader constituencies by way of both representing and
constituting them as publics.[3] To make that point, one does not need
to invoke high-minded ascriptions such as NGOs being the "conscience
of the world" (Willetts 1996) or the "conscience of humanity" (Annan
2006). If NGOs are to be citizens' voices at the tables of institutional politics and beyond, then we need to ask to what degree they actually communicate with citizens. How does an NGO develop and sustain relationships
with its constituency and broader publics? Does it organize citizen input
and public engagement? Does it debate its positions publicly, and is it
thus visible for others to see and for citizens to join in? Evidently, modes
of communication in and with publics vary. NGOs can encourage citizens to write checks; they can ask them to volunteer; they can also enable
them to join in public advocacy and speak up. My local PTA has a choice

---

has pointed out, this would mean that working for women's rights would qualify as a
public interest, but working for the "rights of one particular group of women" would
not (2004: 63). A public status, in my view, is ascribed in the discursive public arena.
Therefore, even a special interest group will attain a "public" identity if and when others
decide to discursively engage with its ideas – be it a business lobbying group or a secret
society. In other words, the "publicness" of an NGO is defined discursively and not as a
self-ascribed status or abstract representational claim of an association.

[3] Jens Steffek has first introduced "public accountability" in regard to international governance institutions (Steffek 2010). I argue that NGOs' public accountability encompasses
the four different modes of transparency, debate, engagement, and activation; for details
see Chapter 4. Knutsen and Brower (2010) employ the term "expressive accountabilities" as constituting the legitimacy of civil society organizations. Yet whereas they define
expressive accountabilities primarily as one-way outreach to gauge constituency sentiment, I submit that the concept of public accountability encompasses NGOs not merely
representing but also *constituting* publics.

of how to communicate with me: It might convince me to give money; it might ask me to bake cakes for school events; or it might organize a public discussion on how we can change education policies. And although most NGOs employ some combination of these different modes of communication, fundraising, organizing volunteer work, and institutional presence seem to occupy a much more substantial part of NGO activities than public advocacy (see, for example, Bass et al. 2007; Kohler-Koch and Buth 2011; Steffek and Hahn 2011). Yet, while fostering certain kinds of citizenship, fundraising and volunteering leave others underutilized.

Kofi Annan's remarks also signal a radical change in the relationship between political institutions and civil society. Whereas governments through much of the 20th century had looked on NGOs as "mobilizers of public opinion in favor of the goals and values" of states' agendas (Annan 1998), in the new century these civil society actors were supposed to turn into legitimate partners of government (e.g., Salamon 1995; Willetts 2000; Gazley 2010). They were to help shape public agendas while being the legitimate voice of civil society at the negotiation table. Indeed there are numerous indicators, from local-level politics to the transnational spaces of governance, that the "era of NGOs" is in full bloom. The implementation of Agenda 21 principles in the 1990s required cooperation with civil society organizations in the global North and global South. Mistrust of government after the breakup of the Soviet Union helped generate a large NGO sector in Central and Eastern Europe. No international organization today operates without some level of NGO engagement (Reimann 2006; Steffek et al. 2010: 100), and neither do national or local governments (e.g., Haus et al. 2005; Powell and Steinberg 2006).

This altered relationship means not only that governments are to develop different modes of engagement with civil society actors; it also presupposes that NGOs adapt to the norms and rules of institutional politics. Some observers have pointed to the dangers of co-optation and mission drift (e.g., Hulme and Edwards 1997; Chandhoke 2003). It seems as though neither governments nor NGOs have much incentive to practice public outreach in a situation where the state can point to NGOs as their proxies for citizens and NGOs can point to policy results. What, then, are the opportunity costs of sitting at the table in terms of public voice? Have NGOs become hollow stand-ins for publics, or are they providing the best mechanisms for citizen engagement with public policy issues? And if, as this book suggests, both dynamics are at work, then what conditions drive one or the other?

THE ARGUMENT

In a nutshell, this book makes three claims. These claims are based primarily on empirical work in Europe and the United States,[4] yet the reader will see the occasional connection to research in the global South, as well as references to fields that are not in the immediate purview of nonprofit or NGO scholarship, such as public sphere and feminist theories. The intent is to create dialogue between different research clusters that share an interest in civil society and the public sphere. Of course, weaving the argument by combining threads of theory and empirical analysis runs the risk that it might satisfy neither theorists nor empiricists. I would counter with C. Wright Mills: "Good work in social science today is not, and usually cannot be, made up of one clear-cut empirical 'research.' It is, rather, composed of a good many studies which at key points anchor general statements about the shape and the trend of the subject" (Mills 1959: 202).

The first general statement is that the public sphere is a key component of civil society; this claim anchors the book theoretically. The next chapter provides evidence that influential theories of civil society sideline its role as a sphere of public debate by focusing exclusively on how associations and social norms are generated. I argue that these theories miss out on the conditions that enable citizens to take their issues into the public arena. Moreover, they cannot explain seeming paradoxes such as the existence of strong associations in societies with weak public voice. Only by making a systematic distinction between organizational density, on the one hand, and public debate culture, on the other hand, can we understand why, for example, the strong web of associations in Japanese civil society has such little public voice and influence (Pekkanen 2006).

The second claim is, in essence, a "public advocacy" argument. It contends that even though both institutional and public advocacy are essential to a democratic culture, it is *public* NGO advocacy that generates citizen engagement and voice. Institutional advocacy, by contrast, tends to be confined to non-public or semi-public contexts, such as government commissions and expert consultations. With late modern societies offering more venues for institutional advocacy, NGOs might see stronger immediate returns if they lobby government officials, brief members of

---

[4] I want to encourage those who might find viewing NGOs through the public engagement lens productive to use that lens in other arenas of the nongovernmental sector.

parliaments, or negotiate with business directly than if they try to organize and sustain public campaigns. Even if institutional advocacy does not produce policy success, there are other factors that incentivize institutional over public engagement, such as resource constraints and reputational gains. NGOs, I argue, face opportunity costs by engaging in outreach and public advocacy.

The third claim builds on a political institutionalist argument. I submit that states and governments play a critically important role in encouraging NGOs to practice public engagement and that therefore the key to a stronger civil society lies not in a stricter separation of state and civil society, but in transparent, interactive, and very public government–civil society relations. My analysis of NGOs operating in various contexts, from the local to the transnational, suggests that the potential for public voice is primarily shaped by state–society interaction. Participation in the public sphere thus rests on governance conditions. These conditions do not just form outward barriers inside which civil society acts independently; they permeate public space and set formal rules and informal tones of communication. They structure information flows and, ultimately, are key to civil society acting as a public sphere.

On a meso level, I put forth a set of three explanatory concepts that define the specific conditions in which NGOs operate in late modern civil societies. All three mark developments that shape NGOs' willingness and capacity to engage in the public sphere: (1) the NGOization of civil society, (2) the institutionalization of advocacy, and (3) NGOs as proxy publics.

The first concept highlights the impact of a specific development in the organizational formation of late modern civil societies. *NGOization* refers to a process by which civic actors from social movements in particular, but also from smaller community groups, are drawn to incorporate and perform as NGOs. Forces that shape NGOization have economic as well as institutional roots. The pull to professionalize meets the need of states, business, and private donors to seek out reliable partners in civil society. Positive feedback mechanisms set in if civic groups or movements NGOize. The returns can be material: A legal status provides better access to funding as well as to consultation or decision-making processes. The returns can also be symbolic, as with increases in communication, insider knowledge, and trust. NGOization might normalize the relationships between civil society actors and governing institutions. However, it also might result in the exclusion of some groups and perspectives that represent less organized interests. In addition, it might lead to insider or client relations between selected NGOs and government (Lang 1997; Alvarez 1999).

NGOization sets the stage for the second conceptual anchor of this study: the increasing *institutionalization of advocacy*. This concept elaborates on a specific connection between government and civil society, arguing that as NGOs become stronger institutional players and are welcomed into civic dialogues with local, national, or transnational political institutions, the incentives to strategically limit public advocacy increase. As they develop, many NGOs come to avoid using their potential to produce and sustain what Jürgen Habermas calls "a critical process of public communication" (Habermas 1989: 232). Contrary to a common perception that highly visible public communication of NGOs increases an organization's institutional clout, the more likely experience is for NGOs to encounter the opposite, namely that too much critical public voice tends to jeopardize institutional leverage. NGOs navigate a trade-off between institutional effectiveness and public voice, and the dominant mode used to resolve this trade-off is to employ the latter only in a very limited way. This might lead to NGOs becoming experts in institutional advocacy and lobbying at the expense of generating broader public debates.

The third conceptual hook addresses what I consider to be the fallout from NGOization and the institutionalization of advocacy: NGOs acting and being perceived as legitimate *proxy publics*. For governments and supranational institutions, NGOs constitute "their" civil society and public, just one phone call away. This study examines how the dynamics of increased returns fostered by NGOization and institutionalized advocacy feed proxy publics and in turn how networked governance can contribute to NGOs' generating stronger public voice and public accountability.

Before elaborating on these arguments, I would like to present briefly what I am *not* arguing. This is to prevent readers from misinterpreting my points and to prevent myself from overstating them.

First, I am *not* arguing that NGOs do not contribute to the public sphere at all. Some NGOs are advocacy organizations that work almost exclusively through public action. Yet the majority of NGOs are much more selective in their public outreach and employ only the occasional strategic communication tool. They are highly strategic in calibrating communication means for specific ends. For the former, generating publics is part of the end in itself; for the latter, it is a tool whose opportunity costs can be high. This book engages with the pulls and constraints that influence NGO public advocacy.

Second, I am *not* arguing that NGOization is always and necessarily bad. The pejorative slant that the concept has received over the past decade (e.g., Funk 2006), which connects the concept to a "sell-out" of movement goals, actually inhibits an analytical perspective that emphasizes configurations and trade-offs; for example, the trade-off between institutional influence and voice, or between professionally stable careers and the navigation of dissent.

Third, I am *not* arguing that engagement in public advocacy will look the same for an urban development NGO and for a globally involved NGO such as Oxfam. Yet I do make the case that all NGOs confront some version of the same pulls and constraints that are embedded in practicing public engagement and advocacy. Steve Charnovitz has identified four pressing issues in the context of internationally operating NGOs that, with some modification, can be applied across the scale, down to the level of urban NGOs: (1) To what degree do legal environments accommodate or inhibit NGO activity? (2) Are governance contexts "rendered more legitimate" if NGOs participate? (3) To whom, and through what kind of procedures, are NGOs being held accountable? (4) How, and to what degree, has NGO participation changed policy outcomes?[5] Whereas policy outcomes are not at the center of this investigation, the first three questions are directly relevant to an assessment of NGOs' public engagement profiles and can inform NGO research from the transnational to the local level.

Fourth, I am *not* arguing that NGOs are the only carriers of public voice. Generally, we consider the news media to be best positioned to articulate citizen concerns while also acting as an interface with political institutions (see, for example, Koopmans and Statham 2010: 5). Yet mass-media-centered accounts of the public sphere tend to focus on elite-driven discourses in established media "arenas" and, as a consequence, award only passive "gallery" status to the majority of citizens and their organizations. The mass media approach to the public sphere does not leave much room for considering the impact of organizational publics, particularly since NGO action is often not reported in the mass media. If publics are made up of citizens joining together to debate issues of common concern, then the organizational publics of NGOs constitute arenas in which such dialogue takes place (see also Bennett, Lang, and Segerberg 2013). These are arenas, moreover, in which citizens can join in and actively partake instead of watching only from the galleries. It also

---

[5] Adapted with modifications from Charnovitz (2009: 777).

would be misleading to conceive of these organizational or issue publics as inward looking and therefore rather marginal contributors to the public sphere. In fact, the publics that NGOs are able to incubate might be more active and engaging than the mass-mediated publics of traditional media.

Last, I am *not* arguing that government is always the solution when NGOs avoid public outreach and engagement. Yet the opposite – freeing the state of all obligations toward civil society and, more specifically, toward making sure that NGOs can actually fulfill their function as organizational publics – is equally shortsighted. Government, so the argument of this book, can either limit or help expand the public voice of the nongovernmental sector. More specifically, it can provide incentives for NGOs to practice outreach, to build and engage publics. In effect, states and other governance bodies play a major role in whether NGOs act as catalysts of, or as proxies for, the public sphere.

Before we turn to the argument more systematically, a few definitions and clarifications of the terms used in this book are in order.

WHAT ARE NGOS?

There is no single widely shared definition of what constitutes an NGO. Much like the term "civil society," the NGO has been one of the moving targets of social analysis in that it describes a phenomenon with unclear boundaries, a multitude of self-proclaimed or associated actors, and an equally hazy set of norms and tasks. Some hail NGOs as leading a "global associational revolution" (Salamon 1993), whereas others see them as an "unelected few" with the "potential to undermine the sovereignty of constitutional democracies" (American Enterprise Institute 2003a). They are perceived alternately as principal agents of a new "subpolitics" (Beck 2007), "wild cards" in politics (DeMars 2005), or as publicly unaccountable interest groups of the third millennium (*Economist* 2000).

The term "NGO" was first used in 1945 when the United Nations made a distinction in its charter between the participation of intergovernmental agencies and non-government associated groups. UN provisions cast a wide NGO net, basically registering every private body that was independent from government control, not seeking public office, not operating for profit, and not a criminal organization (Willetts 2002). For the UN, the U.S. Presbyterian Church is as much an NGO as the International Transport Workers Federation or the Indian Society for Agribusiness Professionals. It is important to point out that the UN did not discover a new species of civic actors, but in a constructivist manner categorized and labeled a broad set of previously active associations. Moreover, this constructivist labeling of the NGO sector was not restricted to truly internationally operating organizations, as some definitions since have suggested. It is a label that has been used to identify civic organizations across the spectrum, from transnational to national, regional, and local associations.

A number of alternative concepts have emerged since the 1950s. Some authors distinguish between grassroots activism (on the local and regional level) and the nongovernmental sector (on the national and international level). Others find the merely negative lineage of NGOs (as in the "non-state" concept) wanting and attempt to replace it with the encompassing term "civil society organizations" (Salamon 1999; Berman 2001). In the United States, the debate is dominated by the term "nonprofit" as opposed to "nongovernmental," which is reserved for the international sphere. Others assert that the terms can be used interchangeably (Steinberg and Powell 2006).[6] Finally, much nonprofit research has been combined in recent years under the header of a "third sector," indicating a specific societal place for NGOs that is different from, and lies between, the public and the private sector or in between state, market, and family (Zimmer 2005).

I opt to retain the label "nongovernmental" organization for two reasons – one related to functionality, the other to semantics. First, the term "NGO" speaks more sensitively to the conflicts that this book explores than the term "nonprofit" or "third sector." The focus on the role of NGOs in contributing to the public sphere and on the give and take between government, institutional publics, and organizational voice is best represented by a term that reflects government–civil society relations. Second, the NGO label has global salience; it is used across Africa, Asia, and Latin America just as much as in the new democracies of Central and Eastern Europe.[7] Because this book attempts to theorize a particular trait of NGOs, I want it to travel well semantically.

---

[6] Linguistic preference for the term "nonprofit" in the United States, as opposed to other parts of the world, might be related to a tradition of economic and political liberalism combined with a more general hesitancy to use, however negatively defined, government-linked concepts.

[7] It is noteworthy that on the local level, the label "NGO" or "grassroots NGO" is quite common in the Global South, whereas local civil society organizations of the Global North have long avoided the nongovernmental label in favor of terms such as "citizen initiative," "association," or "civic group" (Roth 2005: 94). This is changing in recent years, with local civic groups increasingly using the label "NGO" themselves as the sector

Most definitions of the NGO sector enumerate certain shared characteristics on which we can build. On the most basic level, NGOs (1) are
not related to government, (2) are not for profit, (3) are voluntary, and
(4) pursue activities for the common good instead of just for their members. In broad terms, these activities can take the form of either providing
services or advocating public policy (see the definition in the Encyclopedia
Britannica[8]).

Based on this broad characterization, we can add more specific NGO
traits that inform both the empirical part and the theoretical argument
of this book.[9] One, NGOs tend to operate at the intersection between
traditional, mostly nation-state, and institutionally bound politics and
newer forms of stronger identity-based, non-party-driven civic engagement. Even though, in legal terms, NGOs must limit their political engagement to what appears to be "nonpolitical" activities, they often *engage in
a form of politics* "outside and beyond the representative institutions of
the political system of nation-states" (Beck 1996: 18). Therefore the nongovernmental sector is credited with playing a central part in establishing
new geographies of political power at the intersection of civil society and
institutional politics. By publicly staying on the sidelines of institutional
political processes, NGOs might fuel a perception that Volker Heins
describes as "a certain aloofness from politics" (Heins 2008: 17). Yet this
public aloofness might be more strategically motivated than a de facto
unwillingness to engage in institutional advocacy. Second, NGOs have a
moral purpose that fuels their orientation toward problems and people
outside of their organization and thus distinguishes the sector's rationale
from that of business and from a reality lens that focuses on profit or other
self-serving individualist motives. Third, NGOs can be *nonterritorial* in
the sense that they are ultimately not bound by nation-states, seek out
different engagements on multiple levels of society, and might act simultaneously locally and transnationally (Heins 2008: 19). Finally, NGOs often
act as *public* experts, distinguishing their activities from those of private

---

gains prominence and as funder rationales base grant making on specific traits associated
with NGOs (see Chapter 2).

[8] Available at http://www.britannica.com/EBchecked/topic/759090/nongovernmental-
organization-NGO (accessed December 4, 2010).

[9] This study's evidence is mostly harvested from NGOs that engage in socially progressive
advocacy. It invites others to test the argument on NGOs with socially conservative or
religious values, as well as on those NGOs with stronger service-oriented profiles or on
corporate-sponsored NGOs.

corporations. NGOs are focused on lending their expertise to a greater public good.

In sum, this book treats an NGO as a voluntary not-for-profit organization that is bound legally to be nonpolitical but can engage in noninstitutional politics, that generates normative claims about a common good, and that acts on these claims as a public expert in variously scaled civic spaces. Again, this is not a normative statement, but an attempt to capture the empirical NGO reality of the early 21st century.

THE NGO BOOM

Although there is no accurate assessment of how many NGOs operate from the local to the transnational level, the sector has expanded substantially in recent years. Between 1982 and 2006, the number of nonprofits in the United States almost doubled from 793,000 to 1,478,000 (Urban Institute 2006). In Germany, in the five years after unification – from 1990 to 1995 – the number of registered associations jumped from 286,000 to about 450,000 (Anheier and Seibel 2001: 74). National surveys have counted more than one million NGOs in India (Sooryamoorthy and Gangrade 2001), 359,000 registered NGOs in Russia (Skvortsova 2007), 55,000 in Poland (Garsztecki 2006), 570,000 in Germany in 2008 (DGVM 2007; Vereinsstatistik 2008), and 161,000 in Canada (Statistics Canada 2005).[10] NGOs are a thriving part of Western market economies, making up 14.4 percent of the workforce in the Netherlands, 11.1 percent in Canada, 9.8 percent in the United States, 6.3 percent in Australia, and 5.9 percent in Germany (Johns Hopkins Comparative Non-Profit Project 2000), although a more recent survey puts employment in the German nonprofit sector as high as 9 percent (Stifterverband für die deutsche Wissenschaft et al. 2011: 6).

The NGO boom in the international arena is also well documented. Between 1994 and 2009, the number of NGOs registered with the UN Economic and Social Council increased from 41 to 3,172 (UN ECOSOC 2009). Since the start of the new millennium, there has been more than a threefold increase in the number of accredited NGOs registered with ECOSOC. The Global Civil Society Yearbook 2004/5 counts 17,952

---

[10] It should be noted that these figures reflect assessments of the overall nonprofit sector and thus include organizations such as hospitals, colleges, unions, and others that in my definition would not be considered to be proper NGOs. Only a few studies distinguish between the overall nonprofit sector and the core nonprofit sector.

headquarters of internationally operating NGOs (Anheier, Glasius, and Kaldor 2004). The Yearbook of International Organizations for 2005/6 cites 51,509 internationally operating NGOs (Union of International Organizations 2006).[11]

What has caused this explosion in organized civil society activity worldwide? There is no single answer to this question: The growth of NGOs has been influenced by political and social contexts, fields of engagement, and scale. For example, assessments of the factors that drive the NGO boom emphasize different conditions for India (economic liberalization and decentralization; Chandhoke 2003), France (the expansive state; Levy 1999; Rosanvallon 2007), and Russia (political liberalization and international donors; Maxwell 2006; Aksartova 2009). The narratives of growth for environmental NGOs differ from those for NGOs promoting the arts. They also vary depending on whether the focus is on local, national, international, or transnational arenas. Because the field of NGO studies reflects this "multifaceted view of NGOs" (Betsill and Corell 2008: 7), it is faced with the challenge of how to aggregate empirically grounded findings into theoretical propositions that travel across geography, discipline, and scale.[12] Moreover, various subdisciplines in the social sciences point to different roots of increases in civic activism, most obvious in the varied answers that theories of social movements, governance, globalization, and communication have to offer. Early accounts of the local and national civic organizing boom in Western societies since the 1960s focused primarily on postmaterialist values of economically affluent generations (Inglehart 1977). Since then, social and cultural bottom-up explanations that interpret the rise of NGOs as a result of increased levels of education and prosperity have taken a back seat to social movement analyses and their focus on the rise of political opportunity structures as the main predictor for activism (Tarrow 1998; McAdam and Scott 2005). These more recent studies have identified organizational dynamics, such as the professionalization of social movements and their

---

[11] For an excellent overview of quantitative data on international NGOs, see Bloodgood (2011).

[12] Theory-building within the international relations literature, taking as its starting point the global arenas of the United Nations, the European Union, the WTO, and others in which NGOs have been awarded some participation rights (e.g., Nanz and Steffek 2004; Martens 2005; Locher 2006; Bexell et al. 2010; Steffek and Hahn 2010), at first sight seems to have little in common with research that attempts to theorize NGOs in the context of urban civil societies (i.e., Berry et al. 1993; Haus and Heinelt 2002). This book, however, works off the proposition that public engagement can be a legitimizing source for NGOs from the transnational to the local level.

focus on identity politics (e.g., Staggenborg 1988; Edwards 2004; Roth 2005), as contributing to the expansion of the nongovernmental sector. In more institution-focused research, specific organizing opportunities generated by liberal states (Walker 1991; Berry 1999) or neoliberal politics (e.g., Fine and Rai 1997; Grant 2000) have gained traction to explain the increase. In the global North, devolution and Thatcher-Reagan–inspired externalization of state functions to civic sector organizations in particular provided incentives to form NGOs (Peterson 1992). Tony Blair's "Third Way" in Great Britain and Gerhard Schroeder's reformed Social Democracy in Germany formulated political programs that encouraged the subsidiary activation of civic organizing not just as volunteer work but also as a new professionalized civic commons. Kim Reimann shows how the political opportunities for the sector have multiplied through extensive state and foundation funding and that, in fact, "it is impossible to understand the explosive growth of NGOs in the past several decades without taking into account the ways in which states, international organizations, and other structures have actively stimulated and promoted NGOs from above" (Reimann 2006: 46). These changes took hold at all levels of government; however, local and transnational political institutions in particular have, while externalizing state or organization functions and program tasks, provided space for nongovernmental organizations to meet and provide input under the umbrella of formal governance bodies (Alvarez 1999; Reimann 2006; Steffek and Hahn 2010).

Finally, engagement and communication patterns among baby boomers have changed in ways that favor NGOs over political parties and traditional interest groups while exposing more fluid, single-issue, and networked mobilization patterns (Lipschutz 1996; Bennett 1998, 2004; Bimber 2003; Flanagin and Stohl 2009). The majority of post-1960s NGOs seem to be better positioned to feed off, and in turn charge, these different social engagement patterns than traditional interest groups (Skocpol 1999a). Yet, although the sector grows in size and seems to gain legitimacy as a major influence on political decision-making processes, governments or governance institutions do not always or unequivocally like the guests that they have invited to the table.

NGO TROPES

The stories that make the headlines tend to zoom in on the adversarial role of NGOs vis-à-vis governments. Here are some snapshots of how contentious NGO–government relations appear to be across the globe:

In Australia, the Howard government instituted a "gag clause" that prevented NGOs that received government funding from discussing their programs without prior government approval (Edgar 2008). In 2008, the successor government reinstituted freedom of speech for the NGO sector.

In Ethiopia, the Civil Society Organization Law of 2009 prohibited any domestic NGO that received more than 10 percent of its funding from abroad from engaging in activities related to "the advancement of human and democratic rights . . . the promotion of the equality of nations, nationalities and peoples and that of gender and religion . . . the promotion of the rights of the disabled and children's rights" (Articles 2 and 14(5); International Center for Not-For-Profit Law 2009: 2).

In Russia, under President Putin, a new NGO law took effect in 2006 that set strict terms for registration and for the acceptance of funds from foreign donors. An NGO may be denied registration, for example, if its activities are deemed to be a threat to Russia's "sovereignty," its "unique character, or cultural heritage" or if it offends the "national or religious feelings of citizens" (Maxwell 2006: 253ff).

In the European Parliament, the European Commission faced criticism for funding NGOs that are critical of neoliberal politics, such as Attac. That NGO had received the comparatively minuscule amount of about 60,000 Euros from Brussels between 2001 and 2003 (Klas 2005). Economically liberal Parliament members asked the Commission to withdraw funding from Attac.

In the United States, Greenpeace struck a deal with the U.S. government after 14 of its members faced felony conspiracy charges for disrupting a test of the antimissile defense system. Prosecutors acquired a legal promise from the NGO not to hold protests at or trespass on military property for the next five years, and Greenpeace agreed to pay $150,000 in fines to the government (Agence France-Press 2002; "National Briefing" 2002).

Many of today's big news stories signal conflict rather than partnership between NGOs and governments. Not only authoritarian states and managed democracies but also liberal political systems seem to be challenged by the increasing power of NGOs. In an attempt to portray and understand this uneasy relationship, news reports often rely on two tropes that have become iconic from the revolutions in Central and Eastern Europe to the resistance movements in Latin America and the Anti-Apartheid movement in South Africa: (1) the struggle of David against Goliath and (2) the image of NGO-based counterpublics.

The media invoke the "David and Goliath" trope by portraying NGOs as often resource poor and marginalized, but vocal public defenders of human rights, democratic ideals, and economic and political equality. Governments, by contrast, are sketched as – at best – powerful regulators and – at worst – as relentless opponents of the nongovernmental sector. This narrative pits political power giants against the aspirations of marginal groups – well-armored state actors against inventive challengers with fewer resources and only a few stones in a sling. However, the relationship between NGOs and governments is more complicated than the David and Goliath narrative suggests.

What if David and Goliath simply live a marriage of convenience? What if they are actually involved in a somewhat symbiotic relationship? By all accounts, the conflict-ridden news stories of government–NGO relations that dominate the press are not the norm, but the exception: More narratives fit the relationship pattern of co-dependency among unequals. When NGOs sit at institutional tables, there is a reciprocal bestowing of legitimacy. In addition to depending on segments of the NGO sector to provide services and perform consultative roles, governments increasingly rely on NGOs for channeling citizen voice and ultimately for legitimizing state action. NGOs give organizational structure to a fragmented, individualized citizenry that seems tired of "politics as usual" and shows stronger affinity for NGO causes than for ideological party alignments. Many NGOs thus are willing interlocutors of government, however vaguely "representing" civil society. NGOs, in turn, are rewarded for establishing and preserving positive ties with government. The rewards tend to come in legal, economic, and political currency. NGOs depend on states for legal protection and often also for funding, as well as for access to institutional advocacy forums and influence-generating contexts. The ties that bind NGOs and governments thus call for closer inspection.

Whereas the David and Goliath trope has recently begun to receive some critical attention (Warleigh 2001; Berry and Arons 2003; DeMars 2005; Heins 2008; among others), a second and related trope has been less explored: It is the narrative that constructs NGOs as the center of vibrant counterpublics. The "counterpublic" trope portrays NGOs as active catalysts of civil society and as committed public actors, organizing their supporters and using media-savvy repertoires for the purpose of communicating concerns of marginalized constituencies. We all have images of such counterpublics in our minds: We might think of Greenpeace activists in their small lifeboats circling around Japanese whaling trawlers, trying to obstruct their activities. We might recall MomsRising.org covering the lawn in front of the Washington Capitol with two miles of clothesline full of "onesies" advocating for paid sick days. We might remember the worldwide demonstrations against the Iraq War on February 15, 2003, when a broad coalition of organizations mobilized 36 million people to attend antiwar rallies.

This counterpublic trope is prominent in policy circles that perceive NGOs as representatives of concerned citizens and as alternative voices to mass-mediated opinion formation. It is cultivated by NGO staff and advocates who claim that giving public voice to institutionally underrepresented causes legitimizes their organizations. And it is reinforced by scholarly work that credits civic engagement with stimulating the public and political voice of underrepresented constituencies (e.g., Asen and Brouwer 2001). NGOs have become shorthand for vibrant civic voice. Again, the analysis in this book complicates this trope. If the number of NGOs is rising globally and if individuals' options to become involved and exercise citizenship have multiplied with the help of a diverse non-governmental sector, why do so many citizens feel detached from public life and politics? Do NGOs do a good job in aggregating citizen voice and producing alternatives to dominant publics?

Closer empirical inspection reveals that NGOs are not sui generis boosters of public voice. Some do not practice advocacy at all and are committed exclusively to providing services. These NGOs play only a marginal role in this book. Yet even NGOs with an explicit advocacy mission might lack the commitment to mobilize their constituents and practice outreach. My argument is that advocacy organizations in today's world of NGOs are prone to prioritizing institutional over public venues in order to influence their environment. As one of my interviewees succinctly put it, "We don't need a public to be effective" (EWL 2007a; see Appendix 2). Are NGOs then just another reiteration of special interests, the embodiment of a new class of lobbyists of the 21st century? Is the sector in danger of producing organized advocates without incubating and engaging wider publics? What does it take to actually strengthen public voice?

THEORIZING VOICE AND ADVOCACY

"Voice" is probably one of the most common and least theorized concepts in the social sciences.[13] It is generally associated with Albert Hirschman's

---

[13] This is not to say that the concept of "voice" is absent from social science inquiries. Quite the contrary: In democratic theories and empirical analyses, for example, it is present

(1970) analysis of political and economic responses to the decline of organizations or political systems. Confronted with the alternatives of "exit" or "voice," people make conscious choices by exercising either their voice option or by deciding to leave. Voice in Hirschman's theory is "any attempt at all to change, rather than escape from, an objectionable state of affairs" (Hirschman 1970: 30). Being vocal means "speaking up" versus "letting go" and, in political terms, choosing active intervention and public communication over silent dissociation from political conflicts.

Representative democracies, in theory, offer numerous opportunities for citizens to speak up and intervene in political affairs; we can for example vote, write petitions, contact our representatives, and attend public meetings. Yet engaging in these activities is often like participating in a silent auction: The event itself is public, but communication and voice are minimized. Most formal ways of participation in political affairs are individualized, almost private, acts. Theories of deliberative and participatory democracy challenge this anorexic vision of political citizenship and propose alternative ways to generate citizen voice. It is in this context that James Fishkin (1997) spreads the idea of deliberative polling and that John Gastil (2008) explores citizen voice as processes of public deliberation. Participatory theorists, in their critique of representative and, to some degree, deliberative solutions to citizen voice, emphasize that social marginalization is often reproduced even in engineered deliberations and that underrepresented constituencies might need alternative venues and forms to speak up. They focus on the substantive inclusion of different groups, rather than on procedural acts of molding their different voices into one (i.e., Young 2001). Deliberative and participatory theories have concluded that settings for activating public voice are not naturally engrained in representative democracies, but instead have to be engineered in ways that go beyond liberal democracy's "default" settings. The concept of voice suggests speaking and taking positions in public. It suggests communication, interaction, and debate, whereas participation might not necessarily have such an overtly communicative and public face. Therefore, this book focuses on voice rather than on participation.

<hr>

in a number of proxies that range from participation or influence to more narrowly defined stand-ins such as voting or protest. I argue here that the concept of "voice" has a rightful place next to these more directed and purposeful forms of expression, because it allows us to see acts of communication that have a lower purpose and effect threshold, but nevertheless are public expressions of citizens who care about issues. An example of such citizen voice would be constituency input on an NGO-initiated blog.

Yet often in the social sciences, voice is simply equated with participation (e.g., Verba, Schlozman, and Brady 1995). When we cast a vote,
we voice our electoral preferences. When we sign a petition, we voice
our concern. When we become members of the Sierra Club, we voice
support for environmental issues.[14] Citizens thus seem to have culturally
engrained and "civic duty" proven ways to assert voice, and we are used
to exercising citizenship within a "dutiful citizen" model (Bennett 2008).
Yet there is mounting evidence that the dutiful citizen voice has lost some
of its appeal. In most Western societies, voter turnout is declining. Political parties as historical catalysts of voter choice are losing members and
credibility. Membership-based interest group organizations are experiencing recruitment problems (Skocpol 1999a; Putnam 2001). There is a
clear trend away from established venues of civic duty and toward more
individualized and personalized expression of voice (Bennett 1998; Delli
Carpini 2004; Zukin et al. 2006), driven by "the presence of multiple participatory styles, in which the relationships between individuals' attitudes
or characteristics and their involvement varies across people" (Bimber,
Flanagin, and Stohl 2012: 33).

More personalized styles of communication also produce different
messages. In general, people seem to be more comfortable with asserting
the personal rather than the social dimension of needs, illustrating what
Hannah Pitkin has termed the difference between "I want" and "I am
entitled to" (Pitkin 1981: 347). Personal grievances make for a better
public narrative than investigations of the social and political context in
which they occur. Media like to disseminate and viewers or readers like
to consume so-called authentic stories that feature the personally affected
rather than the politically committed citizen. As a result, Nina Eliasoph
finds, citizens tend to avoid publicly minded debate and instead have
learned to speak about entitlement more in privatized, or what Goffman
has termed "backstage" arenas (Goffman 1959; Eliasoph 1998).

This is where the nongovernmental sector comes in. Even though
most NGOs today are not traditional membership associations, the
sector's self-image is based on speaking up for collective entitlements.

---

[14] Casting such a wide and formal participation net, Sidney Verba, Kay Lehman Schlozman,
and Henry Brady in their 1995 study on "Voice and Equality" reached the conclusion
that altogether, in the United States "only a very small portion of the public, 5 percent"
could be deemed as "totally inactive" (Verba, Schlozman, and Brady 1995: 83). Yet
from a perspective that emphasizes the shortcomings of citizens' engagement in public
life, it is doubtful to what degree the measured activities are adequate proxies for citizen
voice.

The women's NGO that pushes for transparency of the ingredients in cosmetics, the fair trade NGO that rallies consumers around buying coffee directly from small producers, or the environmental NGO that mobilizes against genetically modified food all act not simply on the grounds of "we want," but on the grounds of "we as citizens are entitled to" or "the citizens we represent are entitled to." As discussed earlier, NGOs advance normative claims toward a common good and act on these claims as public experts. Thus they are well positioned to generate, moderate, and synthesize "frontstage" public debate and to articulate and represent social grievances and entitlements to political institutions. In other words, they can produce or enhance the collective voice of their – real or imagined – constituents and amplify it into organizational voice in the public arena.

What do we know about how this organizational voice is being generated? Debra Minkoff and John McCarthy have provided an excellent overview of existing research on the organizational dimensions in social movement organizations and argue that much of this work has "developed independently from organizational theory" (Minkoff and McCarthy 2010: 291). Most studies, moreover, focus on organization ecology and its impact on organizational decision making, with little attention being given to how the environment influences an organization's public voice. Organization theories, if they address voice at all, tend to focus more on internal processes of speaking up than on the public voice of an organization. They construct voice as "the practices and structures that affect who can speak, when, and in what way" *within* an organization (Putnam, Phillips, and Chapman 2006: 389). Questions of external communication tend to be examined as "PR" activities, aimed at the marketing of messages. Yet NGO voice is more than a collection of press releases and staged PR events. Kenneth T. Andrews and colleagues recently argued that "civic associations provide a key mechanism through which citizens exercise voice by combining together to make claims in the public arena" (Andrews et al. 2010: 1196).[15] Whether and in which contexts NGOs speak up tells us something about their role in the public sphere. Whom they publicly address, how they organize dialogue and engagement of

[15] In contrast to the approach presented here, though, Andrews et al. equate voice with recognition, resulting in voice being operationalized as the extent to which "leaders are called upon by the authorities, the media, and the public for their support, resources, or information" (Andrews et al. 2010: 1208). Although voice and recognition are clearly related, not all voices are recognized equally by dominant institutions. Frequently, civic voices are being ignored or marginalized by dominant media and/or authorities.

constituents, and to what degree they are open to broad citizen input are all indicators of their capacity to nurture publics.

Whereas voice refers to speaking up in an undirected and general sense, advocacy means employing purposefully directed and instrumental voice. In advocacy, NGOs use voice with a specific intention and target in mind. In the broadest terms, any attempt to influence political decisions on behalf of an imagined or organized community can be termed advocacy. Some scholars distinguish between "rights-based" advocacy and "civic" advocacy (Boris and Mosher-Williams 1998) or between "political" advocacy that is directed at political institutions and "social" advocacy that tries to influence public opinion (Jenkins 2006: 309). Although these distinctions capture a vital difference in the location, direction, and targets of advocacy, I submit that we would be hard pressed to call some civic advocacy contexts, such as the civil rights movement, not rights-based or all public opinion campaigns non-political. These distinctions reflect a traditionally narrow way of understanding politics, in which what we see as political shrinks to the confines of government. However, many NGO campaigns today combine political and social advocacy; they expose institutional as well as civic features. To characterize these campaigns as nonpolitical is to dismiss the public sphere as a nonpolitical space of influence and the mobilization of constituents as a pre-political act.

This book suggests a different way to look at advocacy, one that distinguishes not between political and social vectors of influence, but instead focuses empirically on distinctive advocacy strategies and tools used to reach an intended outcome. The two modes of advocacy that best capture the role of NGOs in the public sphere are *institutional* and *public* advocacy. Institutional and public advocacy stand for different ways to seek influence, different repertoires of action, and different communication practices (see Fig. 1.1).

Institutional advocacy is the attempt to influence decision making by gaining some degree of insider status in institutions or in organizations that initiate, prepare, legislate, or execute policy change. Institutional advocacy strategies are primarily tailored to secure access to, and build relationships within, a given governance body or arena. NGOs might try to gain legitimacy by providing expertise, or they might build on a reputation of being effective project implementers to gain institutional leverage. The aim is to work constructively inside institutions to achieve policy success. Primary communication practices are the sharing of expert knowledge, insider debate, and lobbying.

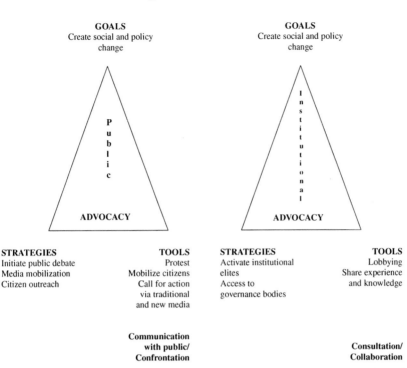

GOALS
Create social and policy
change

P
u
b
l
i
c

ADVOCACY

GOALS
Create social and policy
change

I
n
s
t
i
t
u
t
i
o
n
a
l

ADVOCACY

STRATEGIES	TOOLS	STRATEGIES	TOOLS
Initiate public debate	Protest	Activate institutional	Lobbying
Media mobilization	Mobilize citizens	elites	Share experience
Citizen outreach	Call for action	Access to	and knowledge
	via traditional	governance bodies	
	and new media		

Communication
with public/
Confrontation

Consultation/
Collaboration

FIGURE 1.1. Public Advocacy and Institutional Advocacy. *Source:* Model adapted with modifications from Pettigrew 1990 and Dechalert 1999.

Public advocacy, by contrast, attempts to achieve policy success by engaging broader publics and, at its most effective, actively stimulating citizen voice and engagement in the process. In its "thick" mode, public advocacy means employing strategies that allow for interactive communication with citizens. NGOs practicing public advocacy thus tailor their communication toward mobilizing, synthesizing, and amplifying citizen voices. In its more information-oriented "thinner" mode, public advocacy might mean utilizing public space by putting up a billboard or running an ad asking citizens to sign on to a predefined campaign or to join a single public event. Overall, public advocacy strategies are less driven by the attempt to gain insider status and more by a focus on outreach and on ways to organize and activate publics.

Institutional and public advocacy are not incompatible strategies to achieve policy change. In fact, NGOs might use both modes in different stages of a project or campaign or even at the same time. Institutional advocacy may gain more leverage if institutions perceive the NGOs as having the strong potential to engage in public campaigns and to have

broad, actively supportive constituencies. In turn, public advocacy repertoires, such as campaigns or protests, can be more effective if, at the
same time, lines of institutional communication are being established and
held open. Optimizing insider/outsider navigation can be essential for
successful NGO advocacy.

However, engaging in parallel insider/outsider advocacy also presents
challenges for NGOs. In addition to having obvious limitations in terms
of resources, competencies, and legal restrictions, NGOs might be faced
with governance conditions that actively discourage or more subtly disincentivize public advocacy. Research on state–NGO relations indicates
that invitations to sit at the table are most likely extended to NGOs whose
message is in broad accordance with government agendas (Brinkerhoff
and Brinkerhoff 2002: 12ff.). NGOs with contentious or radical agendas, by contrast, are invited less often to the table. Compounding this
institutional selectivity of who gets to be included is the fact that most
governance bodies exhibit an informal code of conduct. NGOs thus might
need to adapt to a specific institutional habitus in order to gain acceptance and trust in a specific governance context. This informal code of
conduct in turn might diminish an NGO's willingness to advocate for
specific politics through advocacy involving public contestation and citizen engagement. Governance conditions therefore are key to an NGO's
commitment to public advocacy and engagement; they can influence the
degree to which NGOs utilize institutional or public advocacy strategies
or a combination to achieve policy success.

BRINGING GOVERNANCE IN

Governance prioritizes process over conventional hierarchy and communicative over authoritative power. In its narrow sense, governance
indicates the departure from a traditional government perspective by
highlighting the arena in which governments network and cooperate
with business and civil society. Or it can mean, in a broader sense,
any kind of management of interdependent actors in which state institutions have become one player among many (Mayntz 1998; Blumenthal
2005). Throughout this book I employ the narrow use of the concept, in
which governance stands for "a broader, more inclusive and encompassing process of coordination than the conventional view of government"
(Peters and Pierre 2004: 77). This definition points to an increased role of
NGOs in generating and implementing policy, as well as in communicating policy in and with civil society (i.e., Warleigh 2001; Edwards 2004;

Boris and Steuerle 2006; Joachim 2007; Heins 2008). NGOs can be included in coordination processes in different ways, and governments still almost exclusively define the arenas and contexts in which they engage with nonstate actors. An "encompassing process of coordination" (Peters and Pierre 2004: 77) with NGOs can mean different things. It might mean being asked to contribute a five-minute statement in a hearing; it might entail providing continuous and extensive expertise over time; NGOs might help write legislation, implement policy, or organize dialogue with civil society. In short, governance contexts do not *have to* create substantially more advocacy chances for NGOs during these coordination processes (i.e., Smismans 2006b), but in principle they can.

Moreover, with the expansion of policy arenas since the 1960s – horizontally for example in the fields of social justice and the environment, and vertically with the rising influence of international organizations – governments have increasingly become dependent on policy expertise residing within the NGO sector and thus have been compelled to establish coordination and communication venues. As late as the mid-20th century, governments did not have environmental agencies, women's policy units, or antidiscrimination offices. Neither did the European Union or the United Nations engage in the elaborate civil society consultations that they organize today. Now, when the European Union asks for civil society input, it calls on European NGOs to be that civil society and to provide aggregate assessments of what European citizens think about an issue. When the United Nations organizes civil society consultations, its main representatives are NGOs. Accepting NGOs as democratic partners is a requirement for states that have joined the Agenda 21 process.[16] In fact, chapter 27 of the Agenda Charter demands that governments take measures to "establish or enhance an existing dialogue with non-governmental organizations and their self-organized networks.... [and] encourage and enable partnership and dialogue between local non-governmental organizations and local authorities in activities aimed at sustainable development" (United Nations 1992).

Inclusion of NGOs in governance is not confined to transnational and national arenas. In fact, the most vibrant and diverse governance arenas might be found in urban contexts where NGOs interact with government not only to secure funds and provide services but also to

---

[16] Agenda 21 was launched by the UN Environment Program and adopted in Rio in 1992. It is to date the most comprehensive global plan for sustainable development and has been signed by 178 governments.

organize community involvement (i.e., Berry and Arons 1993; Duncan and Thomas 2000; Haus and Heinelt 2005; see also Chapter 5). NGOs thus can be spotted as participants in City Hall hearings and in regional development councils. However, as in other arenas, there is no guarantee that local governance actually fosters substantially more involvement of civil society actors. As we explore in Chapter 5, governance can also mean consultative arrangements with a small number of privileged insider NGOs at the expense of the vast majority of local civil society actors. Local governance can take place in contexts with set rules and ultimately rely on pro forma symbolic inclusion processes. Yet, on the other hand, local governance arenas can enable NGOs to become public advocates and practice citizen engagement.

To sum up, governance is certainly no panacea for generating stronger NGO publics. Although government rationales for inviting NGOs to the table vary just as much as NGOs' reasons to sit down at it, one shared interest is to gain legitimacy by representing interested and affected publics. NGOs that are included in governance may function as catalysts of the voices of these publics. This book investigates the validity of such claims.

The cases presented later will advance the following propositions on how governance modes might influence the degree to which NGOs employ public advocacy. NGOs tend to incubate, engage with, and mobilize publics most frequently under two governance conditions.

First, and this is the condition we are most familiar with, NGOs often choose to rely on public advocacy if they are shut out of, or are strongly marginalized in, a specific high-stake governance arena. If they are denied insider status, NGOs might use public advocacy to increase pressure and have their voice heard. Social movement research has built on this paradigm, arguing that a central condition for the emergence of social movements is exclusion from decision-making processes and lack of voice (Tarrow 2005). Likewise, research on transnational advocacy networks suggests that protest mobilization, most often organized by NGOs, occurs across borders if direct access to national decision makers is blocked (Keck and Sikkink 1998). In these cases, it is the *institutional outsider status* that generates public voice.[17]

The second condition, which is less researched and acknowledged, is that NGOs can focus on generating publics if and when governments

---

[17] This is not to dismiss the fact that some NGOs build their reputation almost exclusively on their outsider status, in which case outreach to and mobilization of publics become a general advocacy strategy, as in the case of Greenpeace.

encourage them to do so. Specific governance modes, more than others, actively enable NGOs to generate public voice. This condition might be perceived as running counter to most liberal theorists' claims that one imperative of a healthy civil society is its distance from government. It might sound equally suspicious to scholars who advance the Foucauldian governmentality paradigm or older regulation school theories. Both, for different and valid reasons, are wary of governments' efforts to strengthen dialogue with civil society and more inclusive decision making.[18] I submit that the capacity of NGOs becoming stronger public advocates lies neither with individual actors, organizations, nor the state alone. It lies squarely in between these forces, but government is at this point the most underestimated promoter, and therefore the least politically targeted motor of this kind of civic renewal.

Yet both these conditions – complete exclusion from institutional venues and active enabling of public voice by governments – are outliers in the overall advocacy topography of late modern societies. Although state actors might accept NGOs at the table, many have little interest in helping NGOs generate public voice. For NGOs, in turn, institutional advocacy has fewer opportunity costs than the mobilization of publics. As a result, public voice of the NGO sector is overestimated and NGOs perform as "proxy publics": In lieu of actually engaging their broader constituencies, the organizations themselves have become stand-ins for citizen participation and public outreach. This might look like a win-win arrangement for both governments and NGOs, but it is a losing proposition for the strengthening of late modern democracy and its publics.

CASES AND DATA

Empirical studies of NGO-driven mobilization tend to focus on prominent, publicly visible, and mostly successful campaigns in the international arena, such as the Greenpeace Brent Spar campaign, the ban on landmines, and the WTO protests, or on abortion laws or migrant rights in national contexts. Yet doing so risks turning NGO public sphere

---

[18] Most liberal theory builds on the idea of the *separation* of civil society and the state to safeguard against state intrusion into spheres of free speech and unhampered associations (see also Chapter 2). Governmentality theories, by contrast, assume that governance is just another "rationale for the practice of political rule" within the hegemonic state (Sending and Neumann 2006; also Lipschutz and Rowe 2005). This book advances a perspective in which certain safeguards against government overreach into civil society are just as necessary as the critical inspection of governance accounts in which the state is considered just one more stakeholder among others and state power has seemingly evaporated within governance.

effects into mere artifacts of peak campaign events. Extrapolating NGO advocacy from these peak moments might limit our understanding of the overall dynamics of NGO communication and action in the public sphere. Instead, the cases that drive and illustrate the argument presented here are drawn from unspectacular places during unspectacular times. They provide insights into routinized NGO action and into the challenges of generating public voice and contributing to the public sphere in a comparative perspective. The study combines deductive and inductive as well as quantitative and qualitative methods to capture NGO voice. In Chapters 2–4, the more conceptual and deductive chapters, the hypotheses and theoretical claims are laid out with references to a broad range of evidence and examples drawn from already available research. Chapters 5 and 6 are painted with a thicker empirical brush: The NGO territory explored there with illustrative case studies spans three polities and ranges in size from the local to the transnational. Germany, the European Union, and the United States provide the core of the data.

Germany and the United States each have strong traditions in theory-building on civil society, fueled by Hegel, Jefferson, as well as Tocqueville's French perspective on democracy in America. Both have historically vibrant, yet very differently structured associational cultures. In Germany, for most of the 20th century, a limited number of primarily state-supported NGOs were cornerstones of an organizationally strong, yet also stagnant civic sector (Anheier and Seibel 2001). In the United States, by contrast, we encounter a multilayered, rather ubiquitous civic landscape with a wide array of organizational diversity and a public/ private mix of funding sources (Skocpol 1999a). Although this statist-pluralist distinction might invite immediate conclusions to the effect that the polyarchic structure of American governance and its more diverse funding sources allow for a stronger NGO role in serving as a catalyst for public voice, this study does not support the state-centered versus pluralist argument. Instead, the findings presented later suggest that the influence of national political cultures is less an independent than an intervening variable. The explanations for whether NGOs function as catalyst or proxy for a vibrant public sphere instead point toward more fine-grained institutional, political, and communicative relationships between governments and NGOs that seem to cut across broad system types such as the corporatist–pluralist one.

A second reason for employing data from Germany, the United States, and the EU is that all three polities have federalized or multilevel governance structures. Multilevel governance has become increasingly central to the nongovernmental sector's operations, forcing NGOs to engage with and adapt to different layers of power, yet also opening up strategic space for advocacy on multiple levels (Risse 2001; Khagram et al. 2002). As NGOs and their networks learn to act on multiple levels of governance, advocacy success might be the result of having created a boomerang (Keck and Sikkink 1998) or ping-pong effect (Zippel 2006), in which several arenas or levels of governance are involved. In Germany, for example, local NGOs have employed European Union directives to bring about policy change in municipalities. NGOs also operate with mixed funding from city, state, and national agencies, as well as the European Union; transnational NGOs and their networks in Brussels, in turn, cooperate with regional or national NGOs (Warleigh 2001; Haus and Heinelt 2002). Studying NGO voice within these multilevel governance structures highlights how differently scaled government–NGO relations invite or regulate advocacy.

I do not claim to cover all NGO advocacy in these three polities. Instead, this book presents an empirical border investigation. It examines NGO advocacy and its public engagement effects at their organizational margins: in the small arena of local advocacy, as well as in its largest form on the transnational level. The study emphasizes local and transnational modes of NGO advocacy because both local and transnational civil societies have in recent years been identified as the most promising sites for reinvigorated publics based on innovative strategies to engage citizens in public deliberation and advocacy (Sirianni and Friedland 2001; Warkentin 2001; Kaldor 2003b; Keane 2003; Nanz 2006). The local level provides highly textured evidence of the role of NGOs as public advocates and, moreover, is commonly perceived as the most fertile ground for studying dynamic environments for civic engagement and political participation (cf. Dahl and the pluralist tradition through Putnam). The transnational level has gained attention for providing NGOs with means to circumvent nonresponsive national governments (Keck and Sikkink 1998) and to enhance their public visibility through association with international institutions. Transnational NGOs are considered to be the seeds of global civil society (Kaldor 2003b). Many national NGOs in Europe and the United States, in contrast, suffer from bureaucratization and from the effects of being close to power centers and having turned into prime lobbying businesses. As a consequence, most of these national "advocates without members" (Skocpol 1999a, 2003) are less prone to employ innovative forms of civic and public communication (Anheier and Seibel 2001). In cases where national NGOs have developed more citizen-oriented forms of advocacy, they tend to cooperate with local NGOs (Skocpol 2003). In short, at this point it is local and transnational NGOs that provide the most stimulating cases for researching NGO voice.

Specific case selection within local and transnational NGO advocacy was determined by a "best fit" model based on two assumptions: One, that NGOs' public advocacy is more salient in issue areas with longstanding politicization, and, two, that it is stronger in issue areas with historically strong associational cultures. Thus NGOs would be most likely to emphasize being catalysts of public voice in policy fields where citizen voice is traditionally strong. I identified urban development and gender as two policy arenas that fit this mold: Both are characterized historically by a substantial NGO presence and by engaged and publicly vocal constituents.

The first case study investigates arenas of public voice of the nongovernmental sector in urban development in three U.S. and three German cities: San Diego, Oakland, and Seattle in the United States and Leipzig, Berlin, and Bremen in Germany. These cities were selected to represent, in a comparative perspective, cities with differing strengths of social capital or civic engagement,[19] thus addressing claims that NGOs might display stronger public advocacy in cities with higher social capital and that in effect, social capital is the prime independent variable in analyzing NGO advocacy. Within each city, I identified one or two "hot" urban development issues according to criteria that are explained in more detail in Chapter 5. Institutional and public advocacy efforts by local NGOs regarding these issues formed the starting point for 60 interviews with NGO, government, and media representatives in these six cities. In the course of follow-up sessions, questions were broadened to include NGOs' role in civil society, their engagement with and means of advocacy, and their interactions with government more generally. I met some interviewees several times in roughly two-year intervals, and others I followed up with phone interviews, thus enabling me to gauge changes in advocacy over time. Although the interviewees were granted anonymity, their general affiliations are identified in Appendix 1. I collected the data between 2000 and 2007. The interviews were conducted using a semi-open format, transcribed, and analyzed. Additionally,

---

[19] For the American cases, quantitative social capital measures were retrieved from Robert Putnam's community survey (Putnam 2002). Such data are not available for Germany. Initial civic engagement assessments for the German cities relied on reports from the Bertelsmann Foundations' Civic Engagement Project CIVITAS, as well as on expert interviews (Bertelsmann 2000).

during several visits to each city, I observed meetings and events; over time I collected printed and online materials, and followed newsletters and blogs to assess to what degree and with what kinds of strategies NGOs practiced advocacy.

The second case investigates transnational women's NGO advocacy in the European Union. Again, the task was to examine the push and pull factors that influence the practices of public engagement and advocacy. I identified five transnational NGO networks in different policy arenas according to size and representativeness and then assembled three data sets. The first set consists of interviews with directors/board representatives and members of the networks. The interviews were structured (1) to gauge strategies to influence frames, policies, and practices and (2) to examine the availability and use of specific resources and tools for outreach and advocacy. I conducted interviews between 2005 and 2008 at two nodes of the networks: with representatives of the central network structure and of member NGOs in Germany, the United Kingdom, and in Poland. The second set of data uses the networks' web presence to investigate how women's NGOs and their networks present their advocacy work via the web and to what degree they utilize web-based tools for public engagement and advocacy. This data set reflects the fact that the web has developed into a fast and low-cost communication tool for strategic action among civic groups (Castells and Cardoso 2006). Because these five NGO networks span multiple European cultures and languages, their websites serve as central and widely accessible focal points for joint discursive frames and collective action.

The third set of data in Chapter 6 consists of network maps generated by the Issue Crawler software developed by Richard Rogers from the University of Amsterdam. The Issue Crawler maps the links among websites and thus provides heuristic evidence of networking activities such as joint agendas, projects, or mere informational exchange relationships. This network tool can be used to assess relative networking strength and gauge the capacity to engage in joint public advocacy. More detail on methods is provided in Chapters 5 and 6 and in the appendices.

I cannot claim to do justice to the empirical variety of NGOs in both countries, in the six cities I compare, or in the civil society arenas of the European Union. Laws, political institutions, governance arrangements, and engrained communication cultures in each locality, country, or supranational arena necessarily differ. Nevertheless, by identifying relevant factors that define NGOs' advocacy capacity in different countries and on different governance levels, my intention is to contribute to a meso-level theory about the role of NGOs as incubators of publics in late

modern democracy. I hope that others will test this proposition in other
empirical contexts.

HOW THE BOOK PROCEEDS

The starting point in the next chapter is an exploration of theories of civil
society. The intent is to capture how dominant theories conceptualize –
or ignore – the public sphere. Building on a critical reading of Jürgen
Habermas's work, the focus is to introduce dimensions of the public
sphere and, more specifically, of organizational voice and advocacy into
civil society theories. In Chapter 3 I explore the idea that civil society's
primary mode of organization in the 21st century is found in the
expanding nongovernmental sector. I argue that civil society is becoming
"NGOized" and that NGOization has implications for voice and advocacy. This chapter also engages with a commonly held assumption that a
large NGOized civil society produces a vibrant civic culture and strength-
ens public communication and participatory democracy. Chapter 4 then
focuses on the governance conditions in which NGOs operate, the institutional constraints they confront, and some successful attempts to practice
public advocacy in conjunction with government assistance. Of particular
interest here are legal constraints that NGOs face when practicing public
advocacy, the insider-outsider dynamics of "speaking up," and perceptions of NGOs as proxy publics. This theoretical framework is then tested
in Chapters 5 and 6. Chapter 5 addresses the question of what enables
NGOs to engage in public advocacy in urban publics in the United States
and Germany. In Chapter 6, I turn from the local to the transnational
level and assess women's NGOs' transnational activism in the European
Union. Finally, the conclusion summarizes my argument that across a
broad spectrum of cases NGOs today serve more as proxy publics than
as catalysts of public voice. Yet, and this marks the "light at the end of
the tunnel," by the end of this book I will also have identified conditions
that enable NGOs to strengthen their function as incubators for public
engagement and advocacy. In more theoretical terms, I argue that the
performance of civil society as a public sphere depends significantly on
institutionalized regulatory frameworks and cultures of governance. As
Charles Tilly recently put it, "We should doubt that associations as such
hold the key to democratic participation. Instead, we should recognize
that the forms of relations between trust networks and public politics
matter deeply" (Tilly 2007: 94).

2

Civil Society as a Public Sphere

[The social scientist's] aim is to help build and to strengthen self-cultivating publics.

C. Wright Mills (1959: 186)

Civil society may be to 21st-century democracies what political parties were to an earlier era: a litmus test for organized citizen voice and participation (Cohen and Arato 1992; Keane 1998; Kaldor 2003a). A vibrant civic sphere, we assume, fosters social and cultural integration and facilitates engagement with a polity. As a result, "strengthening civil society" has become a formula for democracy frequently cited in government commissions, by donor agencies, as well as in the democratic transition and development literature. Whereas some theories emphasize civil society's role as a buffer against autocratic regime intervention, global economic neoliberalism, and social injustice (Cohen and Arato 1992; Rosanvallon 2007), others identify it as a source of economic wealth and personal happiness, guaranteeing economically favorable exchange conditions and a meaningful life to members of its community (Bellah 1985; Wolfe 1989; Putnam 2001).

Even though civil society is generally assumed to be good for democracy, the specifics of how civil societies might contribute to various properties of the public sphere are much less developed. Frequently, broad assumptions are made without much attention to how civil society and strong democratic publics are inherently linked. Terms such as "the public sphere of civic engagement" (Paterson 2000: 51) or the claim that civic engagement will somehow automatically endow strong civil societies with vibrant publics speak to this neglect.[1] Yet even the most cursory glance at history and politics reveals that there is no automatic link between civic engagement and democratic public voice. In Nazi Germany, powerful civic groups helped mold public opinion into a "one-man voice" propaganda spectacle (Armony 2004), and a staged civil society provided the backdrop for silencing dissent. In Japan, a web of potent civic associations serves as election machinery for political candidates, but not as the provider of large-scale independent public voice (Pekkanen 2006). In the United States, during the Obama administration's town hall meetings on the proposed health care reform, organized Tea Party critics hijacked the microphones and shut down debates (Media Matters for America 2009). In short, not all modes of publicity originating within civil society are positive, not all associations allow for plurality of public voice, and not all public forums encourage and enable debate.

Although some theories of civil society tend to neglect the public sphere,[2] much focus has been put on civil society's role in building associations and in generating common norms and values. Why does this bias toward community and norm generation matter? On the most basic level, it influences citizenship practices and informs what we teach children or students about how to be good citizens. Do we highlight the importance of community and norm generation? Or do we emphasize the value of constructive dissent, communicative action, and contributions to public discourse? To put it differently, do we encourage volunteerism for the sake of association and helping others? Or do we put just as much emphasis on speaking out and on the conditions that enable citizen voice? On a theoretical level, the "association and common good" bias tends to nourish the idea of civil society as a pre-political space from which economic and political forces can be successfully bracketed. In effect, we often encounter an "idealized, one dimensional version of the concept" (Cohen 1999: 56) that stresses face-to-face community in a non-agonistic pre-political realm of society; voice and advocacy are not part of that narrative.

---

[1] Michael Edwards, the former director of the Ford Foundation's Governance and Civil Society Program, noted this lack of focus on the public sphere as part of a somewhat "lazy thinking" in civil society theorizing (Edwards 2004:10).

[2] A number of civil society theories *do* put emphasis on the public sphere dimension (e.g., Fraser 1992; Cohen 1999; Chambers 2003; Edwards 2004; Alexander 2006).

The focus of this chapter is to bring the public sphere back into civil society debate and thus establish conditions that make NGOs not just civic but also public actors. I offer two routes by which we can re-import the public into concepts of civil society: a historical path and a theoretical path. Historical evidence suggests that early modern civil society did not grow exclusively out of pre-political associations, but that it has deep roots in the idea of voice, citizens' public engagement with politics, and modern state-making of the late 18th and early 19th centuries. I argue that public and political advocacy were historically an integral part of emerging modern civil societies. In contrast, the civil society debate in the aftermath of the revolutions of 1989 highlights how civil society and the public sphere have been separated in their most recent theoretical iterations. Specifically, the theoretical turn toward communitarianism and social capital has obscured the public sphere mode of civil society. Based on this historical evidence and theoretical reassessment, I reframe the current civil society debate to include voice and advocacy as not only a potential effect but also as an integral part of the design and assessment of a democratic civil society. I then consider the implications of this reframing for the study of nongovernmental organizations.

A HISTORICAL APPROACH

Notwithstanding recent waves of attention, civil society is not a new concept. Its oldest iteration goes back to Aristotle's notion of *societas civilis* (cited in Kaldor 2003a: 23). In its modern and liberal version it is a term of the old Europe (Kocka 2006). Advancing in step with the establishment of 18th-century bourgeois society and enlightenment ideas, it provided a platform for the rights-based aspirations of bourgeois men who envisioned not just a society free of censorship and repression but also a state that would actively value participation by its citizens (Zaret 2000; Lang 2001; Barker and Burrows 2002). Historical investigation provides evidence for questioning civil society's persistent image as a purely association-based, pre-political, apolitical, or even anti-political realm set apart or in opposition to the state. Early modern civil societies were built on claims to publicity and to political advocacy, and both these claims showed civil society and the emerging modern nation-state to be strongly interrelated. The struggle to establish civic associations in 18th- and 19th-century Europe was thus, at its core, a *public* struggle in which organizational claims to voice and advocacy played a prominent role.

Publicity

Across late 18th- and early 19th-century Europe, bourgeois citizens articulated their right to form associations not simply as a right to meet, but specifically as a civic right to publicity.[3] "The big slogan which now everybody shouts... is 'publicity,'" rhymed German poet Samuel Buerde (1789, cited in Hölscher 1971: 157). The associational revolution that swept through the continent during this period was not new. People had assembled before – in guilds, around the bread oven, in pubs, and at markets. What was new was the attempt to bring strangers together and encourage them to communicate and debate as a public. The right to assemble was articulated as an inherent civic right to partake in public affairs. "Publicity" became its rallying call and a synonym for freedom of speech and bourgeois liberties, often invoked with a reference to Kant's enlightenment claim that all actions that affect the rights of others are wrong if their maxim is not consistent with publicity (Kant 1996 [1795]: 347).

The articulation of this right to publicity took many different forms: Patriotic associations advertised with the slogan that publicly educating citizens on the constitution was crucial for a nation's well-being. Civic groups disseminated their messages by staging public events with speakers, food, drink, and entertainment. Newspapers printed series of treatises on the principle of publicity, and censored editors or journalists retaliated by publicly demanding their right to publicity (Lang 2001). Democrats and liberals invoked publicity in courthouses, in the media, in parliaments, in bars, and on the streets. Without publicity and public agency, there would be no justice (Splichal 2002: 111). Thus, the democratic order that European bourgeois activists fought for was directly linked to the principle of publicity. Finding one's voice and expressing it were perceived to be key to a democratic civil society reigned by "critical publicity" (Habermas 1989 [1962]).

Others argued that publicity needed educated citizens. Because majorities of European populations in the early half of the 19th century could not read, conditions for adequate public judgment seemed frail. Yet liberals countered that, whether educated or not, citizens would do democracy a service by forcing others to defend their position publicly and would

---

[3] For an analysis of early associations in Germany, see Dann (1984); for Belgium and the Netherlands, Ertman (2003); for England and Germany, E. Hellmuth (1990); for Great Britain, Clark (2000); and for an overview of civil society in Europe during the 19th century, see Bermeo and Nord (2003).

learn the practice of active citizenship in the process. English philosopher John Stuart Mill expressed this sentiment, arguing,

> The notion is itself unfounded, that publicity, and the sense of being answerable to the public, are of no use unless the public are qualified to form a sound judgment. It is a very superficial view of the utility of public opinion to suppose that it does good only when it succeeds in enforcing a servile conformity to itself. To be under the eyes of others – to have to defend oneself to others – is never more important than to those who act in opposition to the opinion of others, for it obliges them to have sure ground of their own. Nothing has so steadying an influence as working against pressure. (Mill 1998 [1861]: 360–1)

Publicity was not just the term of democratic trade across early 19th-century Europe. In Tocqueville's rendering of American civil society, publicity likewise turned out to be more than a marginal afterthought. What Tocqueville admired in the American landscape of associations was that "men had bound themselves *publicly*[4] to a cause" (Tocqueville 1945 [1835]: 114); in other words, citizens expressed public commitment and used public communication arenas to articulate their allegiances and opinions. When Americans form associations, Tocqueville wrote, they become "a power seen from afar, whose actions serve for an example and whose language is listened to" (114). Community in civil society thus is not a self-serving ideal, but has two public dimensions: It consists of people signaling publicly that they identify with a cause, and it produces public power, exemplary action, and messages that travel in the wider public sphere. Interpreting Tocqueville's fascination with American civil society as purely community oriented, as exercised in neo-Toquevillian theory (see the later discussion), does not do justice to the emphasis he puts on its public appeal. It is not the bounty of American communities per se, but their public face and public spirit that catch his eye.

Politics

A second noteworthy feature of early 19th-century civil society was that it was neither pre-, nor a-, nor anti-political. Instead, its expansive organizations engaged in ongoing negotiations among themselves and with government about what "politics" and "political" were in the first place and about how "civic" and "political" should relate to each other. Some associations perceived the individual, the civic, and the political to be organically tied together. Gymnastics clubs of the early 19th century, for

---

[4] Emphasis added.

example, were generally not based on an individualized notion of personal fitness, but on the idea that they would turn men into active citizens of their polity (Clark 2006: 351ff.). They did not just provide opportunities for physical exercise but also offered practice in political citizenship through sponsoring reading and discussion groups or by organizing public events at which candidates for office presented themselves. Others used the communicative venues of reading societies and guild meetings to organize member debating forums and public discussions (Dann 1984). Emerging civil society, populated by an increasing number of associations and publications, performed intricate strategic dances with authorities. These dances were aimed at carving out space for a repertoire of actions that actors claimed were merely civic and not political in a state-defined manner, but in effect redefined the political itself.

Specifically, groups that promoted liberal or democratic ideas in countries with monarchic or absolutist regimes used the claim to nonpolitical activity to broaden their arenas of involvement in public affairs (Darnton and Roche 1989; Lang 2001). When an editor sought approval from government authorities for publishing a newspaper or a pamphlet, the claim to engaging in "nonpolitical" activity was what initially prevented all too harsh censorship. When women's groups came together to bake for the poor or to sew clothes for the army in need, their aspiration to nonpolitical, purely social activity belied the fact that their activities spoke to the politics of needs, to questions about distributive justice, and to the fact that they devised the category of "deserving and needy" in their own view. As Mary Ryan puts it for 19th-century American women's societies, "If social life was divided between male and female, public and private, the history enacted on each side of that shifting border was deeply politicized" (Ryan 1992: 273). In other words, the cover of being nonpolitical served well to strengthen civil society while holding interference from government at bay. Yet strategically employing the tarnish of "nonpolitical" is not the same as *being* nonpolitical.

Governments all over Europe tried to defend their institutional monopoly over politics, while civil society action corroded this monopoly and not just demanded but also actively organized participation in public affairs. Wary governments, as in the case of the administrators of Württemberg in southern Germany in 1849, worried that "the masses [would get] used to seeing the real [political] forces in arbitrary meetings, party associations, clubs and the like" and that this would "destroy the already limited understanding of state order and citizen representation" (cited in Lang 2001: 213; see also Dann 1984). In effect, what

came to be known as the "age of associations" – the network of clubs
and philanthropic, civic, professional, and cultural associations – was
"the arena, the training ground, and eventually the power base of a
stratum of bourgeois men who were coming to see themselves as a 'uni-
versal class' and preparing to assert their fitness to govern" (Fraser 1992:
114). Beyond the bourgeois class, worker groups began to explore voice
through their civic associations; rural populations organized to protest
price increases for bread, demanding dismissal of politically nonresponsive officials – in short, claiming the right to political voice was the
conduit of early civil society and not its antidote. The antidote was politics defined as merely institutionalized government. A core strength of
early modern civil society was that it disputed this narrow conception of
politics.

State

The third noteworthy aspect of this short historical exploration is the
involvement of the modernizing state in shaping and sustaining civil
society. In fact, civil society and the state were never strictly separate
spheres. While trying to rein in the association revolution and its critical
voices, modernizing governments across Europe at the same time confronted the need not only to accept but also to some degree embrace
their emerging civil societies (Lang 2001; Clark 2006). This was often
not an altogether cozy embrace. In part, it was merely the result of realizing that censors, police, and laws could not fully repress emerging civic
spheres. Yet to some degree, governments also started to rely on civil
society in the tumultuous transitions from absolutist Ancien Regimes to
modernized constitutional polities. To gain legitimacy, modernizing states
needed intermediary structures that could help communicate policies and
develop public opinion around government agendas. State actors envisioned aggregate audiences that would serve both as recruitment pools
and as critical echo chambers for government policies and that would
become accountable partners in promoting and executing policies. Agri-
cultural associations, women's charity clubs, and reading societies served
as interpreters and activators for state policies. Moreover, accommodating bourgeois interests in political participation during a period of rapid
expansion of trade and industry provided a bulwark against more radical
workers' interests (Scambler 2001: 3).

Across Europe, states not only guaranteed the institutional framework
for civil society but also took part in facilitating its growth (Levy 1999;

Lang 2001).[5] Governments had a functional interest in grooming emerging civil societies, and this grooming could be just as restrictive as it could be enabling. Although the notion of a "government-enabled" civil society at first sight has a more continental European than an Anglo-American ring to it, it developed on both sides of the Atlantic. Even though we tend to interpret Toqueville's exploration of the state of civil society in America as a purely "bottom-up" take on the importance of associationalism to fostering and sustaining democracy, recent research has pointed to the fact that "government made all that 'volunteerism' possible" (Skocpol 1996: 2). According to Skocpol, the evidence as to when, how, and why civil society flourished in American history points straight to the emerging modern state. It was government-sponsored and implemented infrastructure, like the network of postal offices, that allowed faster communication and networking among citizens and their associations. It was in the interest of members of Congress to facilitate news dissemination by legislating cheap newspaper postal rates and increasing the frequency of delivery to remote areas of the country. Likewise, the associations that Tocqueville visited functioned as mediators between state and civil society. Many were not just local, but developed around citizens who aimed for party offices and government posts. In effect, civil society, even in its American heyday from the 1820s to the 1840s, was marked by government facilitation.

We can draw three broad conclusions from this historical exploration: (1) claims to publicity and to participation in public debates are an integral part of civil society, (2) association-building in particular needs to be complemented with attention to who gets to have voice and at whose expense, and (3) governance conditions matter. Ultimately, specific state–society relationships fuel democratic politics in what Iris Marion Young calls the continuous attempt to "link state institutions and civil society in a way that reinforces each other's virtues" (Young 2000: 157).

Yet the civil society that today speaks out of foundation brochures, municipal volunteer day celebrations, and classroom textbooks rarely makes these connections. There, the emphasis of civil society development tends to be rarely on citizen voice and reciprocally enabling state–society

---

[5] At times, this interest in expanding a "controlled" civil society produced hazardous endeavors. In Germany, state governments tried in the early half of the 19th century to establish seemingly "independent" newspapers whose editors and journalists were in fact on governments' payroll (Lang 2001: 161). Buying off editorial opinions and spying on associations were an integral part of how governments engaged with civil society.

relations, but most often on the personally fulfilling element of individu-alized civic engagement – that is, "volunteering feels good"[6] – or on the role of the civic sector as compensating for government failure. Why did public voice and the idea that civil society can enable government, and vice versa, take back stage in civil society debates?

THE REVIVAL OF CIVIL SOCIETY

After its ascendancy in the late 1800s to mid-1900s to public discourse, the concept of civil society lay dormant for more than a century. Indus-trialization, two world wars, and the emergence of large-scale collec-tive action from labor to civil rights movements prompted a focus on class-based, national, and ethnic cleavages and thus highlighted the fric-tion within, rather than the democratizing substance of, civil society. Distributive struggles over economic and political resources took center stage. Theorists and practitioners sponsored "society" as the adequate unit of social analysis, trying to capture social developments by way of intersecting forces such as the economy, ethnicity, and family – forces that most theorists did not consider to be part of civil society (Anheier 2004). Not until the 1980s did the term "civil society" resurface in the transitional movements in Central and East European countries and in the mobilization against military dictatorships in Latin America. In these contexts, it became key to the antidictatorial critique of societies that had been stifled under the hegemony of one party, of organized state associa-tions, and an omnipresent secret police. By the 1990s, a similar attempt to count on civil society for democratic renewal occurred in India, as well as across Africa (Chandhoke 2003: 21).

In the Central and Eastern European countries, the term "civil society" was reintroduced to capture the attempts of Solidarność in Poland (Arato 1990), dissident movements in Hungary and Czechoslovakia, and civil rights groups such as the Neues Forum and Democracy Now in the GDR to form associations and generate a civic infrastructure in their countries. The early proclamations of these groups were not about toppling their regimes; they were about state–society relations and about voice: voice that would break the silence surrounding large clusters of Central and Eastern European (CEE) niche societies, voice that would challenge the

---

[6] The combination of both "volunteering" and "feels good" brings up more than 2.1 million results in a Google search. The combination of "volunteering" and "public voice" has merely 900,000 hits (accessed February 1, 2012).

monopoly of quasi-feudalist dictatorial state publics, voice that might ultimately break down the walls that shielded the ruling political elites from their citizenry. New Forum, the first dissident group in the GDR to go public, opened its founding statement of September 10, 1989, with this observation: "In our country, the communication between state and society is obviously troubled" (Gray and Wilke 1996: 6).

Dissident movements across Central and Eastern Europe took different paths in addressing this breakdown of communication. In the GDR, activists tried to engage the authorities by demanding press freedom and a seat at the decision-making table; in other countries, and much earlier than in the GDR, disillusioned leaders abandoned attempts to institutionalize communication with the regime and instead focused energies on generating an alternative civic universe of associations. Václav Havel in Czechoslovakia and Adam Michnik in Poland prioritized social self-organization over interaction with the state. They insisted on the non-political community-building character of their movements. In fact, civil society was to be the space of *anti-politics* (Kaldor 2003a: 4), a sphere in which autonomous citizen voice could grow in a "parallel polis" rather than in direct communication with the government. Havel promoted "independent self-organisation" as "an area in which living within the truth becomes articulate and materializes in visible ways" (Havel 1985: 65). Most of the intellectual leaders of the "associational revolutions" of 1989 framed their strategies within a collective action paradigm that highlighted civic consolidation and solidarity over public political communication and advocacy.

Strategically, many Eastern European intellectuals' focus on association seemed to be appropriate responses to the threat of political repression. Yet in theoretical terms, the emphasis on association over voice remains paradoxical.[7] Would a civil society, made up of inward-looking associations, have been able to topple the CEE regimes? It is not associations per se, but their orientation toward communicating issues to a larger public that produced the momentum for change. Without voice and advocacy or, to put it differently, without a public sphere element, 1989 might have looked quite different. The tipping point of the old regimes was not the associational practices of dissident groups in their

---

[7] In Latin America, neither activists nor intellectuals shared this restrictive version of civil society (Alvarez 1999; Wampler and Avritzer 2004: 294). Yet arguably European and North American theorists of civil society were more influenced by the end of the Cold War and the developments in CEE countries than by the Latin American movement struggles.

niche environments as such – the tipping point was reached when these associations decided to leave their niche and go public: to squat at the Danzig shipyard in Poland, to hop on trains to Hungary and onward to the West in the thousands, to protest every Monday on the streets of many Eastern German cities, to occupy embassies and public squares. When Solidarność was legalized as a union representative in Poland in 1980, this meant the end not only of the monopoly of party-related organizations but also of party control over the public sphere (Adloff 2005: 11).

In sum, it was the public advocacy mode of civil society that became the driving force behind the East European revolutions. It was the publicly displayed decision to choose voice over silence, or exit, within CEE countries that gave credence and political power to these developing civil societies. Independent association and networks of trust are therefore necessary, but not sufficient anchors for conceptualizing civil society. It is civil society in its mode as a public sphere that provides the stimulus for social change.

WRITING THE PUBLIC OUT OF CIVIL SOCIETY

We have established that the "parallel polis" idea of the 1980s might have facilitated a lopsided understanding of civil society – one that marginalizes public advocacy in favor of strict disengagement with the state and of building small-scale autonomous and solidarity-oriented associations. Yet in theoretical terms, this solidarity-focused vision of civil society has found widespread resonance in the debates of the past two decades. Communitarian and social capital theories of civil society, in particular, have shaped discourses on civil society with paradigms that tend to marginalize or "write out"[8] the politically engaged public. What makes these discourses important for our purpose is that they do not just stay within the confines of universities and conference rooms; they influence how governments and donor agencies perceive or "construct" civil society actors and, more specifically, shape interaction with the nongovernmental sector.

In communitarian terms, civil society is made up of communities and associations that are not political and that "foster competence and character in individuals, build social trust, and help children become good

---

[8] I owe this term to Jane Jenson (2008). She investigates the processes by which women are written out of EU policy imperatives; I focus on the arguments by which the public is written out of civil society narratives.

people and good citizens" (Elshtain 1999: 13). It is based on norms of trust and solidarity in a "space of uncoerced human association" (Walzer 1995: 7) that people enter "for the sake of sociability itself" (16). Alan Wolfe calls this a focus on the small-scale world of intimacy (Wolfe 1989: 38) and face-to-face community, and Nathan Glazer refers to it as the "fine grain of society" (Glazer 1998: 103). Within these tightly woven social structures, citizens can learn solidarity-based behavior that in turn is supposed to strengthen the foundation for democracy.

Public voice and advocacy are rarely addressed in communitarian versions of civil society. All matters requiring interest mediation are externalized to other spheres such as politics and the economy, turning civil society itself into a semi-privatized moral school for solidarity-based citizenship. What remains unclear is how these solidarities are being communicated and negotiated, for example, during times of conflicting interests and priorities. Sociability, as Neera Chandhoke has observed, can rapidly "dissolve when it comes to competition over the resources and the symbols of collective life" (Chandhoke 2003: 31). Yet if we encounter a public at all in communitarian territory, it is an intimate and locally bound public that dispels any notion of it being a contested site of different voices. Local associations somewhat organically find their way into local media, which in turn shape the debate that essentially reflects the community: "The fact that important issues are decided locally enhances the importance of local media, which in turn focus the debate on these issues by those affected" (Taylor 1998: 48). Problems such as media access, economic constraints on communication, or how to generate translocal solidarities are sidelined in communitarian theories. We encounter a civil society that ultimately could just as well thrive without larger and competing publics.

A second contribution to writing out the public sphere can be attributed to the past decades' "onward sweep" (Mayer 2003) of the social capital paradigm. In most general terms, theories of social capital assess civil society with a set of indicators aimed at measuring the strength of its community-building associations (i.e., Edwards, Foley, and Diani 2001; Putnam 2001). Social capital "is about capacities for cooperation that are embedded in associations" (de Haart and Dekker 2003: 155). Associations are credited with generating trust, norms, and networks, which in turn become predictors of democratic salience and economic prosperity (Putnam 2001). In Robert Putnam's shorthand, the more choral societies and community picnics, the higher are government responsiveness and economic well-being.

What makes recent social capital theories so appealing is that they indeed provide the first systematic empirical measurements for assessing the overall state of civil societies (i.e., Edwards et al. 2001; Minkoff 2001; Hooghe and Stolle 2003). It is of interest here how these concepts capture public voice and advocacy, which can be extrapolated most clearly from survey-response–focused social capital literature. On the basis of the Social Capital Community Benchmark Survey that Robert Putnam and the Saguaro Seminar released in 2002, we understand social capital to be a composite survey measurement, encompassing about one hundred different measurable variables that can be grouped in eleven "facets"[9] (Putnam 2002). Yet in the context of our exploration of the writing out of the public sphere, the social capital index presents us with two somewhat related problems. One, social capital proxies capture individual membership in associations, but never associations themselves. We get information about whether an individual joins an NGO or how many groups he or she is part of, but we do not learn anything about the conditionality that informs this NGO's actions in civil society nor the role of individuals within them. The proxies empirically capture a sphere of individual joiners, but not how joining a particular association conditions agency and communication or how different forms of civic organizations enable or restrict voice and advocacy. In effect, survey-focused social capital proxy measures gauge individual membership and not collective voice. They are fueled by methodological individualism and ultimately convey an atomistic notion of engagement in civil society (Skocpol 1996).

A second methodological decision that erases the public in survey-oriented social capital theories pertains to the kinds of measurements offered to gauge civic strength. Of the one hundred measurements that the social capital index offers, the following table presents those with the most salience in regard to voice and advocacy. Only seven call on individual voice and advocacy (see Table 2.1). The vast majority of measurements, by contrast, assess civic strength through variables that capture an individual's associational ties, trust, and norm generation and depend only on the "passively participating" or "dutiful" citizen. Reading

---

[9] "The 11 different facets of social capital found in the Social Capital Community Benchmark Survey include two dimensions of 'social trust' (whether you trust others), two measures of political participation (electoral political participation and participation in protest politics), two measures of civil leadership and associational involvement, a measure of giving and volunteering, a measure of faith-based engagement, a measure of informal social ties, a measure of the diversity of our friendships, and a measure of the equality of civic engagement at a community level" (Putnam 2002: 2, fn 3).

TABLE 2.1. *Proxy Measurements for Voice and Advocacy in Putnam's Social Capital Community Benchmark Survey, 2002*

Facet	Measurement	Facet	Measurement
Electoral participation	Knows U.S. senators from state	**Protest politics**	Signed a petition
	Daily newspaper reader		Attended a meeting/rally
	Interest in politics		Participated in demonstration
	Registered to vote		Participate in labor union
	Voted in last election		Participate in ethnic/other organization
Civic leadership	Formal group involvement		Participate in political group
	Served as officer/ committee		Belong to local group that took reform action
	Number of times attended meeting		
	Number of times attending town/school meeting		
Associational involvement	Number of formal secular group involvements		

a newspaper, for example, although it certainly speaks to an interest in public affairs, does not by default generate opportunities to express one's ideas in a public arena. Formally belonging to the American Automobile Association, likewise, does not gauge whether this person ever speaks out about climate change or has asked an organization to do so on his or her behalf. In short, if civil society is measured through individualized and for the most part passive associational linkages, then the quality of civil society as a public sphere is not adequately captured. The implication is that a strong civil society in survey-oriented social capital terms might, in fact, be based on multiple one-time, comparatively passive, and perhaps simply monetary declarations of support for a civic cause.[10]

---

[10] Some social capital literature relies less on individual-level surveys and instead uses aggregate data of civic organizations (i.e., Stolle and Rochon 1998; Minkoff 2001). Yet even though these authors clearly take collectives as their starting point, their proxies for measuring social capital (i.e., density of members in associations or associations themselves, association type, capital) do not explicitly speak to civil society in its mode as a public sphere. If social capital is measured in terms of sheer density of associations, we might miss not only the actual diversity of actions within and by associations but

Along the same lines, we can diagnose dense networks of associations across the United States, from the national to the local level; yet associational density does not measure the degree to which these associations contribute to their local, regional, or even national or transnational publics. Focusing our analytic lens on civil society as a public sphere, by contrast, means taking into account the governance conditions in which associations decide on strategies for action, as well as the means of communication by which they engage citizens and incubate publics.[11]

In sum, writing out the public sphere in social capital theories is a direct consequence of the premise that generating civic trust and norms within a nation of strong associations fuels a vibrant civil society. Social capital theories tend to de-emphasize conditions that enable these networks of trust to aggregate citizen voice, carry it into larger civic arenas, and practice public advocacy. This is not just a theoretical problem that stays confined within academic conference circles. The dominant social capital discourse of recent years has had repercussions for how states, parties, foundations, and other philanthropic donors have conceived of and sponsored civil society in Berlin, Baltimore, and Baghdad. A major effect of operationalizing civil society assistance on the basis of the social capital paradigm has been "association overload" – the creation of civic landscapes that display layers of NGOs, alliances, and networks, all founded for the sake of investing in social capital production. This overload might lead to the appearance of a dense civil society, but tells us little about civic voice or the ability to strategically join forces to practice effective public advocacy (Petrikova 2007; Browning 2009).

CIVIL SOCIETY AND POLITICAL SOCIETY

As we have established earlier, writing out the public sphere might occur as fallout from theoretical attempts to shield civil society from becoming overly politicized.[12] Liberal theories, in particular, remain acutely

---

also in more specific terms how associations navigate between institutional and public advocacy.

[11] New information technology, for example, has created the potential for more frequent and denser vertical communication between NGOs and constituencies. However, it has also facilitated the rise of new and highly professionalized NGOs that employ radically different modes of communication within, among, and beyond associations than traditional membership NGOs (see Chapter 3).

[12] Margret Somers calls this the "metanarrative of Anglo-American citizenship theory" (Somers 1995: 2320). Its reach today extends far beyond its origin.

sensitive to state intervention and insist on strong barriers between civil society and the political system. In normative terms, a benign realm of voluntary association is posited against the harsher realities of a political society dominated by institutional actors who attempt to influence politics. Whereas the former is said to sharpen our sense of morality in independent associations, the latter is driven by instrumental rationality and provides the connections to representative government (Wolfe 1989: 180). Instead of constructing civil society and the state as different aggregates within a range of forms of social organization, liberalism tends to present an artificial dualism in which "civil society is believed to be the realm of popular freedom because it is declared autonomous from and prior to the state, spontaneous in its workings, self-activating and naturalistic" (Somers 1995: 232). Thus liberal theories construct a "great dichotomy between a vilified dangerous public realm of the state (always lurking behind the tamed government of the people) versus a noncoercive voluntary and pre-political (hence private) realm of (civil) society" (232).

Yet even if civil society is perceived not as private per se, but as a realm in between public and private spheres, it comes across merely as a "public-lite." John Rawls claims that "the reason of associations in civil society is public with respect to their members, but nonpublic with respect to political society and to citizens generally" (Rawls 1993: 220). In his view, associations provide "publicness"[13] to their members because by joining an association, they leave the intimate privacy of their home and family. Yet at the same time and in contrast to associations in which citizens exercise political citizenship, such as parties or parliaments, civic associations remain private assemblies, organizing the personal lives of their members. Theorizing civil society as a sphere in between public and private fortifies the limited publicness of civil society, offering private citizens temporary and occasional public status, but at the same time keeping civic associations out of political society. Citizens "go public" as individuals by leaving the intimate sphere of their family, but they do not form publicly recognized collectives in civil society. In Rawls's theory,

---

[13] I use the term "publicness" here in conjunction with the more established term "public sphere." Whereas the German term "Öffentlichkeit" combines aspects of a *sphere* as well as a specific, namely public, *property* or characteristic of a setting, we need two terms to demarcate the difference in English, namely *public sphere* and *publicness*. For example, Theodor W. Adorno's 1964 Frankfurt School article has been translated into English as "Opinion Research and Publicness" (Adorno 1964 [2011]).

"churches and universities, scientific societies and professional groups," for example, are nonpublic expressions of civil society and belong to what he calls the "background culture in contrast with the public political culture" (Rawls 1993: 220). This liberal reflex to shield areas of society from public and political intervention has consequences for theorizing and practicing citizenship. In theoretical terms, walling off civil society tends to turn a blind eye to the constructions of publicness within its confines and, in particular, to the interaction between civil society and the state. In practical terms, separating civil and political society leaves political agency squarely within the dominion of institutionalized political actors and government.

The perspective advanced in this book is that neither political society nor civil society is essentially public or private. Nonstrategic domains of solidarity and association can establish public voice, and strategic debate in political society might happen behind closed doors and in privatized settings. A neighborhood street party can ignite the spark for collective action, while simultaneously political negotiations on the same issue take place between parties and unions in City Hall in back rooms and never acquire publicness. The feminist theory debates of the last two decades have shed light on the forces that continually *construct* public and private and thus the power relations within the realm of civil society (Scott 1988; Fraser 1992; Landes 1998). As Jude Howell has pointed out, the "concern with autonomy leads analysts to focus more on the boundaries between regimented sectors than on their permeation by social relations" (Howell 2007: 429).

In sum, the expulsion of the political public from civil society needs to be framed within a broader context of depoliticizing citizenship. The liberal claim to privacy or semi-publicity of civil society brackets questions about the spaces and the conditions by which voice and advocacy are constituted, trained, and practiced in this sphere. Jean Cohen has forcefully concluded that "without the concept of the public sphere, civil society talk will remain hopelessly one-sided and analytically useless" (Cohen 1999: 59). Without the concept of the public sphere, the analysis of NGOs misses a central dimension of how these organizations channel and condition public voice and advocacy. Yet the limited perspective of influential civil society theories on the public sphere is only one obstacle to understanding the role of the nongovernmental sector within a framework of civil society. Another obstacle is created by approaches that convey an overly narrow view of the public sphere itself.

BRINGING THE PUBLIC SPHERE BACK IN

Civil society and public sphere theories tend to promote a tacit division of labor: Some respected theories within the civil society paradigm write out public voice and concentrate on associations; working within a public sphere paradigm, meanwhile, often results in a focus on the media at the expense of associations. Historically, the most influential attempt to ground the associational public sphere squarely within the realm of civil society was made by Jürgen Habermas, who argued that civil society's institutional core "is constituted by voluntary unions outside the realm of the state and the economy and ranging from churches, cultural associations, and academies to independent media, sport and leisure clubs, debating societies, groups of concerned citizens, and grassroots petitioning drives all the way to occupational associations, political parties, labor unions, and 'alternative' institutions" (Habermas 1992: 453). Civil society's centers are nongovernmental, noneconomic, and voluntary associations that anchor the communication structures of the public sphere in civil society. What specifically should be noted here is that the function of associations goes beyond establishing networks of trust and solidarity. Habermas conceives of associations as *public* actors that ideally aggregate and disseminate citizen voice and provide space for public engagement. Moreover, in its mode as a public sphere, civil society generates debate and carries issues from the margins to the centers of power that might otherwise never get to be on the radar screens of institutional politics: "Through resonant and autonomous public spheres [it] develops impulses with enough vitality to bring conflicts from the periphery into the center of the political system" (Habermas 1992: 330).[14]

Who or what creates these impulses? The most common answers point to the mass media, assuming that only what makes it into the mass media is "truly" public. From this assumption, it is just a stone's throw to the idea that the media *are* the public sphere or that "the public sphere is what the media make of it" (Risse 2010: 115). Support for this equation comes from empirical work that exposes the limited influence and power of all forms of publics that are not mass mediated (Donges and

---

[14] Whereas Habermas argues for the power of democratic discourse to deliver these impulses, Jeffrey Alexander (2006) rejects the notion that purely rational discursive practices devoid of emotional and cultural attachments can create a democratic civil sphere. For Alexander, "publicness is a social and cultural condition, not an ethical principle; it points to symbolic action, to performance, to projections of authenticity" (2006: 16).

Jarren 1999: 62). Yet conflating the public sphere with the mass media poses a number of normative and analytical problems. One obvious normative problem is that it reifies and reproduces media hegemony and thus validates mass media voice without adequately examining the filtering processes involved in media content. Traditional media, for example, "index the sources and viewpoints in the news according to perceived power balances among factions within political institutions" (Bennett 2010: 107). Hence, what is voiced in mass-mediated publics is filtered through mechanisms that attribute relevance according to institutional power. Failure to examine these power and status filters thus invites ignorance regarding those publics that congregate beyond the reach of the mass media or that operate in alternative arenas of public communication. Moreover, it leaves unexamined the motifs for their outsider status. Certain publics might be sidelined by the mass media, whereas others will not even want to get mass media attention or will use alternative media to distribute information and organize mobilization for their issues.

A second area of concern regarding the media approach to the public sphere is that it tends to operate with the assumption that the public audience is primarily passive (Trenz 2002: 36). If the public sphere consists of what the mass media report on, then the role of citizens is for the most part receptive or, at best, "monitoring" (Schudson 1998); that is following closely the media reports on issues they are concerned with. A more active citizen role in constructing and sustaining publics tends to get marginalized in the mediated public sphere paradigm.

Finally, constructing the public sphere as exclusively mass mediated takes little account of the radical changes in the contemporary media environment. New information and communication technologies have revolutionized the way we interact and mobilize for civic causes (Bimber, Flanagin, and Stohl 2005). Many publics today do not rely on traditional mass-mediated communication spheres to pursue collective goals. In fact, the very same audience member who is the seemingly passive recipient of traditional media messages might in other contexts decide to employ voice and be an engaged member of a subpublic. Therefore, solely referencing the mass media as the public sphere actually limits our understanding of the conditions that shape public voice and advocacy.

In broader terms, the public sphere may be defined as the composite of real and virtual arenas in which private citizens come together to give voice to matters of public concern or common interest (see Habermas 1962; Fraser 1992; Lang 2001). Much like civil society, it is a contested concept that combines normative and empirical elements. Thus, every examination of the public sphere raises questions about the quality of democratic life such as: Who should be participating, in which form, how regularly, and toward which end? What kinds of resources are necessary to partake in the public sphere? What should a public process of democratic debate look like and aim for? Different theoretical traditions have given different answers to these questions (Ferree et al. 2002) that pertain directly to the place that civil society actors have in the public sphere and to the voice of NGOs in the democratic process.

Traditional liberal theory generally finds the public sufficiently represented in the voting act and supports knowledgeable elite participation that competes in a free marketplace of ideas. It "economizes the attention of men as members of the public, and asks them to do as little as possible in matters where they can do nothing very well" (Lippmann 1925 [1993]: 189). Liberal theories thus find the public well served by elections, free competitive private media, and the occasional meeting of elite expert publics. More recent accounts of liberal theory, as we have established earlier, value associations primarily because they generate social capital, and not because of their capacity to aggregate public voice and advocacy. Viewed through the lens of liberalism, NGOs are useful as long as they provide civic infrastructure and moral orientation. Yet if they expose too strong a public voice, they tend to be framed as rogue and unaccountable actors that challenge and at times undermine state sovereignty and are neither institutionally nor publicly legitimized to speak on behalf of citizens (Spiro 2007).

Other theories question whether such a thin public platform provides adequate legitimacy and cohesion in late modern societies. Participatory, deliberative, and constructivist models of the public sphere all share a normative call for "deepening democracy" – albeit with somewhat differing actors, stages, and therapies in mind.[15] Participatory theories conceptualize the public sphere as a realm that citizens should use to maximize participation in all decisions that affect their lives. "Self government by citizens rather than representative government in the name of citizens" (Barber 1984: 151) can be achieved through "an evolving problem-solving community" that is open to all. These communities preferably link themselves into existing decision-making processes and

---

[15] For a recent and encompassing overview of these concepts see Ferree et al. (2002), Chapter 10.

operate simultaneously as insiders and outsiders.[16] The nongovernmental sector could be seen as well positioned to generate, organize, and professionalize such problem-solving communities. Yet whereas participatory theories emphasize organizational inclusion and empowerment in and through the public sphere, they give less attention to the settings and conditions for communication. Critics have pointed out that participatory theories neglect the actual forms in which communities assemble and the exclusion processes inherent in hierarchical communication structures.

Discursive or deliberative theories, by contrast, specifically highlight the communication practices and conditions that enable debate. Discursive theories ask what helps citizens "sort out self-interested claims from public-spirited ones" (Gutmann and Thompson 1996: 43; see also Mutz 2006; Gastil 2008). For our purpose, they help focus attention on the internal communication structure and the discursive forms in which NGOs seek to generate or contribute to publics. Deliberative theorists, such as Jürgen Habermas, insist on the relevance of debate formats in which citizens can achieve consensus based on rationality, reciprocity, respect for other arguments, and truthfulness. Hence, according to the discursive model of the public sphere, NGOs need to adhere to deliberative processes that guarantee open access and achieve argumentative closure by employing those norms.

Constructivists, although they share an emphasis on discursive practices, are skeptical about the possibilities of achieving consensus and reaching closure in public debates. Moreover, they dispute Habermas's claim that there is and, even more importantly, that there should be ultimately only one public sphere. They point, for example, to feminist counter- or subpublics that have generated voice and advocacy from relatively powerless positions on the margins of a masculinist public sphere (Benhabib 1992; Fraser 1992; Young 2000). "Subaltern counterpublics [construct] parallel discursive arenas where members of subordinated social groups invent and circulate counterdiscourses to formulate oppositional interpretations of their identities, interests, and needs" (Fraser 1992: 123). These groups' identity hinges specifically on *not*

---

[16] Workplace participation, for example, combines the public display of workers' expertise and voice with internal negotiations (Bachrach and Botwinick 1992). Other participatory forms, such as town halls, range in scope from advisory bodies to actually providing the forum for self-governing of communities (Mansbridge 1983).

having a large and consistent voice in dominant media discourses, on *not* seeking consensus and fast closure of a debate. Instead, through their organizational capacity, they provide "structural solutions to the problem of marginal communication" (Herbst 1996: 125).

At the same time, dominant forms of communication frequently silence other voices by setting standards of dispassionate, rational discourse attuned to a bourgeois habitus. Constructivism challenges these theories of the public sphere to rethink the artificially drawn boundaries of the public and private, as well as the fencing off of the political sphere against all those who are not part of the institutional political system. Marginalized groups, in particular, are seen as providing specific voices that institutions frequently refuse to hear and media do not report, and that therefore politics neglects to take into account.

NGOS AND THE PUBLIC SPHERE

A constructivist model of the public sphere, I submit, might be best equipped to provide analytical tools for assessing the role of NGOs in late modern publics. Constructivism positions NGOs not just at the margins of an established and mass-media-dominated public sphere, but acknowledges that NGOs and their networks might form subpublics or issue publics that act to some degree independently of dominant media, and make strategic decisions as to when and how they engage with the debates in other publics. I use the terms subpublic and issue public interchangeably, as they both reference "a communication and networking process in which various actors come together in defining an issue and establishing a configuration of actors connected to that issue" (Bennett, Lang, and Segerberg 2013). Moreover, a constructivist model of the public sphere awards legitimacy to NGO advocacy on grounds not only of expertise but also of engagement with uncrystallized interests at the margins of society that might, or might not, adhere to conventional repertoires of public expression. By taking into account forms of advocacy that run counter to dispassionate rational discourse, constructivism provides recognition of multiple forms and venues of expression. It recognizes Greenpeace's acts of civil disobedience just as much as human rights NGOs negotiating at the United Nations. Hence, a constructivist theory of the public sphere enables analysis of the conditions under which NGOs do or do not operate as (1) central communicative actors within mostly non-mass-mediated subpublics that (2) provide an organizational context for citizen voice and thus organize the "publicness" of civic concerns by (3) directing advocacy at different levels of the political or economic system via (4) discursive and nondiscursive means of expression.

NGOs Avoiding the Public

Although I propose that we treat NGOs essentially as public actors, some caveats are in order. One, there are associations that do not even aspire to contribute to public deliberation and advocacy because they see their mission in arenas other than organizing voice and influencing policy, such as service provision, entertainment, or mere socializing. Such NGOs might attain "publicness," for example, if they engage their constituents in debate about their mission or if they are challenged from the outside, but for the most part they do not actively seek it. Two, there are associations that shun public voice because of fear of appearing "too political" or "too polarizing." In effect, they discourage what Nina Eliasoph in her study of associational cultures has called "frontstage" public communication (Eliasoph 1998): communication that employs more generalized, political, and principled talk. Eliasoph cites the story of Charles, an African American member of the Parent League and local NAACP representative, who wants to activate fellow parents to deal with a teacher who used racially disparaging language. Yet instead of investigating the issue, his fellow Parent League members divert attention by stating in different iterations that the incident should go "through the proper channels" (Eliasoph 1996: 276). Members of the group are hesitant to connect the issue to a larger problem and to discuss its implications for the group and beyond. In fact, they attempt to turn it over to other "channels," clearly not conceiving of themselves as an adequate public body to address it. Moreover, throughout the discussion, Charles gets the impression that he is too political and does not use the proper meaning-making rhetoric in the group. In sum, this voluntary parent association suppresses public deliberation rather than nurturing it. Eliasoph illustrates "how people can create a sense of 'the public' that paradoxically shrinks their own meaning-making powers" (276). The public, so to speak, is forcefully placed elsewhere, even though the Parent League clearly has a public communication mission. In Eliasoph's analysis, this case "shows a paradoxical situation, in which committed, concerned citizens tried to do good precisely by hushing public-spirited conversation in public" (276).

She continues,

Thus, rejecting abstract, political, or principled talk was, paradoxically, volunteers' way of looking out for the common good. Volunteers assumed that if they want to show each other and their neighbors that regular citizens really can be effective, they should avoid issues that they considered "political." In their effort to be open and inclusive, to appeal to regular, unpretentious fellow citizens without discouraging them, they silenced public-spirited deliberation – which was just what someone like Charles thought the group needed to have in order to involve new members. This creation of "the public," this civic practice, itself dissipated the public spirit from public settings. (Eliasoph 1996: 279; see also Eliasoph 1998: 63)

If the public spirit of associations is so fragile, then what are the conditions under which associations develop public voice and advocacy? Or, to rephrase Thomas Risse, how do we know an associational public when we see one (Risse 2010)? This, as pointed out earlier, is a different question than probing the policy influence or issue salience of NGO politics. It focuses less on outcome than on modes of communication and strategies that enable public debate. Before we turn to the next chapters for a closer exploration of the actual conditions that constitute, shape, and limit NGO voice today, I end this discussion by proposing a conceptual framework for analyzing NGO publics that is anchored in their communication practices.

Communication Repertoires of NGOs

On the most general level, we can assume that a public exists if actors communicate about the same issue, at the same time, using similar frames (see Habermas 1998: 160; Bennett 2009). If Oxfam UK and SHRO, the Sudan Human Rights Organization, both publicly criticize the politics of the Sudanese government and employ a genocide frame, they would analytically qualify as a public. At the same time, the minimal requirements of this definition could be met with a single press release by each organization during the same time period. Hence, attention to the specifics of communication practices is required. To gauge the actual strength of an associational public, a more fine-grained set of quantitative and qualitative data is needed that assesses (1) the actual *density* of communicative ties, that is how often an issue is being communicated about at the same time using similar frames; (2) the *modes* of communication, that is whether the debate takes place primarily within the organization, between organizations, or also between organizations and nonmember

**Communication modes
of associations** ⟶ **and their targets**

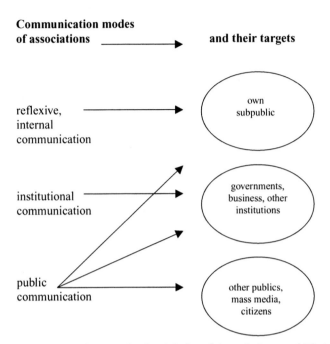

FIGURE 2.1. Communication Modes of Associations and Their Targets.

citizens, and (3) the *target* of communication, that is who the public debate is directed at and specifically whether the task involves mobilizing and enabling citizens for action.

NGOs are continuously involved in scaled modes of communication (see Fig. 2.1). An NGO might primarily communicate with its members – I refer to this mode as the practice of *internal* or *reflexive communication*. It might communicate directly with institutions or organizations that it is trying to influence, for example by offering expertise or consultation or contesting information and thus engaging in what I refer to as *institutional communication*. Finally, it might use means of communication to engage in *public communication* practices to gain support from a wider array of citizens and to engage with those who are not part of their subpublic.

These modes of communication are by no means exclusive; in fact, civic activists tend to utilize them simultaneously. Yet from a public sphere viewpoint, they are not all equally "loud" and visible and not all equally inclusive. Even within these communication modes, NGOs make choices as to the degree of publicness that a communication will gain. Communicating within one's subpublic might take place in rather closed communication circuits, such as in chapter meetings of member organizations. Or it might take place via blogs or Twitterstreams that are, in principle, accessible to others and maybe even posted to encourage wider debate. The institutionalized communication circuits of expert publics with their targets tend, for the most part, to be closed to others and often strategically even avoid going public because of possible repercussions. Yet, at times, if an NGO takes the expert's seat in institutional hearings, its communication officer might invite other NGO representatives or the media into the audience. In contrast, public communication modes by default involve broader outreach into untapped segments of an NGO's constituency and beyond. Hence, they tend to put more emphasis on broad visibility of public messages. Public communication repertoires of NGOs can, but do not necessarily involve traditional mass media. New media, in particular, have to some degree displaced traditional mass media as the prime public communication means. Moreover, NGO publics with such dense communicative links do not rely on incorporating a wide array of voices within *one single* public sphere. Strong NGO publics can be small, removed from dominant discourses, and formed solely to "invent and circulate counterdiscourses to formulate oppositional interpretations of their identities, interests, and needs" (Fraser 1992: 123). Ultimately, it is the combined strength of these three modes of communication that accounts for strong NGO publics. If NGOs use exclusively reflexive and institutional communication repertoires, their legitimacy is in jeopardy.

CONCLUSION

The task of this chapter was twofold. First, it provided evidence and an explanation for the tendency to expunge the public sphere from civil society and in turn downsize the public sphere to a media public. Second, the argument recommended that we "write" the public sphere into conceptions of civil society and situate the nongovernmental sector squarely within that public sphere mode of civil society. For civil society to be more than an empty euphemism for a gentler, better world, it needs to be held accountable, not just to what norms it fosters and what kinds of association it promotes but also to what kinds of publics it generates. In contrast, not strengthening civil society in its public sphere mode creates a "a democratic time bomb" (Smismans 2006: 6) that breeds disappointment for those interested in meaningful associations, in citizen voice, and in seeing accountability and representativeness as outcomes of discursive interaction. Therefore, enhancing individualized social capital, which is the main civic engagement paradigm that currently informs community development policies across the world, is not an adequate response to strengthening anemic civil societies. At the same time, calls for the revival of associationalism miss the mark if they merely employ civil society as an arena in which declining state functions can be compensated for by activating citizens. The proliferation of voluntary associations "could easily advance parochial interests instead of serving democracy" (Tilly 2007: 86). It is only in the context of the debates within a public sphere that NGOs become accountable actors, able to engage citizens in public affairs.

Hence, assessing the role of the nongovernmental sector in the public sphere is not equivalent to measuring policy influence and outcome, and it is also not adequately captured by assessing their media presence. NGO publics have proliferated at the margins of, or sometimes even outside of, elite mass-media-driven public spheres. They use new means of communication that have the ability to connect members, supporters, and issues with greater frequency and depth, and possibly with a greater potential for activism than provided by traditional media. Density, modes, and targets of NGO communication have been identified as measurements that gauge how much an association contributes to civil society in its mode as a public sphere.

At the same time, not all NGOs are equally committed and strong enablers of publics. In the democratic tranformation literature, in particular, NGOs have recently acquired a reputation for turning into technocratic operatives and for actually contributing to the decline of public engagement.[17] In this view, NGOs have become neoliberal stand-ins for empire-building interests, shortchanging those who are invested in building strong civil societies. How then did the NGO sector come to be perceived as the equivalent of civil society, and what are the implications for its role in the public sphere?

---

[17] See the debates in the Uganda NGO Forum at http://ngoforum.or.ug (accessed February 1, 2012).

3

The NGOization of Civil Society

> Witness the tragedy that has befallen the proponents of the concept ["civil society"]: people struggling against authoritarian regimes had demanded civil society; what they got instead were NGOs.
>
> Neera Chandhoke 2003: 9

In 2006, the U.S.-based Kettering Foundation commissioned a study from the Harwood Institute for Public Innovation to assess how "public-oriented" advocacy organizations operate.[1] The results are addressed in more detail later, yet Harwood's summary can serve as a guidepost for this chapter. It asserts that advocacy-oriented NGOs "find themselves enveloped in a profound and airtight gestalt of inwardness, planning, and professionalism" (Harwood Institute for Public Innovation 2009: 4); in other words, "nongovernmental institutions are being colonized by governmental ways of doing business" (21). NGO advocacy, according to this study, is shaped primarily by inner-organizational processes and, more specifically, by a Weberian-style rationalization of bureaucratic power. In their efforts to secure organizational reproduction, NGOs are compelled to streamline and minimize input from external constituencies other than through donations. As a result, engaging with publics and channeling their voices become increasingly difficult tasks.

This somber assessment casts doubts on the widely shared assumption that the nongovernmental sector is an overall effective public voice

---

[1] The report is based on a two-year, participant observation relationship between the Research Institute and ten NGOs with an intermediary or advocacy role (Harwood Institute 2009).

of citizens' concerns, as well as an increasingly powerful counterpart of the neoliberal state. In 1992, the British Westminster Foundation for Democracy, established by the Blair government to strengthen democracy in development aid, asserted, "NGOs play a key role in creating civil society. Their focus on mobilizing resources, providing services, undertaking research and public education, while also providing advocacy for membership organizations and people's associations, gives NGOs an unparalleled liaison role between civil society and government" (cited in Henderson 2003: 74). In the past two decades, researchers have produced a wealth of research that depicts NGOs as being "facilitators" (Warkentin 2001: 4) or "harbingers" (Minnix 2007) of civil societies, laud NGOs as civil society's most important and defining actors (Gosewinkel et al. 2003: 33), or apodictically argue that NGOs simply *are* the carriers of a transnational or global civil society (Gellner 1994; Lane 2008). Within European Union institutions, as I discuss in Chapter 6, NGOs are seen as prima facie expressions of a vibrant civil society (EU Commission 2002), as hubs for civic engagement, and as central voices in European multi-level governance. A similar NGO-constructed civil society appears in the workings and documents of the United Nations and its agencies.[2] To some degree, the equation of civil society with NGOs is actively co-produced by NGOs in need for legitimacy. NGO representatives "typically argue that they represent the collective interests of the general public and underrepresented groups" (Jenkins 2006: 307). It is obvious, however, that a set of normative and prescriptive assumptions inherent in this equation are quite problematic. As early as 1997, Shelley Feldman dissected attempts to "conflate NGOs with civil society" (Feldman 1997: 64) and asserted that constructing NGOs as the sole proprietors of civil society might not do justice to the complex relationship between the two entities. In Feldman's account, this uncritical equation ignores the facts that (1) there can be oppositional relationships between NGOs and civil society, (2) there are civic interests not represented by NGOs, and (3) many NGOs have become part of a neoliberal service sector of state-devoluted activity and could be thus seen as part of an extended state (65). Feldman's critique points to the structural position of NGOs vis-à-vis states, markets, and society and to the importance of analyzing the ties that bind organizations

---

[2] Sarah Henderson cites numerous cases that exemplify this equation. The World Bank, for example, in 1995 renamed its NGO liaison officers "civil society specialists;" the United Nation's Development Program followed suit in 1996, changing the name of its NGO Unit to the "Civil Society and Participation Unit" (Henderson 2003: 67).

to these sectors. Following these early clues, research within international relations, development, and comparative politics has identified an array of problematic assumptions about the nongovernmental sector, culminating in Paul Wapner's assessment after reviewing the literature on NGOs in 2007:

> Today, the discipline's love affair with nonstate actors is starting to wane. Scholars are realizing that most nonstate actors are not what they seem to be. Rather than being progressive agents of change that are animated by altruism, nonstate actors span the political spectrum and, in terms of their engagements, are much like other political actors. They are self-interested entities engaged in advancing their own agendas... often non-democratic, hierarchical groups concerned with their financial and publicly perceived longevity. (Wapner 2007: 85)

In short: The worlds of research and politics have become somewhat disillusioned with NGOs.

Yet rather than bemoaning the end of a "love affair" and turning this disappointment into a diagnosis of the sector's outright failure, we need to situate NGOs within the constraints and opportunities that shape their actions. Neither normative extreme – lifting NGOs onto the civic pedestal as the sole torch bearer of civil society or identifying them as mere pseudo-governmental agencies, in essence firms clad in altruistic cloaks – does justice to the sector's achievements nor to the systemic constraints that inform its norms, strategies, and actions. The approach developed here, by contrast, wants to shed light on the conditions that influence NGOs' organizational structure and in particular on the relationship between governance, organizational properties, and advocacy. To reiterate the theoretical frame established in Chapter 1, governance conditions are shaped both by formal constraints, such as regulations and laws, and by informal constraints, such as norms and conventions regarding access, behavior, and speech (see also North 1990: 4). These constraints, in turn, positively or negatively sanction certain forms of advocacy that NGOs might employ. To better grasp the set of formal and informal conditions that influence NGO advocacy, this chapter introduces a theorem called *NGOization* of civil society.

The NGOization of civil society (Lang 1997) marks a shift from rather loosely organized, horizontally dispersed, and broadly mobilizing social movements to more professionalized, vertically structured NGOs. This shift not only has lasting effects for mission, goals, management, and discourse cultures of civic actors but it also influences advocacy strategies and ultimately the properties of the publics that NGOs seek out or try to generate. The concept of NGOization has been employed to capture civil society conditions in such different political contexts as Germany (Lang 1997), post-Yugoslavia (Bagić 2006), Croatia (Stubbs 2007), Russia (Aksartova 2009), Romania (Grunberg 2000), Latin America (Alvarez 1999), Nicaragua (Borchgrevink 2006), Israel (Herzog 2008), and Palestine (Smith 2007).[3] Although I believe there is a rationale for why the concept has resonated more in states that are enmeshed in various democratization struggles,[4] I do make a case for its relevance in Western societies as well. The argument proceeds in three steps. First, I introduce the concept of an "NGOized" civil society and explore conditions for its emergence. In this context, I also engage with the predominant organizational frame employed by social movement research – the social movement organization (SMO) – and address some limits of the SMO frame for the study of civic organizational change. Second, I present evidence and examples of NGOization. Finally, I spell out the implications of civil society becoming "NGOized" by focusing on three developments: the turn from publicity to public relations, the change in symbolic resources that trade activism for advocacy, and the emergence of accountability questions.

WHAT IS NGOIZATION?

NGOization is perhaps best considered to be a "sensitizing concept . . . an idea that suggests directions along which to look" (Blumer 1954: 7) when we are trying to understand early 21st-century civil societies and their advocacy cultures.[5] It refers to the process by which social movements

---

3 Whereas early NGOization research put more emphasis on government-induced pulls for NGOs to professionalize and institutionalize, new analyses based in the global South, in particular, tend to conceptualize NGOization more in terms of a neocolonial and externally induced mechanism by foreign donors – and consequently try to identify conditions in which activists move "beyond NGOization" (Alvarez 2009).

4 First, civil society actors during political transformation processes might be more sensitive to matters of co-optation or, in more subtle iterations, to a reframing and containment of radical messages within an omnipresent state. Second, until very recently, much of European as well as U.S. academic debate seemed split in half with little connective tissue in-between: Social movement scholars, by default, used the "social movement organization" frame for all organized groups; nonprofit scholarship, in turn, rarely connected the organizational form of NGOs to issues of broader social change.

5 Blumer distinguished sensitizing concepts from definitive concepts that refer "precisely to what is common to a class of objects, by the aid of a clear definition in terms of attributes or fixed benchmarks. . . . A sensitizing concept lacks such specifications of attributes or benchmarks and consequently it does not enable the user to move directly to the instance and its relevant content. Instead, it gives the user a general sense of reference and guidance

professionalize, institutionalize, and bureaucratize in vertically structured, policy-outcome–oriented organizations that focus on generating issue-specific and, to some degree, marketable expert knowledge or services. Emphasis is placed on organizational reproduction and on the cultivation of funding sources. It frequently results in increased recognition and insider status in NGOs' issue-specific policy circles. One effect might be the containment and reframing of more radical messages; another effect might be an orientation toward institutional advocacy and away from public displays of dissent. Large transnational networks, just like smaller community or grassroots groups, experience the pull to consolidate, incorporate, and "behave" as NGOs in order to be treated as legitimate players by donors, business, or in governance contexts. The resulting organizational forms might vary: The large transnational movement might create an umbrella NGO with networks of members and affiliates, and the small local initiative might incorporate with a formal legal status but with very few resources. Yet in effect both are being pulled, even though with varying incentives, in the direction of professionalization, institutionalization, and bureaucratization. The pull to NGOize is created by various incentives: economic – funders demand accountability; social and career based – civic actors want salaries and other forms of adequate compensation to reflect their often substantial time commitment; legal-bureaucratic – states convey a tax-exempt charity status based on specific forms of registration; and political – formal organizations have more consistent credibility with political actors and the media than do loose associations, and invitations to sit at government tables come more frequently today than even two decades ago.

In the process of exploring what fuels NGOization, three caveats are in order. First, NGOization is treated as a likely, but not inevitable stipulation of civic life in the early 21st century. Unlike the concepts of resource mobilization or political opportunity structure that have long been cornerstones of social movement studies, I do not consider NGOization to be or become the centerpiece of a theory of either social movements or the public sphere. It is a sensitizing and process-tracing concept that enables us to pinpoint conditions that affect the public roles of many NGOs from the local to the global level. Thus, the idea owes more

---

in approaching empirical instances. Whereas definitive concepts provide prescriptions of what to see, sensitizing concepts merely suggest directions along which to look" (Blumer 1954: 7).

to Bourdieu and Garfinkel than to more strictly predictive theories in the social sciences. NGOization describes a culturally and politically mutable tendency rather than a narrowly confined path. Because it is mutable, it might have different iterations and be fueled by different processes in different global or local constellations.

Second, NGOization is not a tightly defined process of the sort that McAdam, Tarrow, and Tilly (2001: 11) describe as a "mechanism," in the strict sense of a "delimited class of events that alter relations among specified elements in identical or closely similar ways over a variety of situations." Rather than a locked-in mechanism, I consider NGOization to be a strong, albeit contingent linkage between macro-level factors and organizational choice that draws on organizational theory, neo-institutionalism, and social movement theory. Thus, it captures a process that plays out to different degrees, in different political and cultural contexts, and among differently situated civic groups. Some civic groups defy NGOization (e.g., Incite 2007) or surpass it (Alvarez 2009). Others, like Greenpeace, counter the effects of NGOization by keeping an explicit commitment to, and getting from their supporters a mandate for, public advocacy. Still other highly professionalized and hierarchically structured organizations are able to capitalize on organizational density to orchestrate an occasionally highly visible public advocacy event, such as the AFL-CIO did during the Seattle WTO protests in 1999. Yet zooming in on such peak groups or events fails to tell a more common narrative of organizational reproduction with a focus on institutional advocacy.

Avoiding a mechanical image of NGOization suggests a third distinguishing quality of this approach: It cautions against perceiving NGOs as somehow uniform and without distinct organizational properties or varied strategic repertoires. Clearly, a number of factors influence NGO advocacy, such as size, legacy of the organizational culture, target, and available repertoires for action. Some groups, for example, rely more on web-based means of communication (Bennett 2002), offering a different array of public information and engagement tools for constituencies than more traditional member organizations that tend to rely primarily on local and regional chapters for communication. In fact, the Internet has been hailed in the past decade as a revolutionary technology to bolster existing publics and create new ones based in the virtual worlds of blogospheres and web 2.0. "New forms of organizations [practice] increasing cooperation between social activist 'outsiders' and 'insider' NGO advocates producing hybrid forms of activism and organization" (Tarrow 2005: 210). Although I do argue (in Chapters 6 and 7) that new communication technologies indeed provide NGOs with much more flexible and activist repertoires to practice advocacy and engage publics, I submit that the fallout from "acting like an NGO" (i.e., establishing and sustaining a professionally staffed, institutionally durable and credible, and bureaucratized organization) influences the core of decision: making about which kind of advocacy strategies and tools are employed to advance contested issues.

Keeping these caveats in mind, the frame of NGOization should not be employed to rekindle debate about an iron law of (non)organizing in social movements. Whereas Piven and Cloward saw formal and hierarchical organizations as antithetical to large-scale and effective mobilization (Cloward and Piven 1984), there is by now plenty of evidence that organizations can mobilize quite effectively and do so with broad engagement tools (i.e., Clemens and Minkoff 2004). One strength of the NGOization frame is that it connects mobilization and engagement repertoires with organizational properties. In other words, it attempts to clarify both the conditions that enable organizations to reach out to publics and the constraints that caution against too loud or too strong public displays. Moreover, advocacy strategies typically involve a subtle "political etiquette" (Eliasoph 1998), and the NGOization frame asks what informs this political etiquette. Hence, the concept of NGOization sensitizes us in particular to managed mobilizations, that is to NGOs deploying acts of publicness without yielding too much voice to constituents and larger publics.

The social movement literature has established the concept of social movement *organizations* (SMO) to capture organized structures within movements (McCarthy and Zald 1987; Lofland 1996; Zald and McCarthy 1997; Caniglia and Carmin 2005; Minkoff and McCarthy 2005). In order to be able to identify the material properties of NGO-ization in more detail, we need to elaborate on distinguishing features of SMOs and NGOs and determine indicators that warrant classification of organizations as one or the other.

SOCIAL MOVEMENT ORGANIZATIONS AND NGOS

Following Deborah Minkoff's definition, I understand a social movement to be any collective effort to change the social structure that uses extra-institutional methods at least some of the time (Minkoff 1997: 780). SMOs then are the organized parts of such collectives. They are organizations that attempt to implement movement goals (780). As early as the mid-1980s, debate among social movement scholars ensued when McCarthy and Zald promoted the idea that the social movements of the 1960s and 1970s were successful only because a new form of social movement organization had installed itself at the core of their operations (McCarthy and Zald 1987).[6] Although McCarthy and Zald viewed professionalization as a central precondition for the success of new social movements and made it a cornerstone of resource mobilization theory, others emphasized the negative impact of elites controlling grassroots movements and the mutations of message and repertoire as a consequence of elite patronage and professionalism. Proponents of SMOs countered this argument by emphasizing that favorable elite intervention granted legitimacy to movement goals and provided the technical base on which to mount legal challenges (Jenkins and Eckert 1986), thereby fostering movement success. Policy success, however, is not the focus of this book, but rather how the organizational properties of civic actors affect the capacity and willingness to create and sustain public dialogue and to employ public advocacy. Assuming that SMO and NGO properties can be distinguished, we can then stipulate that the process by which more movement-oriented groups turn into or are replaced by more professionalized and effectiveness-oriented groups makes a difference for strategies of public advocacy and outreach.

Table 3.1, adapted and modified from Rothschild and Whitt (1986), captures ideal-type differences between SMOs and NGOs. In a nutshell, NGOization means for social movements and their organizations that (1) authority moves from the collective into individuals; (2) charters and legal frameworks bind more than substantive ethics of the organization; (3) cooperation gives way to more delegation and control; (4) personal trust is replaced to a degree by instrumental relations; (5) recruitment takes place with an eye on competence rather than shared values; (6) salaries tend to trump normative and solidarity-based incentives; (7) horizontal stratification is replaced by hierarchical stratification; and finally (8) the organization moves from the minimal division of labor into a system with a strong division of labor.

To be clear, these juxtapositions do not indicate strict properties, but ideal-type categorizations that will hardly ever appear in the pure form that the table suggests. NGOization being a process, some organizations exhibit traits of both an SMO and an NGO. Moreover, some NGOized

---

[6] For social movement research's response to the SMO theory, see for example Jenkins and Eckert (1986) and Minkoff and McCarthy (2005).

TABLE 3.1. *Ideal-Type Differences between SMOs and NGOs*

Dimensions	SMO	NGO
Authority	Authority resides in the collectivity as a whole; it is delegated, if at all, only temporarily and is subject to recall. Compliance is to the consensus of the collective, which is always fluid and open to negotiation.	Authority resides in individuals by virtue of incumbency in office and/or expertise; there is hierarchical organization of offices. Compliance is to universal fixed rules as implemented by office incumbents.
Rules	Minimal stipulated rules; primacy of ad hoc, individual, or collective decisions; some calculability possible on the basis of shared substantive ethics.	Formalization of fixed and universal rules; calculability and appeal of decisions on the basis of correspondence to the formal, written charter.
Social Control	Social controls are primarily based on personalistic or moralistic appeals and the selection of homogeneous personnel.	Organizational behavior is subject to social control primarily through direct supervision or standardized rules and sanctions, secondarily through the selection of homogeneous personnel, especially at top levels.
Social Relations	Ideal of community; relations are to be holistic, personal, of value in themselves.	Ideals of impersonality; relations are to be role-based, segmental, and instrumental.
Recruitment and Advancement	Employment based on friends, social-political values, personality attributes, and informally assessed knowledge and skills. Concept of career advancement not meaningful; no hierarchy of positions.	Employment based on specialized training and formal certification. Employment constitutes a career; advancement based on seniority or achievement.
Incentive Structure	Normative and solidarity incentives are primary; material incentives are secondary.	Material incentives compete with normative and solidarity-focused incentives.

Dimensions	SMO	NGO
Social Stratifications	Egalitarian; reward differentials, if any, are strictly limited by the collectivity.	Isomorphic distribution of prestige, privilege, and power (i.e., differential rewards by office); hierarchy justifies inequality.
Differentiation	Minimal division of labor: Administration is combined with performance tasks; division between intellectual and manual work is reduced. Generalization of job functions; holistic roles. Demystification of expertise; ideal of the engaged amateur.	Maximal division of labor; dichotomy between intellectual work and manual work and between administrative tasks and performance tasks. Maximal specialization of jobs and functions; segmental roles. Technical expertise is exclusively held: ideal of the specialist-expert.

Source: Adapted with modifications from Rothschild and Whitt (1986: 62).

organizations might decide that the strategic paths they embarked on are not adequately reflecting their membership or goals and might move in the direction of movement organizing. As a general trend, however, many organizations that in the 1970s and 1980s served as carriers of social movements with an SMO profile have since developed a stronger NGOized footprint. The *NAACP*, for example, historically a central SMO for the U.S. civil rights movement, today embodies more properties of an NGO. Jenkins and Eckert show, in their study on African American SMOs, how professionalization and elite patronage have shaped these organizations and in effect contributed to their demobilization. Without sustained indigenous mobilization, they argue, excluded groups cannot count on professionalized organizations to advance their interests (Jenkins and Eckert 1986: 825).

Other SMOs try hard to avoid any resemblance to being an NGO. The French-rooted and European-based SMO Attac, for example, is adamant about not turning into a hierarchical organization that lacks a vibrant constituency. In the words of Christophe Ventura, Attac's international office secretary, "Attac is really *not*[7] a nongovernmental organization, or NGO. The big difference between an NGO and us is that we are an

---

7 Emphasis added.

organization with a real base. We are not a club of researchers or activists. We are a civic movement" (cited in Ancelovici 2002: 440). Just like the Harwood study mentioned earlier, Ventura articulates the features of an inward orientation and lack of a constituency base as critical differences between Attac and an NGO. He portrays Attac as an outward-oriented movement whose members are not part of an exclusive club, but who intend to make their voices heard and mobilize publicly for their change agenda.

Some NGOs might even externalize part of their public advocacy by participating in movement organizations. The Attac Germany membership base, for example, includes large NGOs like *World Vision* Germany. World Vision is a Christian relief organization focusing on children and poverty. In its self-presentation and in its campaigns, there is no equivalent to the voice of social justice, protest, and resistance that Attac uses. Being part of Attac might allow the German chapter of World Vision to "outsource" voice and advocacy efforts that its board of directors would not deem appropriate for the image of World Vision itself.

In other scenarios, movements cooperate with NGOs and thus, to some degree, externalize the demands for a professionalized and media-savvy presentation of their campaigns. For example, the Mexican Zapatista movement was successful in persuading international NGOs such as Human Rights Watch to carry their message (Bob 2005). Human Rights Watch, in turn, leveraged its professionalized advocacy expertise to enhance its own activist advocacy profile.

In effect, civil societies host multifaceted civic organizations and alliances, among them SMO/NGO hybrids as well as NGO-movement cooperations. The argument here is not intended to deny existing diversity, but rather to sensitize the reader to an aspect of organizational change that is poorly understood: The push-and-pull factors by which specific properties of NGOs disincentivize certain kinds of publicness. This is not equivalent to claiming that NGOs "sell out" or are doomed to marginalization. In fact, there is certainly evidence that, for example, the relocation of the U.S. women's movement organizations "inside the beltway" has led to greater institutional legitimacy, getting former "outsider issues" on the congressional agenda (Disney and Gelb 2001: 66; also Banaszak 2010). Hence, NGOization might in fact increase policy success at the expense of generating viable publics.

The three central developments that signal the onset of NGOization are professionalization, institutionalization, and bureaucratization – and these in turn shape the advocacy repertoire of civil society actors.

I consider each separately and then analyze the effects they have on public voice.

PROFESSIONALIZATION

According to German sociologist Max Weber, professionalization, like bureaucratization, is an aspect of the rationalization of modern society (Weber 1947). In an abstract sense, it signifies the authority of institutionalized expertise over the authority of other claims, be they coercive or moral in nature. Through this authority of institutionalized expertise, NGOs have advanced from being suspicious outsiders to government to being frequently welcomed at negotiation tables and in institutional decision-making settings (i.e., Clemens 2006). NGOs have not just learned to voice their claims in the language of knowledge producers, but they have also successfully bolstered their organizations with the resources needed to make well-founded, thoroughly documented claims that are sought out by governments. Susanne Zwingel, in her study on CEDAW (UN Convention on the Elimination of Discrimination Against Women), identifies these nongovernmental experts as "crucial to enhance [the] learning processes of state actors" (Zwingel 2005: 56). The authors of *The 21st Century NGO*, likewise, attribute "well advanced professionalization" to NGOs in the Northern hemisphere and an "early stage" professionalization to those in the global South (SustainAbility 2003: 14). It is primarily in their function as professional experts that NGOs gain public and institutional recognition.

Professionalization started in NGOs that primarily provided services and were well positioned to be incorporated into new public management initiatives in the 1990s (Anheier 2009: 1084). Yet in recent years we see a second wave of professionalization, primarily among advocacy NGOs. Elisabeth Clemens (1997) analyzed how the adoption of more structured organization features enhances coordination, serves to decrease external criticism, and in turn increases legitimacy (see also Caniglia and Carmin 2005). Organizations learn to streamline their operations, establish hierarchical structures, and increase their salaried employee base. Overall, the NGO sector today accounts for about 6 percent of employment in OECD countries (Anheier 2009: 1082) and 9.7 percent of the workforce in the United States (Wing et al. 2008: 14). Such economic and social success depends on, and in turn reinforces, the establishment of businesslike operations with a professional work ethic at the core.

The professionalization of the NGO sector alters organizations and individuals alike. Organizational development is geared toward maximizing resources and toward increases in the number of salaried employees and in fundraising activities. A stronger division of labor and the turn toward more hierarchical structures support these goals. In terms of individual agency, by contrast, professionalization can be seen as a habitus – that is as a set of co-produced dispositions that generate practices and perceptions of NGO members (Bourdieu and Wacquant 1992: 53). Professionalized NGO workers have shed a persistent image, anecdotally reinforced in many policy contexts, that stereotypes them as Birkenstock-clad norm entrepreneurs trained in "being demanding, impatient, stubborn, and overly aggressive on their single issue" (McDonald 2004: xiii). This is not to say that the more professional habitus keeps NGO workers from being creative, innovative, or idealistic. Yet the habitus confines these traits "within the limits of its structures, which are embodied sedimentation of the social structures which produced it" (Wacquant 1992: 19; also Hopgood 2006: 217). In other words, professionalization, while promising policy success, demands adaptation to institutional norms and structures as well as to a policy field's language and terms of trade.

By contrast, there is evidence that in civil societies that lack professionalization, policy influence of NGOs is low. A case in point is Japan. In his study on Japanese civil society, Robert Pekkanen shows how a rather active, but merely locally organized and volunteer-based civil society lacks the means to exercise institutional influence and ultimately forfeits political power (Pekkanen 2006). The "relative lack of professionalization of Japan's civil society organizations" (33) does not mean that its civil society is small. Yet it fosters dense local volunteer networks at the expense of professional advocacy. Thus, even a high density of local organizations cannot make up for organizational professionalism and continuity, provided by paid full-time staffers and by division of labor. The pull to professionalize, Pekkanen concludes, is directly related to institutional influence, because "not just formation and development of social movements, but institutionalization of these movements into organization is a key variable that affects the development of civil society" (167). The pull to NGOize, then, is reflected in the kinds of institutionalization processes that civil societies encounter.

INSTITUTIONALIZATION

Institutionalization is the second component of NGOization. Institutionalization of movements can appear in three related contexts:

(1) organizations' need to build durable institutions, (2) the political opportunities to participate in institutional settings of government, and (3) movement actors having inside careers in government agencies.

In its first, "inner-organizational" meaning, institutionalization encompasses all attempts to stabilize an organization. It refers to organizations' development of consistent norms, functions, and routines so as to secure their survival. The decision-making process becomes a fixed set of steps laid down in a charter, routines for repetitive actions become engrained through institutional learning, and measures are taken to guarantee that the survival of the organization does not depend on the presence of specific individuals. Institutionalized movements pay more attention to resources and to internal organization-building, leading some movement scholars to argue that investing in new organizations may direct resources away from protests (Piven and Cloward 1984; Koopmans 1993) or increase interorganizational competition (Tarrow 1994; Minkoff 1997). Organization-building also contributes to NGOs' openness to interact with government. In effect, "the higher the degree of organization of civil society actors, the greater is the likelihood of their behaving co-operatively towards the state and international organizations" (Take 1999: 19).

The second meaning of institutionalization refers to the political opportunities created by shifts from government to governance. From the local to the transnational level, NGOs increasingly are being invited to participate in institutional settings such as formal and informal consultations or expert commissions. NGOs take part in parallel conferences to UN meetings, they testify at legislative hearings on the national level, and they sit on municipal boards and commissions. There tend to be rewards for this kind of institutionalization: An organization's reputation can be enhanced by being visible institutionally; its members typically feel recognized and validated by decision makers; and there tends to be increased policy success associated with overt institutional voice, providing organizations with enhanced legitimacy to speak for certain claims. At the same time, sitting at the table increases the pull to adjust agendas from what is considered to be right to what is considered to be feasible; advocacy thus tends to refrain from taking more principled positions and instead concentrates on the appropriate means to move one step further toward any given end.

In a third iteration, institutionalization can mean that movement supporters trade outsider for insider status and enter career tracks in political institutions. In the process of becoming government insiders, they still tend to share movement goals and support movement agendas, thus helping "institutionalize" that agenda in the inner circuits of political decision making. In gender politics, for example, the term "femocrats" refers to those feminist activists who get jobs within the state and thus carry movement goals into institutions or adopt feminist movement goals during their careers (Kantola and Outshoorn 2007). Both Lee Ann Banaszak, in her study of the U.S. women's movement inside the federal government (Banaszak 2010), and John Skrentny, who analyzed the institutionalization of the civil rights struggle in the 1970s as a successful "march through the institutions" (Skrentny 2003), emphasize the relevance of institutional insiders who push for social change.

Institutionalization thus provides continuity, proximity to governance arenas, and partial insider status to civil actors. In all three iterations, institutionalization advances movement goals and enhances political influence. At the same time, it has been argued that in this process, movements "often adjust their goals in order to better fit their resource environments and survive" (Campbell 2005: 41; also Kriesi 1996). Yet just as importantly, movements and their organizations adjust strategies and tools to reach certain goals. NGOization as institutionalization thus contributes to a refocusing of *advocacy*; it redirects advocacy from public arenas into institutional advocacy venues that have been opened up by new governance modes and enhanced by institutional allies. In effect, altered forms of agency might alter an organization's engagement with its publics. And even though NGOs might be cognizant of this pull and make due effort not to let institutionalization suffocate public outreach, that pull is difficult to resist (i.e., Take 1999: 20).

BUREAUCRATIZATION

The third element of NGOization is the turn toward a more bureaucratic organization of movements. Just as with institutionalization, the process of bureaucratization "begins with environmental pressures" (Meyer and Brown 1977: 365). When welfare states decided to externalize substantial service provision to outside providers, social movement organizations were on the frontline of receivership of those contracts. This produced what McCarthy and Zald termed "bureaucratization of social discontent" (cited in Jenkins and Eckert 1986: 813) – meaning that social ruptures felt by poor and marginalized people became encapsulated and insulated in individualized caseworker files and administered largely through nonprofits that, in that process, bureaucratized their operations. However, service providers are not the only organizations to tend to develop bureaucratic structures. Advocacy organizations likewise are encouraged by their environment to bureaucratize their operations. They are expected by funders to establish formal accountability chains; by conveying charity status, tax authorities require detailed bookkeeping of financial transactions and internal monitoring of the "dos" and "don'ts" related to tax-exempt status (see Chapter 4). Civic organizations therefore feel pulled to instill predictability, functional hierarchies, and monitoring in their operations. The trade-offs may concern the terms of inclusion of constituencies and larger publics. Jenkins, in line with previous studies, argues that "bureaucratic structures provide technical expertise and coordination essential in institutional change efforts but are less effective at mobilizing 'grass roots' participation. Decentralized structures maximize personal transformation, thereby mobilizing 'grass roots' participation and ensuring group maintenance, but often at the cost of strategic effectiveness" (Jenkins 1983: 542).

Employing case study methods as well as large-scale aggregation, social movement and nonprofit researchers have substantiated the claim that "organizational survival hinge(s) on conformity to institutional conventions" (Minkoff and Powell 2006: 596). The cases that Minkoff and Powell present span such diverse organizations as large SMOs, neighborhood groups, feminist service agencies, and community-based AIDS organizations in the United States. Other studies have come to similar conclusions regarding the "adaptive pressures located in broader opportunity structures" of political institutions (Minkoff and McCarthy 2005: 291). In sum, incentives from "outside patrons" tend to "encourage routinization and professionalization" (Walker and McCarthy 2010: 319) and thus fuel NGOization.

If NGOization is induced to some degree by outside patrons through their funding requirements, then one of the prime incentives for SMOs to professionalize, institutionalize, and bureaucratize is to acquire legitimacy in the eyes of potential donors. We can also assume that, for most NGOs, increases in funding will in turn produce even stronger commitments to professionalization, institutionalization, and bureaucratization. Therefore, one strategy to uncover NGOization footprints is to examine the finances of organizations in civil society.

501(C)(3) TAX RETURNS IN THE UNITED STATES: CAPTURING NGOIZATION

I start with the hypothesis that the more the financial volume of an organization increases, the more professionalized and bureaucratic it will be compelled to become in order to run a stable operation. Hence, smaller organizations that double or triple their budget in a short period of time would need to make similar adjustments in the same direction (i.e., establishing more division of labor, increasing hierarchies, hiring more professional staff) as larger organizations that dramatically increase their revenue. Yet obtaining financial information directly from civic organizations tends to be difficult. A competitive environment generates an understandable reluctance to share details regarding donors, government-sponsored programs, or salaries. For the United States, however, it is possible to deliver "spot checks" of the footprint of NGOization. Every charitable organization with a 501c(3) status, receiving funds greater than 25,000 USD per year, is required to file Form I-990 with the Internal Revenue Service.[8] The tax returns of organizations filing I-990 forms are public records and have been made accessible through the Guidestar database.[9] To substantiate the claim that NGOization occurs across a wide range of organizations from the local to the national and global level, we examined the tax returns of a sample of 64 national, statewide, and local NGOs in the United States from 1998 to 2005.[10] For the national/global sample, we analyzed 34 of the 200 largest charities based in the United States as listed by *Forbes* magazine in 2005.[11] Additionally, we sampled the 10 largest national organizations in the areas of housing/urban development and women's issues. After excluding those organizations that did not provide full tax return information for each of the eight years, five organizations remained in each policy field. For the statewide sample, we took organizations based in Washington State

---

[8] This stipulation means that we could not access data of smaller neighborhood groups with a yearly income below 25,000 USD. Yet we provide clues in Chapter 6 that point to NGOization even among these smaller actors (see also Andrews et al. 2010).

[9] The Guidestar database can be accessed at http://www.guidestar.org. Being a relatively recent database, it is not fully comprehensive and thus provided constraints in the sampling procedure. Our sample is thus not representative: We consider the results it merely exploratory.

[10] This taxonomy is not related to outreach. A local organization might be engaged in a project in Asia or Latin America. It captures a primary support structure based on how organizations define their support base as local, regional, or national in scope.

[11] Because our interest is in public interest advocacy NGOs, we excluded from the Forbes 200 sample all purely professional organizations, hospitals, museums, libraries, and religious organizations. The remaining sample was checked in terms of availability of tax data on the Guidestar database. This led us to the present sample consisting of 34 organizations. For their support with data collection, coding, analysis, and presentation I owe special thanks to Elisabeth Lyons, Garrett Strain, Aspasia Bartell, Amanda Reynes, Henrike Knappe, and Elizabeth Zherka.

that were registered with the Global Washington initiative, which brands itself as a catalyst for development organizations based in the state.[12] We selected a random sample of 23 organizations and collected data from 6 state-based organizations whose tax returns were available in full over the same period from 1998 to 2005. For the local sample, we chose 10 housing and urban development NGOs in each of three U.S. cities[13] and collected data from 4 to 6 organizations in each city that had available all I-990 files for that same time period. Even though there is some debate about the accuracy of reporting and the saliency of filing categories (Krehely 2001), we understand tax documents to be one meta-level measure to assess financial conditions and organizational development of the NGO sector. For our sample of 64 NGOs, we extracted data on income, employment, fundraising, and lobbying.

Giving to nonprofits rose sharply through the 1990s. Even though "the subsequent downturn in the stock market tempered the rate of increases" (Berry and Arons 2003: 2), our data show that, even during harder economic times, the financial volume of 501(c)(3) organizations rose steadily, driven both by increasing government and foundation contributions and direct public support in the form of charitable donations. In fact, charitable giving in the United States dropped for the first time in the past two decades only in 2008, when it declined by 2 percent over the past year (Center on Philanthropy 2009). The 1998–2005 tax returns speak to something akin to "turbo-professionalization" from the local to the national and global level, showing organizations, on average, more than doubling available funds in the course of eight years. During those eight years, total income of the 34 large national and global U.S.-based NGOs climbed from 2.6 billion to almost 6 billion USD (see Fig. 3.1). They received the lion's share of this income, roughly 5 billion USD in 2005, in the form of donations and foundation grants. During the same period, management and general expenditures roughly doubled from 152 million to 324 million USD. Similar levels of increases can be observed in NGOs on the local level and among national urban NGOs. Only national women's NGOs show a slight dip in income in 2004, after almost doubling their revenues in the previous six years. Even more pronounced,

---

[12] The Global Washington Initiative was founded by the University of Washington, the Seattle International Foundation, and Washington State University to bring together public and private partners engaged in global development across Washington State. Details at http://globalwa.org.

[13] I chose the cities in which I did the empirical fieldwork for Chapter 5. For a detailed profile of Seattle, San Diego, and Oakland see also Chapter 5.

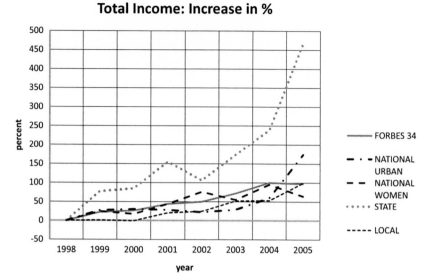

FIGURE 3.1. Increases in Income for National, State, and Local NGOs, 1998–2005, from baseline 1998 = 0, in Percentages. *Note*: N = 64. *Source*: I-990 data 1998–2005, Guidestar database.

the Washington State organizations in the sample increased their income over eight years by more than 450 percent.

Over the same time period, expenses did increase (see Fig. 3.2), but not to the degree that income rose, suggesting NGOs' responding to the pressure to deliver cost-effective returns on grants, fees, and donations – pressure that tended to be translated into organizational restructuring with increased professionalization, institutionalization, and bureaucratization.

Another indicator of turbo-professionalization of the nongovernmental sector is its employee structure. Figure 3.3 shows the overall increases in management and general compensation for top management, board of directors, and general staff. This category refers to all salaries related to providing overall administration to an organization (i.e., preparing for and holding board meetings; working in office management; dealing with personnel issues, accounting, and investment activities). These are salaries that secure the stability of an organization and, although there certainly will be some overlap, are treated on the I-990 report form separately from program building and implementation, as well as fundraising.

All types of organizations, except for national women's organizations, nearly doubled their management salary expenses over the eight-year

Total Expenses, Increase in %

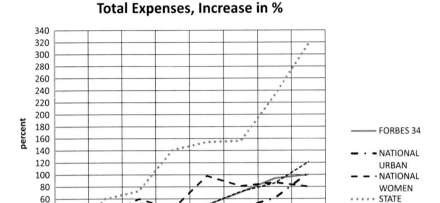

FIGURE 3.2. Increases in Expenses for National, State, and Local NGOs, 1998–2005, from baseline 1998 = 0, in Percentages. *Note*: N = 64. *Source*: I-990 data 1998–2005, Guidestar database.

Management and General Compensation: Increase in %

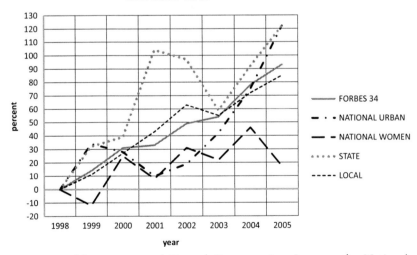

FIGURE 3.3. Management and General Compensation: Increases for National, State, and Local NGOs, 1998–2005, from baseline 1998 = 0, in Percentages. *Note*: N = 64. *Source*: I-990 data 1998–2005, Guidestar database.

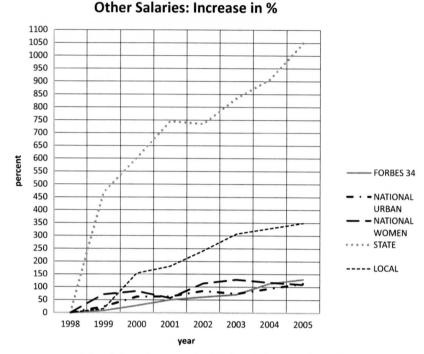

FIGURE 3.4. Other Salary: Increases for National, State, and Local NGOs, 1998–2005, from baseline 1998 = 0, in Percentages. *Note:* N = 64. *Source:* I-990 data 1998–2005, Guidestar database.

period. Interestingly, Washington State NGOs' core salary expenses did not reflect their 450 percent increase in overall income, for which an explanation might be found in Figure 3.4. This figure tallies the salaries for all employees not included in the key management and general compensation category, whom we can assume to be staff added for specific tasks or on a temporary basis. It shows clearly that Washington State NGOs tried to manage turbo-professionalization not primarily with an increase in key managers, but by employing 11 times more additional midlevel staff in 2005 than in 1998. The *Forbes* NGOs also increased this nonessential staff, albeit by a comparatively lower 350 percent, whereas the other NGOs reported increases between 100 and 150 percent.

Turbo-professionalization is also reflected in increases in fundraising. As in the previous figures, Washington State NGOs had massive increases in fundraising expenditures from their baseline in 1998: Figure 3.5 shows increases of almost 1,600 percent over their baseline. The local and national urban development NGOs had 500 percent and 190 percent

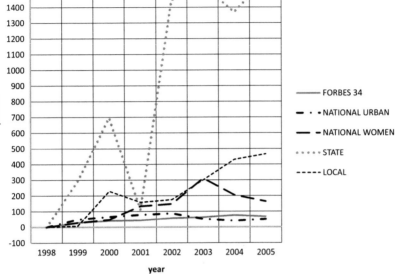

FIGURE 3.5. Fundraising Expenditures: Increases for National, State, and Local NGOs, 1998–2005, from baseline 1998 = 0, in Percentages. *Note*: N = 64. *Source*: I-990 data 1998–2005, Guidestar database.

increases, respectively. National women's NGOs, as well as the Forbes NGOs, had only a modest 80 to 90 percent increase. In the Forbes NGOs, the fact that we see only a small increase might be attributed to historically large fundraising budgets. In the case of the women's NGOs, either relatively modest income increases might not bring in enough funds needed for more fundraising, or there might be deliberate efforts to focus limited funds on other arenas besides fundraising. Although we cannot answer this question, the point of this spot check I-990 analysis was to provide indicators for the increased focus on organizational stability by U.S.-based NGOs from the local to the national/global level during the past decade. Turbo-professionalization is evident in impressive increases in income, management, and salaried staff. One of the root causes of the "inward orientation" that the Harwood Study proclaimed might be the intense effort to cope with the massive expansion of these organizations.

Although the data unveil an empirical footprint of NGOization, bringing together NGOs of different sizes and missions in a sample that tracks raw financial data has its drawbacks. A global player such as Habitat for

Humanity operates in a very different environment from a Seattle-based local NGO such as Bahia Street. Moreover, solely assessing financial volume does not provide us with narrative about the dynamics inside such expanding organizations. Fortunately, a number of qualitative studies that have explored the internal fabric of SMOs and NGOs relate some of the tensions entailed by a move toward professionalized structures. *Amnesty International* is an organization that traditionally relied on individual volunteer work and direct action such as letter writing and activist researchers. Stephen Hopgood has documented in detail the frustration within Amnesty International during its professionalization phase: "At the beginning, there was no meaningful distinction between staff and members; all were unpaid. As the staffers were transformed into employees, they kept (and passed on) a commitment to the ethos that was not professional but vocational ('not a job, but a life choice'). It was a calling" (Hopgood 2006: 16). This culture changed with professionalization and the integration of employees who had "commercial skills," but not necessarily the "heartbeat" of an activist. Today, the "keepers of the flame form a kind of amateur (vocationally oriented) profession inside a bureaucracy" (17), evident in one exasperated activist's outburst in 2003: "I don't know when or what moment they handed the flame to a small number of paid staff!" (10). Even though reliance on professionalized voice does not eclipse the moral claim-making of Amnesty, its privileging of expert and commercial knowledge over moral claims in recent years has stabilized the organization and has opened entry into institutional governance arenas. Other advocacy NGOs also have experienced these tensions. Jeff Atkinson relates how Oxfam uses its ability to conduct surveys and research to open up formerly closed political doors (Atkinson 2007), thus supporting organizations in the global South that do not have the same "capacities and skills to research and use evidence in policy processes" (2006 report of the Overseas Development Institute cited in Atkinson 2007: 69) while at the same time presenting itself as a desirable ally to political institutions. Professionalization, institutionalization, and bureaucratization serve Oxfam and others as a conduit for internal reproduction and external legitimacy.

NGOIZATION IN EMERGING CIVIL SOCIETIES

NGOization is not limited to Northern or Western societies. A similar "intensifying push towards greater professionalization" (SustainAbility 2003: 25) of civil society is at work in the political transformations of

Central and Eastern European (CEE) states and Eurasia. In these parts
of the world, NGOization is primarily driven by foreign donors such
as Western governments and philanthropic foundations. Epistemologies,
structures, and institutions of Western civil society are imported and
mapped onto rather unsettled and culturally diverse civic landscapes. A
case in point is Russia, where the post–Cold War era saw a massive
international interest in democratization brought about by the establishment of a domestic civil society (Mendelson and Glenn 2002; Henderson 2003; Hemment 2004, 2007). After 1989, thousands of NGOs
were created with the support of foreign donors. By 2007, the Committee on Statistics of the Russian Federation reported that there were
at least 665,000 registered noncommercial NGOs operating in Russia
(Klitsounova 2008: 2).[14] In the decade between 1992 and 2002, the U.S.
government alone funded democracy and civil society projects in 12 post-
Soviet states costing almost a billion dollars (U.S. Department of State
1995–2003). Between 1992 and 1998, USAID provided approximately
92 million USD to civil society in the former Soviet Union; George Soros'
Open Society Institute supported Russian civil society with more than 56
million USD, and many other foundations such as the McArthur and the
Charles Stewart Mott Foundation added to this new civic wealth (Henderson 2003: 7).[15] In addition, the European Union contributed yearly
budgets of 30 million EURO for the development of Russian civil society
in 2007 and 2008 (Sholkwer 2009).

As Sada Aksartova observed during her fieldwork on Russian NGOs,
Western donor influence fostered Russian NGOs' embrace of a similar
style of professionalized office and employee culture as their Western
counterparts, albeit on a much lower financial scale: "Salaries measuring
in the hundreds, not thousands, of dollars, although modest by Western
standards, put employees of such NGOs in relatively high-income brackets locally. No less important are the physical surroundings afforded by
Western grants that include well-appointed office space in a nice location
equipped with computers, faxes, photocopiers, etc." (Aksartova 2005: 4).
The insignia of professionalism contributed to the legitimacy that in turn
was needed to acquire funding. An article in an online Russian magazine,

---

[14] The accuracy of this data cannot be confirmed because it is unclear how many registered
NGOs are indeed operative.

[15] Henderson quotes a USAID official's explanation that "civil society at that time was
either nascent or nonexistent in most countries of the region.... We decided early on that
vigorous USAID support for local nongovernmental organizations would be a critical
element of strengthening civil society in the region" (Henderson 2003: 7).

giving NGOs advice about how to obtain a grant, is quite explicit about the appropriate appearance and employees' habitus in a successful NGO operation: "Your organization must have an office. The office should have a respectable, European look. It must have a fax machine, Xerox, computers, Internet; it should be clean and comfortable, and you should treat visitors politely. In short, your office would resemble a business office but be a bit more modest. It is important not to overdo it" (cited in Aksartova 2009:5). The matrix for this piece of advice was donor expectations: The donors expected to encounter an upwardly mobile, fully service-oriented, professional environment exhibiting all the regalia of a trustworthy business enterprise.[16] Moreover, the outward symbols of professionalization were complemented by Russian NGO workers' efforts to develop a professional habitus. In consequence, agencies like the NGO Development Center in Russia evolved from serving as general clearinghouses for NGO-related matters to teaching more specific person-to-person skills such as "managing effective meetings, time management and training for administrative staff" (SustainAbility 2003). They helped create what Henderson calls a "civic oligarchy" (Henderson 2003: 9), thus reinforcing economic inequalities instead of addressing them.

For international donors, quantifiable indicators of success were "NGOs established, people trained, photocopying machines distributed, websites created, Internet accounts used, projects conducted, reports issued etc." (Aksartova 2005: 7). Thus, the formula that signals "money well spent" to donors was the formula that only organizations with a high level of professionalized operations could employ:

> Once an NGO succeeds in winning a multi-thousand-dollar grant, it is understandably determined to continue winning them in the future because few other opportunities in Moscow . . . guarantee similar levels of economic security combined with similar moral rewards. This is not to cast doubt on NGO activists' commitment to what they do or to overstate material benefits. . . . Rather, the point is that the conception of what constitutes the NGO is wedded to a particular style of work that was made possible by – and, for the time being, would be impossible without – multi-thousand-dollar grants provided by foreign aid agencies and Western foundations. Any other mode of functioning becomes unimaginable, and great efforts are expended on cultivating relations with the donors and assuring the NGOs' organizational survival. (Aksartova 2005: 6)

---

[16] I identify these regalia of trustworthiness later in the context of what Habermas calls a "refeudalization" of the public sphere (Habermas 1989). Publicity production in this refeudalized public relies on attributes similar to the publicity of feudal societies such as insignia (the Xerox machine), dress and demeanor (the professional), and rhetoric (donor speak).

With organizational reproduction at the core of an NGO's mission and the sources of funds for stabilizing its operation relatively limited, much energy had to be devoted to a set of endeavors that have not been created endogenously, but have been blueprinted off the "civil society" charts of the West. As Sarah Henderson observed in her fieldwork on Russian women's NGOs, "In visiting groups' premises, it was obvious that women's groups spent an inordinate amount of time producing material for the Ford Foundation in order to prove that they had been active with their grant money. The groups became so focused on producing 'results' for the foundation that they rarely stopped to consider the qualitative impact of their work; nor were there any incentives to do so" (Henderson 2003: 142). The same sentiment was shared by interviewees for the case study in Chapter 6 in Poland. One interviewee estimated that about 50 percent of NGO working time goes into the reproduction of the organization proper (KARAT 2008; Appendix 2). "Professional NGOs propagated by American donors are vehicles for specific conceptions of associationalism and state-society interactions for which often there is no pre-existing vocabulary and literal translation is impossible" (Aksartova 2005: 12).

Even though the research on Russia demonstrates the massive effort to invest in an NGO-led civil society, resonance in the population has been limited. A survey in 2001 indicated that 55 percent of Russians had never heard the term "civil society" and that 74 percent of Russians could still not name a single charity (Henderson 2003: 55). The types of organizations that were built and supported by international donors, following the blueprints of the West, were often considered elitist, upscale, and uncommitted to the real lives of Russians. No doubt, Russian NGOized civil society has helped establish a politicized and well-trained professionalized class of citizens – citizens who take on enormous risks in their encounters with the structures of a managed democracy. Yet the need to establish legitimacy by focusing on a limited range of activities within a professionalized environment, driven substantially by donor requests, might have inhibited a more public-spirited and outreach-oriented focus of this sector of Russian civil society. The donor-defined mandate was geared less toward public engagement and more toward establishing a professional civic entrepreneurial class.

This orientation, in turn, did not bolster the perceived presence of NGOs in Russian public life. In a countrywide study in 2006, 68 percent of Russians said they did not feel protected by the law, yet only 4 percent would turn to human rights NGOs for assistance in case of human rights abuses (Klitsounova 2008: 4). Less than 10 percent of Russians in a representative poll think that NGOs should even be active in the areas of human rights and in supporting citizen initiatives and local self-government (Klitsounova 2008: 5). What Klitsounova calls a "failure of public communication" is a failure to practice substantial public advocacy and outreach. This lack of NGO engagement with constituents' needs and the lack of efforts to stimulate the growth of Russian publics are co-produced by donor rationales mitigated by NGOization processes. The turn from such "institutional monocropping" (Evans 2004) – that is, the imposition of institutional blueprints – to the idea that public debate and exchange have to be at the center of any trajectory of social change and democratization has been slow to take root in major donor communities. A similar criticism is leveled at NGOs from the global South whose focus on donors, instead of on their grassroots constituencies and their groups, is considered by many analysts to be "the greatest threat to southern NGOs' ability to act as effective intermediaries, and to empower grassroots groups as part of civil society development" (Edwards 2004: 86).

THE EFFECTS OF NGOIZATION

NGOization has mixed consequences for the sector's performance. As policy influence tends to increase, publicness – but not necessarily publicity – suffers. On the positive side, the focus on developing professional expertise and acquiring adequate resources for turning the NGO into a stable organization can support moral claim-making with fact-driven claims. Being seen as competent and reliable experts in governance arenas might facilitate access to institutional contexts; this access in turn can mean more informed NGO strategies on how to achieve policy success. The argument presented here does not dispute these gains; instead, it points toward a more ephemeral, less tangible consequence that has implications for civil society and the public sphere. NGOs that attempt to influence political institutions, while preserving their organizational footprint and their good standing in governance contexts, will be compelled more often to choose means involving expertise in internal negotiations rather than means that involve controversial public campaigns or other tools to activate constituencies. Moreover, what actually constitutes an NGO "constituency" might come to be defined as one's donor community rather than as those affected by an NGO's action. Increased efficiency can be seen in management, campaign organizing, and lobbying, yet substantive contact with constituents and larger publics might be reduced (Frantz and Martens 2006: 127).

In sum, the pull to NGOize has consequences for the kinds of publics that NGOs stand for and contribute to. Professionalizing, institutionalizing, and bureaucratizing one's operation might lead to a preference for PR instead of public engagement. In terms of advocacy, NGOization suggests a focus on policy change by institutional negotiation among experts rather than by involving NGOs' constituencies.

Public Relations Replacing Public Engagement

NGOization tends to increase strategic dimensions at the expense of substantive dimensions in the relationship between organizations and their publics. This change might be reflected in the way internal discussions are managed, as well as in the actual productive engagements with affected constituents. As noted in the Harwood study cited earlier, the "inward" perspective of NGOs signals the disappearance of publicness and the packaging of messages in terms of publicity or PR concepts. Unlike the publics of social movements, whose internal debates for the most part "have been out there for all to see" (Taylor 1998: 48), NGOized organizations privilege boardrooms and closed door meetings for discussions about crucial issues such as strategies, message, and organizing tools. They use strategic communication tools to address constituents and communities; in effect, PR often replaces substantive discursive engagement (Evers 2009). If the majority of events or interactions with selected publics are meticulously crafted in message and display, then chances of creating a "listening" environment and getting real input from these publics are reduced.

PR experts Morris and Goldsworthy (2008: 125) argue that the credibility and influence of campaigns run by NGOs are based on their "perceived altruism" and thus on the notion that NGOs indeed are made up of careful listeners who take up causes on behalf of others. Yet in an era of increasing competition among NGOs for public attention and money, crafting a message that speaks "altruism" might become more important than actually engaging in altruistic behavior. NGOs, moreover, have an image advantage in comparison with private business or governments in that their PR techniques and messages are much less challenged than those of business or political institutions: "The notion that NGO actions are selfless, in contrast to profit-obsessed corporations or power-hungry politicians, is pervasive, and is reflected in the greater degree of trust they attract. It gives them enormous PR clout, and so it is certainly time for critics of the role of PR in contemporary societies to subject NGOs to more searching examination" (125).

As early as the 1960s, Jürgen Habermas interpreted the turn from critical publicity to PR in terms of a "refeudalization of the public sphere." In a refeudalized public sphere, he argued, "publicity loses its critical function in favor of a staged display; even arguments are transmuted into symbols to which again one can not respond by arguing but only by identifying with them" (Habermas 1989: 206). NGOs might actually be well positioned to combine symbols with communicative substance. They are mostly run by people who deliberately choose careers in a civic sector over business; they stand for causes that are in some subpublics' interest; and they work "on behalf of," instead of for their own profit. Yet, refeudalized conditions of the public sphere are incentivizing the NGO sector to forfeit public voice in favor of putting massive energy into creating symbols – not necessarily but often at the expense of substantive dialogue. I submit that refeudalization is generated by a specific incentive structure and by a focus on policy success under conditions of limited resources within basic neoliberal paradigms. NGOization provides disincentives to foster resource ties with an NGO's publics that go beyond donations.[17] "Representative publicity of the old type is not thereby revived; but it still lends certain traits to a refeudalized public sphere of civil society whose characteristic feature . . . is that the large-scale organizers in state and society 'manage the propagation of their positions'" (200). PR of NGOs thus does not "hold court" in a strict sense, but at the same time, if solely publicity focused, it does not genuinely engage constituencies. Under conditions of NGOization, an organization's overall concern is with finding venues to display its public prestige.

Large NGOs employ professional PR firms; small NGOs often hire PR consultants for specific projects. Oxfam United Kingdom, for example, in 2008 hired Weber-Shandwick, one of the leading global PR agencies with

---

[17] McAdam and Scott analyze the effect of resource dependence within the U.S. civil rights movement: "The embrace of more radical goals, tactics, and rhetoric by two of the Big Five – the Congress of Racial Equality (CORE) and the Student Non-violent Coordinating Committee (SNCC) – exposed both to the dangers of external resource dependence, leading to the wholesale withdrawal of liberal financial support. Neither group was able to offset this loss with stronger resource ties to the black community, thus depriving the movement of much of the tactical energy and innovation that had fueled action campaigns in the early sixties" (McAdam and Scott 2005: 34).

128 offices in 78 countries, explicitly to "reinvigorate its engagement with the British public" (Cartmell 2008). Weber Shandwick's lead consultant explained that the agency would "use its expertise to build Oxfam into more of a lifestyle brand." One outgrowth of the strategic consultancy contract was Oxfam's launch of a new branding strategy in April 2008, coded as "Be Humankind." As the journal PR Week interpreted the contract with Weber-Shandwick, "this marks a deliberate attempt to move Oxfam's focus away from world problems, towards good news stories, focused on solutions" (Cartmell 2008: 1).

Civil society advocacy tends to relocate from publicly visible places into conference rooms, hearings, and testimonials. Conversely, the "public face" of many civic organizations comes to be defined by professionalized PR logic. This might be an effective way to advance a specific change agenda, but as we look toward not only effectiveness but also citizen voice in civil society, the question of "who speaks, where, for whom?" needs to be the focal point of any investigation into the NGO sector's democratic quality. The most visible NGOs have recruited professional "brand managers" to "enhance the clarity of thinking and communications behind NGO brands" (SustainAbility 2003: 16). Even in organizations that have historically resisted any sign of co-optation and alliances with states or accepting state funding, the brand has taken central stage in relations with their publics: Hopwood finds in his study on Amnesty International that

the movement now talks of the Amnesty brand, the commodification of its hard-won status, [which] seems an almost sacrilegious association of something so pure with the ultimate profanity – money. There is, for example, an Amnesty Platinum Visa Card, available to IS staff and Amnesty International United Kingdom (AIUK) members (described as 'attractive, silver and bearing the AI candle logo'). I mentioned the word brand to a former and very senior IS manager, who visibly blanched and said 'so people use that language now, really? (Hopgood 2006: 10ff.)

Although civically committed NGO workers might struggle with the corporatizing logic underlying some of these PR strategies, that logic seems to be the way of the future, in effect producing a rather "flattened out version of civil society" (Chandhoke 2003: 9).

One of the most recent examples of "publicity takeover" is the worldwide *TckTckTck* campaign for climate justice under the sponsorship of former UN Secretary-General Kofi Annan. The campaign, which brought together scores of celebrities and powerful transnational NGOs, is in fact

managed by two global advertising agencies[18] whose other clients include
Novartis and Aventis (two major biotech corporations), Shell and General Electric (two major conventional energy giants), EDF (the world's
leading nuclear power company), and Unilever and Nestle. Other Tck-
TckTck corporate partners are *Coca Cola* and *RBS*, the main financier
of the Canadian tar sands projects.[19] These corporate sponsorships led
activists to express profound frustration at what they perceived to be
undue influence of PR experts:

> The mainstream environmental movement is no longer led by visionaries,
> thinkers, activists. (Was it at one time? I would like to think so.) It is clearly
> being shaped and defined by advertising firms. From top to bottom – it is being
> led by advertising executives – people whose expertise is ensuring corporate profit
> and growth at every quarter. I would argue that the mainstream environmental
> movement is no longer based on truth. In the past activism was based on what was
> 'right' both ethically and morally – not on what the polls stated public perception
> would be. Today, polling is now done by most of the bigger NGOs before they
> message anything. Imagine the information Euro RSCG could collect through the
> TckTckTck campaign to give their other clients valuable insight of the millions
> of concerned citizens showing interest for the environment.[20]

Within the environmental movement, there is increasing concern over
what is called "greenwashing" – the adoption of NGO PR avatars by companies to foster engagement, while at the same time employing economic
strategies that are based on exploitation of the environment. Whereas
some NGOs insist that such coalitions are instrumental in moving environmental issues from the green table into practical settings, others scrutinize and criticize not only the compromises these strategies inevitably
entail but also their effects on publicness and public perceptions of the
NGO sector. NGOs thus walk a fine line as they employ strategic communication tools to reach out to broad constituencies. Doing so might
mean forming alliances with powerful partners who bring the money for
these tools to the table, while facing strategic decisions about public advocacy strategies that might target these very companies that are campaign
allies.

---

[18] Havas and EuroRSCG. RSCG, according to the 2008 Advertising Age Global Marketers
Report, has 233 offices across the globe, specializing in advertising, digital, marketing,
PR, and corporate communications.

[19] In tar sand projects, petroleum is extracted out of partially consolidated sandstone
and in the process generates massive greenhouse gases. Major sites are in Canada and
Russia. Part of the communication on "the wrong kind of green" can be found at http://
thewrongkindofgreen.wordpress.com/2010/03/14/communication-to-tcktcktck-partner
-sustainable-environment-ecological-development-society-seeds-india-feb-10th-2010/.

[20] Activist comments on a blog; see fn. 14.

From Activism to Advocacy

A second and related effect of NGOization is that movements-turned-NGOs tend to switch their communication and action repertoire from activism to advocacy.[21] Advocacy conjures images of experts who assess specific spheres of influence and target specific goals and institutions. Activism, by contrast, at times might make specific demands; often, however, activists raise their voice without direct instrumental implications (see Chapter 1). Activists might question power without offering immediate alternatives, or they might challenge the political process as such. When culture jammers subvert the *Nike* logo to unsettle the company's brand, or when students across Europe stage sleep-ins at their universities to protest the commodification of public education, specific policy goals take a back seat to a more general contestation of perceived hegemonies of cultural and economic paradigms. In such events, what Lipschutz calls the "repoliticization of constitutive politics" takes place. Constitutive politics addresses the very terms of participation in a political system. Emphasizing constitutive over redistributive politics means to refuse to be solely concerned with the limited alternatives that redistribution of social goods provide and instead to demand renewal of the very foundations on which late modern polities are built (Lipschutz and Rowe 2005; Lipschutz 2006: 49ff.).

Employing advocacy frames instead of activism frames thus signals more than a shift in political strategy. It indicates a changing relationship not only with political power but also with an NGO's constituency and with wider publics; it signals a tendency to practice *speaking for* instead of *engaging with*. This shift frames engagement with constituents in terms of a *contract to represent* rather than a coming together of critical voices. And it compels NGOs to offer pragmatic policy solutions within the confines of existing policy options instead of pursuing more general social, economic, and political change agendas. In terms of NGOs' professional ethos, it entails a "growing tension between a "24/7" and a "9–5" approach" (SustainAbility 2003: 25), oscillating between commitment to a social and political cause and a professionalized, more disengaged work ethic.

---

[21] Mary Kaldor distinguishes between an activist conception of civil society embodied by social movements and a neoliberal conception represented by NGOs (Kaldor 2003a). Whereas NGOization certainly fits the neoliberal paradigm in its tendency to commodify social injustices (Rai 2004), there are also NGOs subverting neoliberal logics (see Chapter 4). NGOs thus are not bound to the neoliberal agenda, but profoundly shaped by it.

Inside more professionalized organizations, the turn from activism to advocacy may result in a more expert-oriented and donor-friendly communication style and a language that articulates social problems in the idioms of donor- and issue-specific expert cultures rather than in the language of public contestation and power. Turning to Russia again, Aksartova finds that NGOization produces a specific linguistic repertoire that organizations learn in order to acquire funds and status: In practical circles it is called "donor-speak." As a native of Russia, she conducted her interviews in Russian, yet many of the catchwords of successful NGO acquisition strategies appeared "anglosized":

My interviewees' speech was peppered with English words, such as grant (grant in Russian), advocacy (edvocasi), fundraising (fandraizing), gender issues (gendernye problemy), etc.... In a typical donor-NGO Russian-language publication... not only examples are drawn from American institutional experience, the style of argumentation is American, many of the words used are neologisms, and even orthography and syntax often follow American rather than Russian conventions. (Aksartova 2009: 171)

Similar linguistic adaptation processes occur among NGOs in the European Union. Certain catchwords such as "work packages," "modules," "best practices," or "good governance," even though their meaning is often not clear even to those initiated in EU rhetoric, are part of the gold standard of grant applications and frequently find their entry into public presentations of NGOs.

The language of advocacy is also connected to a certain style of presentation, consisting mostly of accounts of "what we did/do for you" instead of "how you can engage with us." The inward direction of organizational reproduction and of donor demands leads NGOs to present cleaned-up success narratives of conferences, meetings, and venues in which the organization represented a specific issue (see Chapter 6). In contrast to activism involving multidimensional goals and often failing to yield measureable results, advocacy is primarily motivated by and follows the logic of success. Even though organization theory has long emphasized the importance of learning through failure, NGOs are in a structurally bad position to admit to failure. There is anxiety about the organization's public reputation, about repercussions such as failing to get new grant money, and, ultimately, about not being able to compete with other NGOs whose reports will confirm that they "successfully" perform the tasks that they have set out to accomplish. In donor logics, failure is not rewarded; therefore it cannot be displayed.

Likewise, governments rarely talk about the failure of cooperation efforts with NGOs (Carothers 2002). In fact, government agencies themselves fall victim to the culture of success, because obtaining higher budgets requires corroborating a success story that serves as legitimacy for the agency. This, in turn, puts NGOs in position as the next in line to put forward legitimizing narratives for why they need to receive further funding. NGOs thus are forced to succeed, because otherwise their funding streams will dry out.

The combination of all these features threatens the saliency of NGO advocacy on three fronts: first, by raising the stakes (e.g., organizational costs and funder dependency) in practicing any kind of advocacy; second, by pushing advocacy toward semi-privatized, institutionally confined settings of government offices and business boardrooms; and third, by equating successful advocacy primarily with policy results and much less with public mobilization. The last problem is exacerbated by government and business making "advocacy without publics" palatable to NGOs; in these institutionalized contexts, they are recognized as "naturalized" representatives of those for whom they advocate.

A report for the European Commission in 2006 on successful partnerships between private companies and citizens' organizations in Europe concluded that in corporate–NGO social-responsibility–oriented partnerships, 56.3 percent of respondents from both sectors stated that the beneficiaries of the partnership – the citizens that were advocated for and that were supposed to profit from these partnerships – had not been involved in the decisions concerning the partnership itself (see Table 3.2). In more

TABLE 3.2 *Involvement of Beneficiaries in Decision Making in Corporate Social Responsibility Partnerships between Private Companies and NGOs in the EU, 2006*

Kind of Involvement of Beneficiaries	All %	Companies %	NGOs %
Asking about needs	33.4	30.0	35.7
Giving feedback	25.0	20.0	28.6
Involvement in project	20.8	20.0	21.4
Indirect	20.8	30.0	14.3
TOTAL	100.0	100.0	100.0

Note: N = 36 partnerships in eight countries.
Source: European Commission, DG Employment, Social Affairs and Equal Opportunities 2006: *Not Alone: A Research on Successful Partnerships between Private Companies and Citizens' Organizations in Europe.* Final Report. Brussels, p. 42.

than half of the cases, the constituents and recipients were involved neither in program building, goal formulation, nor execution of corporate
social responsibility programs (European Commission 2006: 41).

The report points out that partnerships in which NGOs represented
constituencies that in turn were never consulted might contain a self-
referential and thus exclusive component:

> This information raises some concerns.... The fact that more than half of the
> partnerships did not involve the beneficiaries in the decision-making process is
> clearly not positive. Moreover, it raises questions on the innovative characteris-
> tics, which partnerships should have. One explanation for this could be that the
> presence of a citizen-based organization might be considered by both partners
> as an indirect element of representation of the voice and needs of the intended
> beneficiaries. Whatever the reason, this is an element that may involve a risk of
> partnerships being self-referential; a risk which should be carefully considered.
> (European Commission 2006: 42)

The same trend toward exclusion of beneficiaries has been found in
a recent survey among managers of development NGOs (see Fig. 3.6).
When asked about their interaction with constituents, almost 50 percent
reported seeing no or hardly any system in place to secure feedback on

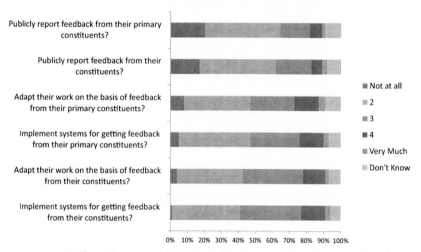

FIGURE 3.6. What Managers of NGOs in International Development Say about
Their Interaction with Constituents. *Source*: Adapted with permission from Key-
stoneaccountability.org, a nonprofit specializing in performance and accountability of the NGO sector at http://www.keystoneaccountability.org/node/365
(accessed April 3, 2011).

their programs from those targeted and primarily affected. Even more managers (63 percent) never or hardly ever publicly reported feedback from their primary constituents.

In both these cases, advocacy status can be assumed and maintained without actually having strong connections and feedback mechanisms in place from one's constituencies. As the next chapter shows, one of the ways to nurture stronger ties between NGOs and their constituents would be for governments and businesses to demand and enable stronger ties with affected communities. These ties should be seen as a major feature of NGO accountability. Yet discussions of the sector's accountability have settled squarely on the donor–NGO relationship, subsequently neglecting NGO–constituency ties and thus the *public* accountability of the sector.

CONCLUSION

Civil society cannot be considered independently of its very material organizational and discursive forms. This chapter has established that the NGOization of civil society entails a restructuring toward more professionalized, institutionalized, and bureaucratized collective action. Because of the imperative of producing policy results, which is supported by funders and reproduced within NGOs, this change in form is often overlooked or legitimized. If NGOization guarantees heightened NGO influence and good policy results, where is the problem? The problem, I argue, is that this change in form has effects on the kinds of publics that NGOized civil society creates, interacts with, and sustains. What has been called NGOs' "nuisance potential" (Donini 2006) is thus often tamed by intra-organizational as well as political and economic logics (Alston 1994 cited in Jaeger 2007). This explains why the 2009 Harwood study finds NGOs enveloped in "inwardness." Engagement with publics is usually defined according to the needs and interests of the organization, and not those of their constituents or communities. Moreover, none of the NGO leaders in the Harwood study saw "community engagement as a core competency necessary to ensure organizational stability" (Harwood 2009: 3). Most funding reinforces the "Organization-First approach" because it is "tied almost exclusively to program expansion and implementation, so funding priorities often determine organizational focus" (4). According to one NGO leader, "There are few grant RFPs (Requests for Proposals) for engagement or community building work. It is very difficult to develop capacities when funding is all about the delivery of programs" (6). Ultimately, donor funding is about "showing impact," and because contributing to public debate is not easily quantifiable, an interviewee consequently states, "No one cares. It's just process" (7). The incentives and structures created by NGOization reward inwardnesss and an "organization-first" approach (18). NGOization thus poses risks to forming and sustaining democratic publics.

4

Limits to NGO Advocacy in the Public Sphere

> We think about how dependent the public is on good government . . . but
> we lose sight of how much good government needs a good public.
>
> David Mathews[1]

Like all organizations, NGOs are learning communities. Hence, privileging institutional over public advocacy takes place within a continuous
reading of an organization's environment and by carefully assessing available options.[2] Chapter 3 focused on the inner-organizational rationales
that are in play as NGOs make decisions on advocacy strategies. This
chapter presents a complementary narrative by exploring broader legal,
political, and social conditions that formally or informally shape NGO
advocacy. These conditions are not equally imposing across different
environments and organizations, and they influence NGOs to varying
degrees. The goal of this chapter is not to make sweeping generalizations
that fault NGOs for not mobilizing publics at all, but rather to understand why a substantial number seems to be more at home in institutional
advocacy arenas despite widely held assumptions about their representing specific constituencies and being their public voice. The four sets
of conditions that, I propose, most contribute to disincentivizing public
advocacy by NGOs are (1) the legal regulatory environment; (2) limited

---

[1] David Mathews, President of the Kettering Foundation, cited in Attafuah (2007: 2).
[2] Organizational learning is based on past successes or failures; thus we can presume that
advocacy strategies depend to some degree on the memory of "what worked" previously
and "what did not." This is in line with the theory of historical institutionalism and
in particular the analysis of path dependency via increased returns and the creation of
positive feedback loops (i.e., Pierson 2000).

technocratic or political perspectives on NGO representativeness or accountability; (3) depoliticized civic engagement practices; and (4) non-responsive media.

In much of the following argument, states, and governments as their primary institutional face, are central actors. It should be noted, however, that the state is not conceived of as a monolithic and autonomous institution, but as linked into multifaceted, changing, and sometimes paradoxical relationships with society. Employing a "process-oriented view of the state-in-society" (Migdal 2001: 232) enables us to see not only how state and civil society continuously make, challenge, and change each other but also how state actors operate inside civil society and vice versa. This is a departure from the strict state–civil society dichotomy that, as we saw in Chapter 2, has dominated most post-1989 analytical frameworks.[3] If states and civil society constitute each other and in doing so can enable or block each other (Chandhoke 2003: 24), then the question becomes what kind of enabling and blocking conditions we can identify that would allow NGOs to – or discourage them from – generating and mobilizing publics. The argument presented here builds on Sending and Neumann's proposal that any attempt to understand the role of organizations in civil society "requires an approach that can theorize about the specific relations between state and non-state actors and about the logic of the processes of governance" (2006: 652). The intention is to contribute to a theory of NGOs in relation to governance by focusing first on legal regulations and accountability challenges, then on the culture of volunteering as a specific citizenship practice encouraged by late modern governance, and finally on the role of the media in awarding relevance to nonstate actors.

LEGAL REGULATIONS

Legal regulation of the NGO sector is still the prerogative of nation-states and will remain so into the foreseeable future. This needs to be kept in

---

[3] Gellner, for example, defines civil society as "that set of diverse non-governmental institutions which is strong enough to counterbalance the state" and "prevent[s] the state from dominating and atomizing the rest of society" (Gellner 1994: 32). In this view, NGOs are part of the bulwark that protects society against the state. The problem of such a polarized conception of states and civil society (which often treats the market as the third independent entity) is that it might conceal more than it might reveal (for a similar point see Smith and Lipsky 1993 and Salamon 1995).

mind, particularly in light of the later discussion on the emergence of a transnational or global civil society. The nation-state prerogative entails decisions as to what is a charitable purpose, what kinds of activities citizens are allowed to support with tax-exempt contributions, and at what point NGOs breach their stated purpose. Such regulatory policies are drafted in national legislatures or executive branches and enforced by government agencies and the courts. Although there have been initiatives within the European Union to establish an EU-based transnational charitable legal status in the form of a *European Association*, none has succeeded so far. In 2006, the European Commission withdrew a proposal for the establishment of a European Association after some member states actively protested and others practiced passive nonengagement (Breen 2008). Of the 27 member states of the EU, only Poland, Slovenia, and the Netherlands allow residents' donations to another member state's NGOs to be tax deductible, 16 member states restrict deductibility of charitable donations to domestic NGOs, and eight states allow cross-border donations as tax deductible in very limited circumstances (57). Across the EU and beyond, nation-states still hold definitional power as to which NGO causes are deemed to be public interest causes and therefore should be supported by the polity through allowing tax deductions. Depending on the country in which they gain official status, NGOs face different sets of legal restrictions that regulate their role as actors engaging in institutional and public advocacy. Generally, NGOs receive charitable tax status through national tax laws or not-for-profit laws. The following brief overview of national laws and their impact on NGOs is intended to provide insight into what exactly is being regulated in the relationship among NGOs, citizens, and the state and how these legal regulations shape advocacy.

In the United States, charitable nonprofits are legal entities under the 1986 Internal Revenue Code § 501(c)(3) if they are founded and operated exclusively for "religious, charitable, scientific, testing for public safety, literary, or educational purposes."[4] Yet charitable status has a price, part of which is restrictions on lobbying legislative bodies at all levels of government. Charities are allowed to educate their constituents, but there is a legal line not to be crossed: They are not to become advocates

---

[4] Internal Revenue Service Code Section 501(c)(3). Not all nonprofits have charity status; some, such as unions or trade associations, are exempt from federal income tax, but are not eligible to receive tax-deductible charitable contributions (Mayer 2011: 3).

for these constituents' causes in legislative settings. As Jeffrey Berry and David Arons forcefully argue in their study *A Voice for Nonprofits*, "What non-profits are not supposed to do is to represent their clients before legislators. Feed them, just don't lobby for better anti-hunger programs. Heal them, just don't try to lobby for changing the health care system. This is the essence of American law on nonprofits" (2003: 4). Moreover, the U.S. regulatory practice is complicated by legal ambiguity: The 501(c)(3) status does not completely forbid lobbying, but only any "substantial" amount of lobbying.[5] The vast majority of U.S.-based non-profits choose not to take any risk: 95% of NGOs that file I-990 forms claim that they do not lobby at all.[6] A survey in 2000 of nonprofit leaders who had filed tax returns with the I-990 form found that more than two-thirds wrongly believed that their NGOs were not allowed to do any lobbying if they received government funding (Berry and Arons 2003). The authors cite comments from interviews that accompanied the survey that reflect a striking level of ignorance or false conviction regarding the ability to lobby: "[We can't] be involved in lobbying as a nonprofit because we receive government grants" (60).[7] This wrong judgment is the result of the ambiguity of the law itself – an ambiguity that has the effect of discouraging public advocacy.

[5] To engage in substantial lobbying and other advocacy activity prohibited to 501(c)(3) nonprofits, charities need to form separate 501(c)(4) organizations that, although tax exempt, cannot receive tax-deductible contributions. It is obvious that only large and highly professionalized NGOs can manage the additional administrative burden involved in such a dual construction of their activity base. Critics therefore argue that the 501(c)(4) status discriminates against free speech by small and less management-savvy NGOs. The "additional burden" being imposed on extensive NGO lobbying and advocacy might also be reevaluated in light of the Supreme Court's *Citizen United vs. FEC* decision of 2010 (130 S. Ct.876) that stipulated the creation of political action committees (PACs) as not adequate to guarantee a corporation's right to speak. The Supreme Court argued here that "PACs are burdensome alternatives; they are expensive to administer and subject to extensive regulations" (Citizens United, 130 S.Ct. at 897; cited in Mayer 2011: 18). Mayer and others expect that the concern for undue burdens on corporations' right to speak might have repercussions on the nonprofit sector, because a similar undue burden might be constructed in having to form a 501(c)(4) nonprofit alongside an NGO's regular operation.

[6] Forty-two percent of all organizations that are registered with the IRS as 501(c)(3) charities submit financial returns (Chaves et al. 2004). These are organizations with a yearly income that is higher than 25,000 USD. Small NGOs that claim charitable status are even less likely to have the legal wherewithal to make sense of how much lobbying they are actually allowed to engage in.

[7] This being an executive from an AIDS organization, it seems safe to assume that this NGO and its constituents would have a significant stake in the development of public policy.

In fact, NGOs can decide to apply for a special status in which they can use a certain percentage of overall expenditures for lobbying;[8] yet where to draw the line between, for example, lobbying and educating legislatures is not at all clear. A number of studies have concluded that, because of such ambiguity, NGOs avoid not only lobbying, but any kind of legislative activity (Berry and Arons 2003; Bass et al. 2007). In fact, the threat of potential noncompliance and the gray zone in IRS treatment of lobbying prevent most NGO boards and directors from engaging in any overt advocacy activity. Regulation thus inhibits NGOs from transforming the public articulation of grievances into the more constructive language of public advocacy for policy change, even though NGOs acquire knowledge and insight in their fields of action from which public debate would certainly benefit. The IRS also forbids all partisan political activities by NGOs, including but not limited to all written and oral expressions of support or opposition to a candidate (OMB Watch 2007: 2). Although this ban on political activities is more than 50 years old, it has no clear definition that would establish workable guidelines for NGOs. Moreover, IRS enforcement of the ban takes place in almost complete secrecy, because the agency is prohibited from disclosing information about its investigations. NGOs thus operate with little guidance on permissible and nonpermissible activities; this level of uncertainty, as OMB Watch concludes, has "deterred them from engaging in genuine issue advocacy and promoting civic engagement among citizens" (1). A sample case cited by OMB Watch is about an NGO client who wanted to put out a press release announcing a presidential candidate's support for one of the nonprofit's policy recommendations. The nonprofit lawyer could not advise his client conclusively on whether this press release was permissible or not (5).

In addition to producing anxiety and reluctance among civic actors to engage in politics at all, such unclear legal regulation has problematic secondary effects. It contributes to depoliticizing a whole array of issues that NGOs deal with by signaling that engagement with these issues

---

[8] Charitable NGOs in the United States can elect to come under a 1976 law that allows them to spend 20 percent of the first 500,000 USD of their annual expenditures and 15 percent of the next 500,000 USD of their expenditures to a total maximum of one million USD per year on lobbying – defined as directed to a legislator or an employee of a legislative body, referring to a specific piece of legislation and expressing the NGO's view on that legislation (Geller and Salamon 2007: 3). Appeals to the public to contact their legislator(s) (known as grassroots lobbying) are subject to a separate cap of one-fourth the size of the restriction on direct lobbying.

is not, or should not be, political. Citizens experience NGOs as acting on social problems while at the same time avoiding taking a political stand on them. Donating to a food bank thus gets cognitively removed from engaging in debate on the politics of poverty and welfare. The present legislation also *disembodies* political practices in civil society by prohibiting NGOs from citing names of politicians running for office and supporting specific policies. This makes it difficult for citizens to recognize connections between politicians' positions and the social problems that NGOs try to address. Supporting salmon preservation is accepted, yet publicly advocating for better toxic waste legislation, by pointing to political candidates who would support such legislation, is not.

Although lobbying legislatures is limited, the IRS does not forbid institutional advocacy behind closed doors or engaging with government agencies or the courts to advance policy goals. Under federal law, "only advocacy before a legislature is considered suspect, lobbying the executive branch or filing a court suit is not considered lobbying" (Berry and Arons 2003: 53). What is the difference between the two activities? Clearly this distinction draws on a controversial understanding that legislative processes are more vulnerable to special interests than the executive branch or the courts. Yet why should organizations that serve broad public interests be allowed less public voice in regard to legislatures than, for example, well-financed private business interests? The public dimension of advocacy is most closely reflected in the legislative process, and if NGOs are not allowed to try to shape legislators' positions, then their role as *public* interest groups is in question.

Whereas Berry and Arons argue that the U.S. IRS code in fact deters nonprofits' participation in public policy making, I would slightly rephrase this conclusion: The tax code does not deter NGOs from employing institutional advocacy strategies within the confines of executive agency consultations and private boardrooms, but it *does* prevent public interest groups from participating in the *public* part of public policy making. Thus, the IRS code communicates that public policy making is policy making *for* the public, not policy making *with* the public. Government agencies often invite NGOs to serve in planning or advising roles. When the Aspen Institute asked, in a random sample survey, about the frequency of different types of policy participation among NGOs, the results pointed squarely to government agencies offering NGOs a seat at the table (see Table 4.1).

More than 75 percent of these NGOs said that government officials contact them with requests for information or support – and more than

TABLE 4.1. *Frequency of Different Types of Policy Participation of U.S. NGOs[a]*

	Never	Low	High
Releasing research reports to the media, public, or policy makers	31.0	47.1	21.8
Working in a planning or advisory group that includes government officials	18.5	39.2	45.1
Meeting with government officials about the work it is doing	15	40.2	44.8
Responding to requests for information from those in government	12.9	26.0	41.0

[a] Percentage of respondents; $N = 1,738$.
Source: Table adapted with modifications from Bass et al. 2007: 164.

40 percent said that this occurs at least twice a month (Bass et al. 2007: 164). This finding suggests that, when invited by government agencies or committees, most NGOs are eager to pursue policy goals within the institutional confines of relatively closed settings; yet in public, legal regulatory frameworks incentivize constraint and avoidance.

Across Europe, NGOs are regulated by similar national laws, involving (1) adherence to constitutional principles and (2) the exclusion of what is considered to be political activities. Adherence to constitutional principles means accepting not only a normative order but also specific modes of political expression. In Germany, a 1984 ruling by the Federal Finance Court, for example, established that charity status had to be revoked if an NGO publicly sponsored nonviolent resistance in public spaces or refused to comply with police orders during a demonstration.[9] In effect, endorsing civil disobedience could cause the NGO to lose its charitable status. For example, a sit-in held in the office of the Family Minister to protest restrictive abortion policies might endanger the charitable status of participating or mobilizing NGOs.

All EU member states have stipulations that threaten NGOs with losing charitable status if they engage in political activities. Yet what constitutes a political activity is defined quite differently from country to country and leaves much room for interpretation. The baseline criterion is that support for political parties is not allowed. Beyond that, Hungary, for example, prohibits involvement in all direct political activities (Moore et al. 2008: 12) without specifying what is deemed political, whereas Latvia only

---

[9] German Federal Court of Justice decision 8/29/84, BStBl 1984 II S. 844.

restricts political activities "which are directed to the support of political organizations [i.e., parties]." German law stipulates that an occasional attempt to influence public opinion is acceptable under charity law, but involvement in "daily politics" is not.[10] What constitutes "daily politics" as opposed to occasional political public advocacy is not clearly laid out in existing law. Thus, establishing demarcation lines for acceptable public advocacy is left to the courts of EU member states, and most NGOs try to avoid the dimly lit territory of political advocacy in the first place.

It should be noted, however, that restrictions of political activities for NGOs are much more severe in autocratic states or in managed democracies. In Ethiopia, the Civil Society Organization Law passed in January 2009 prohibits any domestic NGO that receives more than 10 percent of its funding from abroad from engaging in activities related to "the advancement of human and democratic rights... the promotion of the equality of nations, nationalities and peoples and that of gender and religion... the promotion of the rights of the disabled and children's rights."[11] In Eritrea, the government issued a proclamation in May 2005 that prohibited all NGOs, domestic or foreign, engaging in relief or rehabilitation from receiving funds from the United Nations or its affiliates, from other international organizations, or through bilateral agreements. Moreover, NGOs are only allowed to operate inside the country if they have one million USD or its equivalent at their disposal, thus effectively closing down all smaller community-led public interest groups (Vernon 2009: 9). As a result, the number of NGOs operating in Eritrea fell from 37 in 2005 to 11 in 2007. In Russia, President Putin introduced revisions to the nonprofit law in 2006 that expanded the grounds on which registration of an NGO could be denied if its "goals and objectives... create a threat to the sovereignty, political independence, territorial integrity, national unity, unique character, cultural heritage and national interest of the Russian Federation" (Bourjaili 2006: 4). Moreover, Russian state agency officials obtained the right to attend all NGO meetings, even those strictly internal to the organization, and required complete funding disclosure. Additionally, as prime minister in 2008, Putin attempted to curb foreign involvement in the civic sector with a decree that effectively removed the charitable status of 89 foreign-based NGOs (Vernon 2009). These organizations also became subject to a 24 percent tax on all grants

---

[10] German Federal Finance Court decision 2/9/2011 IR 19/10; also §52 German Fiscal Code.

[11] Articles 2 and 14(5) Ethiopian Nonprofit Law, cited by International Center for Not-for-Profit Law (2009, 1(1): 2).

they made inside Russia, thus squeezing their operations from two sides. Yet although it is not surprising that autocratic systems would be particularly sensitive to the role of NGOs as critical civil society voices, it is much less obvious why democracies limit political advocacy of the nongovernmental sector and quite successfully rely on "anticipatory obedience" by NGOs eager not to jeopardize their charity status.

Few states have taken steps to clarify the public advocacy role of NGOs with the intention of expanding their rights to engage in politics. Yet discussions and resulting policies in Australia and the United Kingdom point to an increasing, albeit contested, public awareness that the present regulations are not adequate when considered in the context of NGOs' roles of organizing civil societies and being the organizational voice for constituency matters. In 1991, the Australian government officially recognized the need to allow NGOs to operate as public interest representatives. The House of Representatives Standing Committee on Community Affairs issued a report that addressed the role of NGOs explicitly in terms of their responsibility to practice advocacy: "An integral part of the consultative and lobbying role of these organizations is to disagree with government policy where this is necessary in order to represent the interests of their constituents."[12] However, when the Howard government came to power in 1996, the official interpretation changed. Prime Minister Howard referred to the NGO sector as "single interest groups," "special interest," and "elites" (see Staples 2007) and took stringent measures to reshape the NGO sector, including the following:

- *Defunding:* During the Howard government, several vocal critics of the government's policy were defunded, many of which were representing the poorest and most disempowered Australians. By 2002, 20 percent of NGOs had lost all their funding, and a further 50 percent faced substantial losses. Some of these funds were redistributed to groups that provided services, but did not engage in advocacy (Staples 2007: 9).
- *Forced amalgamation:* Some organizations that had been critical of government policies were pushed by officials to merge with more mainstream NGOs. For example, radical feminist groups were forced, under threat of defunding, to merge with other, non-gender-specific groups. The *Association of Non-English Speaking Background Women* was defunded and advised to "mainstream" its advocacy through the Federation of Ethnic Councils. Yet this association had been created

---

[12] Parliament of the Commonwealth of Australia 1991; cited in Staples (2007: 4).

specifically because women felt that they were not being heard in the male-dominated councils (Staples 2007; also Sawer 2002: 45).

• *Altered contract relationships:* Changes from government provision of core funding to purchaser-provider contracts hit networks or peak groups that tended to serve a range of NGOs within a subsector, providing them with information and advocacy tools, as well as determining group positions on specific policy issues. In the purchaser-provider model, the core of the government–NGO relationship is a service that is being provided, in effect abolishing advocacy funding for NGOs (Staples 2007).

• *Confidentiality clauses:* These clauses, which were included in most contracts that NGOs had with the Australian Federal Government, required "that the organizations not speak to the media without first obtaining the approval of the appropriate department or minister" (Staples 2007: 10). They also prohibited publicizing any agreements with government and required that media releases and the like be cleared by the agencies of the Commonwealth (Sawer 2002: 46).

It took the successor Ruud government, in 2006, to undo these overtly repressive policies and enter into a more cooperative relationship with the NGO sector.

Criticism of restrictive NGO provisions also led to policy change in the United Kingdom, where the discrepancy between encouragement of democratic participation by community organizations and restrictions on their public voice had attracted considerable criticism. The traditional focus in the UK, as across Europe, had been to encourage "volunteering or grassroots community work rather than 'upward' activism through...forms of advocacy" (Dunn 2008: 53). The 2006 Charities Act's definition of public benefit did not include political activities, which it defined quite broadly as covering "any activity or purpose which furthers the interests of a political party or cause or which seeks to change the laws, policies, or decisions of UK or other governments" (Dunn 2008: 54). Just like other national regulations of the NGO sector, the Charities Act operated with a tacitly understood gray territory: Consultative functions of NGOs, for example, could be interpreted as nonpolitical activities, as opposed to activities aimed at changing legislation. As discussed earlier, vague language on what constitutes political action tends to result in NGOs treading very cautiously around political issues in public. Moreover, it disproportionately affects the activities of small NGOs, which have few resources to withstand possible legal tax challenges (Berry and Arons 2003; Dunn 2008; Lang 2009a). As a consequence, in the UK as elsewhere, only a limited number of large sector organizations tended to have regular consultative access to political institutions.

In 2007, a *Government Advisory Group on Campaigning and the Voluntary Sector* was formed in the UK with the intent to spur "legislative reform to change the definition of 'political activity'" for the voluntary sector (Kennedy et al. 2007: 1). The advisory group's report recommended enhancement of a legal framework that "recognizes the unique role that the sector is playing in articulating peoples' views and promoting political debate" (Government Advisory Group 2007: 2) and thus called for "clarification of the law and for an opening up of the legal rules to allow all political activities save support of political parties" (Dunn 2008: 57). Moreover, the report highlighted the relationship between engagement of the public and liberalized rules for political engagement of NGOs, because "advocacy of a range of opinions would itself be valuable and beneficial to the community, as the best means of promoting democracy" (Government Advisory Group 2007: 16). It concluded that the mission of the law should not be to protect the public from political activity by NGOs – by contrast, "the law should encourage the public to participate in democratic processes through such organizations" (16). Hence, the report suggested a radical departure from the prevailing government tradition to "protect the public" against political activities from the NGO sector. In recommending new guidelines to the existing law, the UK Charities Commission voted in favor of adopting the Government Advisory Board's recommendations in March 2008. It is noteworthy that nothing has changed in the overall legal framework for NGOs. Only the guidelines for interpreting what constitutes acceptable political activity in the United Kingdom have been clarified, thus allowing for a stronger, more confident voice of the NGO sector. To date, to my knowledge, no other European country has followed suit.

In sum, even though most countries' charity laws condone some political activity, the gray areas and unclear margins, as well as the fear of potentially severe repercussions when transgressing these margins, make public political advocacy a potentially hazardous activity for NGOs. Nonprofit sector research points out that restrictions of political activity tend to promote a culture of tacit self-censorship and ultimately limit the capacity of NGOs to advocate for social change and engage publicly with public policy (Berry and Arons 2003). As the changing debate in the United Kingdom signals, governments can encourage the nongovernmental sector to use its voice for public and political advocacy. Yet in most governance contexts it is taken for granted that NGOs tread the waters of public political advocacy very carefully and are ultimately at the mercy of the goodwill of government agencies. This stifles dissent and discourages NGO advocacy and politicization of civil society matters.[13]

ACCOUNTABILITY DEBATES

A second factor that constrains NGOs' public advocacy, as well as their engagement capacity, concerns the particular frames that have been employed in recent debates about representativeness and accountability.[14] Whereas it is widely accepted that NGOs do not operate within a *narrow* traditional representational paradigm (they are not being voted in and out of office),[15] they are often asked to answer to more loosely defined representational claims ("whom do you speak for?") in their institutional and public principal–agent relationships. When the International Monetary Fund and the World Bank prepared for their annual meeting in Prague in 2000, *The Economist* published a lengthy article on groups that they identified as fueling the "backlash against globalization," arguing,

The increasing clout of NGOs, respectable and not so respectable, raises an important question: who elected Oxfam, or, for that matter, the League for a Revolutionary Communist International? Bodies as these are, to varying degrees, extorting admissions of fault from law-abiding companies and changes in policy from democratically elected governments. They may claim to be acting in the interests of the people – but then so do the objects of their criticism, governments and the despised international institutions. In the West, governments and their agencies are, in the end, accountable to voters. Who holds the activists accountable? (*The Economist* 2000)

---

[13] Politicization, in this context, is used in two related ways. One, it implies raising political awareness or involvement and thereby the salience of issues – that is, its participatory dimension. Two, it refers to the agonistic dimension of the political process; it indicates conflict and debate (Mouffe 2005; see also in a neofunctionalist tradition Schmitter 1969). NGOs struggle with the capacity to politicize on both accounts: with how to achieve salience of issues when participation often is limited to institutional actors at the expense of broader public involvement and with their limitations on taking part in agonistic public debate around some policy issues for fear of overstepping legal restrictions.

[14] For an overview of this debate see Jordan and van Tuijl (2006). Accountability questions, according to Jordan and Van Tuijl, are on the rise for three reasons: There is a rapid growth in the numbers and size of NGOs, they attract more funds, and they gain a stronger voice in shaping public policy (4).

[15] See, for example, Peruzzotti, who argues that "analyses that simply stretch the concept of political representation to civic associations overlook the crucial differences between these two types of organizations" (Peruzzotti 2006: 44).

In such accounts and across all levels of governance from local to global arenas, NGOs have come under scrutiny for exerting what is perceived to be undue influence. If they are not elected, then how can they claim to represent civil society? Although recent research has emphasized both the normative and technical differences between representation and accountability schemes (Charnovitz 2005; Jordan and van Tuijl 2006; Peruzzotti 2006; Vedder 2007), NGOs have been struggling with the perception that they lack both representativeness in a narrow sense and accountability to constituents in a wider sense. They have not been able to embrace and capitalize on the idea that their accountability derives its mechanisms not from institutional politics, but from interaction with civil society constituencies, which, in principle, "leave[s] great room for creative and innovative action, allowing... NGOs to challenge present identities or existing constituencies without being concerned about electoral accountability or due process" (Peruzzotti 2006: 48).

In addition to the challenges they face regarding formal representational mechanisms, NGOs also tend to find themselves increasingly under scrutiny for not delivering results. A recent example is the public dispute over how the Red Cross and other NGOs distributed donations after the Haiti earthquake of 2010. Human rights advocates and the media criticized that, two years after the disaster, "more than a half million Haitians are still sleeping under tarps, often in camps without enough water or toilets" (Page 2012: 1). A PBS documentary titled *Haiti: Where Did the Money Go?* placed responsibility for still lingering inhuman living conditions squarely on the international NGOs on the ground. Filmmaker Michele Mitchell claimed that "when you give money to a do-good organization, you expect them to do good with it. We need to do better." NGOs in this case are presented as a disappointment when it comes to "fixing" social ills. They are being made singlehandedly responsible for the lingering catastrophe, while considerably less attention is given to the political, economic, and social context in which they try to "do good."[16]

---

[16] The limits of constructing legitimacy in the language of efficiency are glaring in this case. Although the Red Cross might well have been able to build more housing and a better infrastructure than it did, and although there can be a legitimate public interest in asking "how many people the NGOs have missed, and why" (*Chicago Tribune* Page 2012), this narrow construction of legitimacy uses an undisclosed, and maybe even unreflected, yardstick: ending the extreme poverty for all affected Haitians. In other words, it assumes that NGOs could have done what governments and international assistance over decades have failed to do. If, to the contrary, public engagement would have been used as a substantial measure in constructing the legitimacy of the Red Cross's and other NGOs' efforts in Haiti, then, I submit, a more realistic assessment of the

Shortcomings in effectiveness are perceived as indicating a lack of legitimacy and as breaking the compact between an NGO and its individual sponsors.

Narrowly formal, highly individualized, and overstated moral accountability claims have succeeded in putting many NGOs on the defensive. In order to construct a more robust, civically embedded legitimacy for NGOs, we need to redefine accountability. One way to view accountability is as the "institutional vocabulary through which ideas of representation, legitimacy, and authorization are represented" (O'Kelly 2011: 256). Yet this vocabulary, as I have argued in Chapter 1, can be based on different dictionaries: It can reflect concerns of representation and authorization within an organization, between an NGO and its funders or donors, or between the organization and its wider stakeholder community as defined by the NGO. In a different perspective, so the argument of this book suggests, acts of NGO outreach and engagement with publics should be put at the center of the accountability debate.

Yet most public debate on accountability at this point is not concerned with NGO outreach to constituencies. Instead, it takes its cues from misused funds, violations of laws, or perceived shortcomings in effectiveness that threaten accountability to donors. The remedies that are offered tend to focus on internal management processes on the one hand, on outcome measures and so-called 'stakeholder accountability' on the other hand. These remedies, in effect, urge NGOs to organize even more bureaucratically and produce even more quantifiable data on internal affairs and external effects than in the past. Although my intention is not to deny altogether the validity of these specific measures of accountability, it seems important to consider the various frames that shape the debate and, in particular, to what degree they address accountabilities to the public.

The first frame is donor accountability. In the 1990s, accountability was primarily raised in the context of "ties that bind" (Hulme and Edwards 1997), articulating discomfort with the dependencies created by an increasing number of NGOs relying on funding from states and private donors. The arguments presented in this debate were not simply that NGOs were silenced by money. Instead, researchers followed the more intricate traces of how donors produced and shaped NGO work and their advocacy. One of the earliest empirical analyses on how

degree to which NGO intervention was legitimate in the eyes of constituents might have emerged. Moreover, with a focus on public engagement as a legitimacy source, the Red Cross could have better communicated and politicized the limits of its interventions with donors as well as with constituents.

donors influence advocacy through funding allocations was Shelley Feldman's account of the "un(stated) contradictions" between NGOs and
efforts to build civil society after independence in Bangladesh (Feldman
1997). Feldman traced the role of NGOs in the privatization and liberalization of a formerly nationalized economy in the broader context
of the neoliberal agenda of development assistance. As NGOs came to
speak for the people and as the NGO sector became legitimized "as
a controlled, organized arena of public debate with institutional and
financial support from the donor community" (Feldman 1997: 59), other
less controllable voices were being marginalized. The "ties that bind"
led NGOs to shift their accountability from constituents to funding
agencies. As a consequence, agendas were tweaked and frames altered
so that they presented a better fit for donors and might secure future
funding more easily. Even if an NGO lost trust within a local community, this did not necessarily mean losing donor support, because
evaluations tended not to look at long-term effects. Accountability to
donors thus resulted in frame adaptation and ultimately became a technocratic assessment of "numbers of beneficiaries and resources allocated and
disbursed" (64).

In the past decade, a number of studies have taken up the question
of NGO and donor relationships, with the vast majority corroborating
Feldman's conclusion by finding strong frame adaptation to donor interests. In the global South, NGOs align their mission to comply with their
mostly foreign and northern donors' emphasis on service provision at the
expense of advocacy (Hudock 1999; Edwards 2004). Structural dependency problems are often exacerbated wherever direct communication
channels are weak. The more that constituents of NGOs and funding
sources are removed from each other, the more difficult it becomes for
NGOs on the ground to satisfy demands from both sides (Chandhoke
2003).

In the global North, some NGO leaders fear that confrontational
political activity will impact their donor or government funding (Salamon 1995; Hudson 2002: 412; Berry and Arons 2003: 74; Bass et al.
2007), that donor dependency produces mission drift (Henderson 2003;
Aksartova 2009), and that donors prefer service provision over advocacy
(Smith and Gronbjerg 2006).[17] Donors, by way of how they frame program calls, already preselect certain agendas, in the process framing social

---

[17] Counterevidence has been provided by Chaves, Stephens, and Galaskiewicz (2004),
who analyze differences in political activism between church congregations that receive
government funding and others that do not. They find either a neutral or a positive

conflicts in ways that tend to establish specific norms while marginalizing others (i.e., Hudock 1999: 33ff.). Grant recipients, in turn, will adapt their frames to funders and, as we have established earlier, there are clear disincentives for NGOs to discuss mismatches of program mission with constituent needs or other failures with their donors. Until recently, for example, Western donors who sponsored programs dealing with violence against women in Russia and Africa did not accept contextualization in terms of class and poverty, but instead only sponsored projects with a clear focus on domestic violence against women (Hemment 2004). Gordon and Berkovitch (2008), in their study of Israeli human rights NGOs, show that international donors not only produce program frames but also incentivize certain strategies over others. Major foreign donors to human rights causes in Israel, they point out, strongly favor litigation over more systematically critical and activist approaches to human rights violations. In sum, donor ties, albeit to varying degrees, influence NGO mission, strategies, and advocacy capacity.

To limit exposure to and the influence of donor interests, some NGOs have policies of not soliciting any funds from potential adversaries in business or government. Greenpeace for example, an NGO that exposes state and business failures in environmental protection, considers independence from state sponsorship a crucial element of its organization. Amnesty International depends on a similar image as not being susceptible to state influence for its ability to critique human rights violations across the globe. And Médecins Sans Frontières avoids donor influence by making it their mission to provide medical care independent of who is a perpetrator and who is a victim in humanitarian crisis situations; it argues that its mission could be jeopardized if it could, however indirectly, be associated with one side of a conflict (Frantz and Martens 2006: 28).

Yet most NGOs are dependent on grants from institutional donors such as governments or foundations and will therefore to some degree adapt frames, strategies, and tools to those favored by these institutions. In recent years, donor prerogatives have come under scrutiny, and "donor accountability" is now discussed not as accountability *to*, but as accountability *of* donors (Bendell and Cox 2006). Yet far more critical inspection is reserved for NGOs, specifically their deployment of funds for programs, services, and advocacy.

correlation between government funding and political activism. Their conclusions, however, might need contextualization, because government funding might make up only a small proportion of a church's budget and thus not influence its agenda to the degree that constant and larger outside donor support does.

A second stream of the accountability debate focuses on inner-organizational accountability, in particular relating to hierarchy and delegation within an NGO and to accountability to external boards. This debate has affected the activities of larger NGOs more than smaller ones, with criticisms regarding financial transparency, unclear hierarchies, and unaccountable decision-making processes resulting in considerable inner-organizational inspection by many NGOs. Frequently, change agendas are drafted and monitored by means of self-regulatory codes and standards (Ebrahim 2009: 889ff.). Yet whereas extensive inner-organizational accountability measures primarily sap labor and energy resources and thus might affect an organization's willingness to engage in public advocacy and outreach indirectly, accountability to boards has been identified as a more immediate and critical issue for NGO advocacy. A discussion among nonprofit leaders in the United States, recorded by the Johns Hopkins Nonprofit Listening Post Project, highlights some of the constraints that board accountability might impose on advocacy and outreach:

Several participants emphasized that they feel inhibited by their boards from getting involved in policy advocacy, and particularly advocacy around the issues that could affect their clientele and community (vs. issues relating to their programs and funding). Providing a clear example of this, Peter Goldberg (President and Chief Executive Officer, Alliance of Children and Families and United Neighborhood Centers of America) noted, "I don't know of many service providing organizations in our field who will address the issue of gun control. Our boards don't want to engage in this type of issue." Explaining the challenge, Mr. Goldberg pointed out that in the human service field, nonprofit boards have grown more conservative over the past twenty years. "This creates a tension in our organizations that is sometimes easier to avoid by staying away from policy and advocacy." (Geller and Salamon 2009: 2)

Two features of boards intertwine to stifle NGO public political advocacy. One, NGOs need to have boards composed of knowledgeable, but also well-networked personalities; increasingly, rich donors and members of business communities are being asked to serve on boards and thus bring profit-making as well as more socially conservative logics to the table. Two, boards are more narrowly focused on mission accomplishment and tend to disincentivize broader social agendas, thus leaving NGO executives prone to neglecting public advocacy and to streamlining accountability measures to fit their internal operations.

This focus on internal accountability finds its academic equivalent in public choice theories that conceptualize NGOs as firms. The "firm" analogy asserts that NGOs operate just like corporations and therefore can be subjected to the same accountability mechanisms as business operations, that is, primarily accountability to an NGO's board and consumers or clients. The firm analogy developed in opposition to accounts that see the NGO sector characterized by norms and thus clearly distinguish it from the state and business sectors, which are authority and profit centered, respectively (Khagram, Riker, and Sikkink 2002). NGO members and supporters, according to norm-centered approaches, "are primarily motivated to shape the world according to their principled beliefs. Of course, many government and business activities are also involved in managing meanings, but for NGOs and movements it is their raison d'être, rather than an ancillary motivation for action" (Khagram et al. 2002: 11). These principled beliefs and the resulting strategies distinguish NGOs from business, and the specific motivations of NGOs influence their choice of strategies and tools. Yet proponents of the firm analogy, such as Sell, Prakash, and Gugerty, disagree. They find that "both business and NGO networks" have "principled as well as instrumental beliefs," and thus it is impossible to distinguish them on the basis of motivations (Sell and Prakash 2004: 151). Moreover, they find that business and NGOs do employ "similar types of strategies" (see also Prakash and Gugerty 2009). By their account, NGO strategies are exclusively determined by the external environment and not by a set of norms that guide their actions (Sell and Prakash 2004: 150). Proponents of the firm approach to NGOs see individuals who support these organizations as making similar choices as when they buy a product.

Many of the findings that Gugerty and Prakash present echo the NGOization theme of Chapter 3, specifically the tendency in the sector to professionalize, bureaucratize, and institutionalize. However, what from a public sphere and democracy perspective might seem problematic is simply the result of rational choices in the "firm" account of NGOs. Thus, NGOs might be well served to institute equally hierarchical management and business administration procedures as the business firm next door.[18] Moreover, advocacy in the firm analogy mutates into a functional strategy to increase returns for "customers" and indirectly the "employees" of the firm. If we follow the firm analogy, then the public is reduced to an aggregate of individualized consumers or clients of NGOs, which they fund as stakeholders and shareholders. The NGO firm's key purposes are to deliver returns and satisfy consumers. Ultimately, citizen consumers

---

[18] Taking the "firm" analogy even further, Pallotta advocates abandoning the charity constraints on the nongovernmental sector altogether so it can make full use of capitalism's virtues in acquiring capital for social causes (Pallotta 2008).

exert market power by "shopping" for the products of the nongovernmental sector. Accountability to the NGO firm thus becomes an internal
management problem; in its marketized form, it becomes a mere reflection
of "consumer" interest in its products. The fact that NGOs are not dis-
tributing surplus wealth among owners or stakeholders is acknowledged,
but not considered to be a salient enough distinction from firms.

The central problem with the firm analogy is that, although it might
capture the professionalized direction in which the NGO sector is being
pulled, expressed for example in stricter board accountability, it reifies
this pull without addressing its potential effects on democratic voice.
Public choice theory and the firm analogy thus "naturalize" the inward-
oriented dimensions of NGOization and the reliance on citizen consumers
rather than mobilized constituents. In the firm logic, institutional advocacy and upward accountability to boards, trustees, and governments are
valid in that they facilitate survival of the operation, and so is the occasional PR campaign. The sector's functions as an assembly of organized
venues for citizen engagement and as an incubator of publics have little
place in the firm logic of instrumental accountabilities.

Finally, a third debate that puts its mark on the accountability issue
includes right-wing attacks on what is perceived to be a left-leaning and
radical NGO sector. As NGOs have increased their influence in policy
agenda setting from the local to the global level, and as relationships with
governments and business have grown (Keck and Sikkink 1998; Take
1999; Warkentin 2001; Berry and Arons 2003; Risse 2004), concern with
NGO politics has risen to prominence. NGOs are credited with having set
major global public policy agendas over the past decade, tackling issues
such as unsustainable debt, environmental degradation, human rights
law, violence against women, landmine removal, and corporate social
responsibility (Jordan and van Tuijl 2006: 4). The success of these NGO
interventions has begun to raise questions from political conservatives
who see NGOs as progressive liberal forces with too much influence and
too little legitimacy (e.g., Anderson 2003; Entine 2003; Rabkin 2003).

Critics associated with neoconservative think tanks have launched
websites to monitor NGO bias and entice donors to demand stricter
accountability and transparency, framed in the language of "neutrality"
and "nonpartisanship." NGOwatch.org, launched jointly in 2003 by the
Federalist Society together with the American Enterprise Institute, the
Rushford Report in Washington, DC, and the NGO Monitor in Jerusalem
all target progressive advocacy NGOs and in particular their participation in global governance arenas. These projects have a similar mission: to

expose what they believe to be biased investments in progressive causes by NGOs that share "a knee jerk demonization of corporations and free market" (Entine 2003: 2) or other "biases" such as pro-Palestinian political positions. As seen through the eyes of this conservative subpublic, the nongovernmental sector is responsible for ideologically motivated and unsubstantiated attacks on the pillars of global capitalism and U.S. foreign policy. Entine, for example, cites the Rainforest Action Network's campaign against Citigroup starting in 2000, which exposed the bank's investments in operations responsible for rainforest destruction, climate change, and the disruption of the livelihood of indigenous peoples: "Clearly, this one issue will not bring a multi-faceted company such as Citigroup to its knees. But it is more than just a mere annoyance; it is reputation management hell" (3) fueled, in his opinion, by "NGO hysteria" (1). Sponsors of NGO watchdogs are mostly right-wing think tanks; NGO Monitor, by contrast, operates as a university-based project in Israel that is co-founded by the Wechsler family foundation.

Assessing the long-term impact of these relatively new conservative watchdogs on NGO advocacy is difficult. What is already apparent is that organizations such as NGO Monitor primarily use legal stipulations attached to charity status to force donors or funders to withdraw from sponsoring certain NGOs. In February 2012, for example, NGO Monitor succeeded in getting a German NGO that compensates survivors of Nazi labor camps to withdraw funding for an Israeli NGO because of its support of the Palestinian right to return (Axelrod 2012). The director of the German NGO argued that it could not support an organization with a political agenda. Even large targeted NGOs, such as Human Rights Watch, find themselves engulfed in a PR war over claims of anti-Israeli positions and actions, and they spend precious staff and financial resources defending themselves (Peratis 2006). Conservative watchdog organizations thus might contribute to a climate of subtle fear, ultimately counting on the self-restraint of targeted NGOs that are motivated to protect their organization.

By some measure, NGOs themselves have become culprits in allowing the accountability debate to shift from seeking legitimacy through broad public engagement to singularly defending their organizational survival (Feldman 1997: 64). By allowing the debate to shrink to inner-organizational and technocratic management strategies, donor engagement, and the occasional public audit, NGOs might be forfeiting chances to substantiate their legitimacy claims with public engagement. This response is even more notable considering that the sector's public

TABLE 4.2. *Trust in NGOs and Other Institutions, 2012*

	United States %	Europe[a] %	Asia[b] %	Canada %	Brazil %
NGOs	58	57	62	66	49
Business	50	40	54	56	63
Government	43	30	46	56	32
Media	45	48	57	54	61

Note: This survey is conducted yearly with 1,950 "opinion leaders" in 11 countries. Opinion leaders are defined as high-income persons with significant interest in media, economic, and policy affairs. Results are based on 25-minute phone interviews.
[a] Europe = UK, France, Italy, Germany, Spain, Poland.
[b] Asia = Japan, China, South Korea, India.
Source: Edelman Trust Barometer® 2012.

reputation overall has been and still is excellent. Despite increased scrutiny from donors, academic critics, and conservative watchdogs, citizens tend to trust NGO integrity, authority, and expertise compared with other institutions. Public opinion surveys indicate that in the United States, Asia, across Europe, as well as in Canada, NGOs are considered more trustworthy than either business, government, or the media (see Table 4.2).

Knutsen and Brower (2010: 600) argue that NGOs might capitalize on this trust by refocusing the debate on *expressive accountabilities* as opposed to mere instrumental accountabilities. Expressive accountabilities are broadly defined as "accountabilities to the community, to mission, and to patrons." They signal an NGO's reliance on broad community outreach to clarify its mission and learn how to implement adequate change agendas while serving their clients. Yet I suggest that expressive accountabilities should include another important dimension of NGO activity, involving not just a one-way focus group approach to gauge constituents' needs that the NGO will then tend to organizationally but also the pledge to strengthen citizen voice along the way through efforts to generate publics. NGO accountability needs to be based on broadly engaging *and* activating constituents, it is in essence *public* accountability [see also Jens Steffek (2010)].

Public accountability, in this view, entails commitment to the activation of civil society discourse with the goal of generating self-sustaining publics. It implies that NGOs not only *represent* but also *constitute* publics by aggregating, amplifying, and strengthening voices that otherwise might not be heard. Public accountability is generated by four modes in which NGOs relate to publics: (1) providing transparency in terms of the organizations' operation, finances, and information on their mission and goals; (2) initiating and sustaining debate that is open, widely accessible, and interactive; (3) promoting active and continuous engagement of constituents and interested citizens in the organization; and (4) enabling constituents to organize public voice and thus serving as catalysts for stronger publics. Generating public accountability in these four modes of transparency, debate, engagement, and activation would radically alter the status of NGOs in governance contexts. If they would be representatives at all, then they would be "interim representatives" (Nyamugasira 1998), speaking for communities while engaging in a process of organizing publicness. This would mean reversing the tendency that Bass et al. (2007: 116) detected among NGOs to go "from mobilizing citizens to representing citizens."

THE VOLUNTEER CITIZEN

If NGOs want to foster stronger public accountability, they need involved citizens who are prepared to engage with an organization in more than a cursory manner. However, a third set of conditions that disincentivize public NGO advocacy and accountability point to the particular citizenship practices associated with NGOized civil society and late modern governance. In the global North, citizenship practices of the early 21st century are captured in images of the consumer and the volunteer citizen. Whereas governments tend to leave the promotion of consumer citizens to the markets – with exceptions, such as former President Bush encouraging Americans to go shopping post-9/11 – there are clear indicators of states' investment in empowering volunteerism. In 2008, 61.8 million Americans – 26.4 percent of the adult population – contributed a total of 8 billion volunteering hours worth 162 billion USD to the United States.[19] From the local to state and national levels, calls go out to citizens to volunteer, and websites such as http://www.serve.gov link potential volunteers to volunteering opportunities across the country. In a time of fiscal hardship, California Governor Schwarzenegger, in 2008, launched a new cabinet position for "Service and Volunteering," the first of its kind in the United States, to encourage Californians to become involved in their communities and the state.[20] There is hardly a city in

---

[19] The data are extracted from the Corporation for National and Community Service at http://www.volunteeringinamerica.gov.
[20] The initiative was portrayed during its launch as completely cost neutral.

the United States that does not have a government-sponsored or endorsed volunteer platform in which volunteering is presented as the prime means to connect to one's polity.

Across Europe, volunteer rates are considerably lower, which enticed the European Union to declare 2011 the "European Year of Volunteering" and to state quite unabashedly in its press release that "volunteering has a great, but so far under-exploited, potential for the social and economic development of Europe."[21] Governments and foundations across the continent have made a tremendous effort in recent years to instill volunteer spirit in a citizenry that is being slowly weaned off the welfare state. Voluntary agencies have been created in many municipalities that are focused on publicizing the idea of volunteering, as well as matching volunteers with NGOs and other organizations. In Germany, there were about 400 such voluntary agencies in 2012.[22] Yet governments are not the only entities intent on bolstering volunteerism. NGOs likewise depend on volunteers signing on for office tasks, campaigns or other activities.

As economies struggle and funding sources diminish, volunteers have become an invaluable part of most NGO operations. Between September 2008 and March 2009 alone, more than one-third of U.S.-based nonprofit organizations reported an increase in the number of their volunteers, and almost half anticipated an increase in their use of volunteers in the near future.[23]

How does the culture of volunteering affect public advocacy and political voice? The available research on this issue is not conclusive. For some observers, volunteerism indicates initiation into a less individualistic and more social way of understanding society; it is seen as the gateway to social activism (Cronin and Perold 2006). In a recent study for CIVICUS, the World Association for Civic Engagement, Cronin and Perold argue that volunteerism and social or political activism feed on each other, and they criticize approaches that have branded volunteering as a mere "bandaid" for social injustices or even as a depoliticizing force in neoliberal societies. Similar studies see volunteerism as "political in a range of ways, including in the power relations it emphasizes or creates, the

---

[21] European Commission press release, June 3, 2009, at http://ec.europa.eu/citizenship/news/news820_en.htm.

[22] Data from Bundesarbeitsgemeinschaft der Freiwilligenagenturen at www.bagfa.de (accessed June 10, 2012).

[23] Data from the Corporation for National and Community Service, "Volunteering in America. Research Highlights," at http://www.nationalservice.gov.

judgments it implies about the social or welfare system in a community, the action or lack of action by governments on a given issue, the life choices of community members, or simply in the emphasis it places on the role of individuals within the functioning of society" (Petriwskyj and Warburton 2007: 83).

In contrast, although researchers who are more focused on public voice and communicative involvement might see merit in volunteer activities, at the same time they note that judgments that are implicit in volunteering lack discursive power. Individual acts of volunteering will not yield change if volunteers' concerns are not translated into acts of "giving voice" and if voice is not transformed into collective public advocacy. Jeffrey Alexander, in his seminal study on civil society, argues,

> Civil associations, such as Mothers against Drunk Driving or Moveon.Org, are...vital communicative institutions of civil life. It is traditional to equate such civil associations with voluntary associations, but I am skeptical about taking this path. Voluntariness characterizes the Girl Scouts, hospital volunteers, and the PTA. Each of these is a good thing, but they do not project communicative judgments in the wider civil sphere. (Alexander 2006: 5)

The criterion that is being employed here is whether volunteer activity emphasizes, or at least includes, the construction of public social or political messages and the dissemination of these messages into wider publics. I call the act of projecting communicative judgments "doing public advocacy." Not that the Girl Scouts or PTA volunteers are by some iron law restricted to holding cookie sales and school fundraisers. They could engage in, albeit limited, public political advocacy to try and alter policies in their district or state. It is the abstinence from "projecting public judgment" while claiming to do good as an individual that makes the culture of volunteering not conducive to public advocacy.

Trying to understand this "strange process of political evaporation" in many volunteer-based contexts, sociologist Nina Eliasoph has provided an intricate account of the lack of public-spirited talk in American civic group contexts (Eliasoph 1998: 7). First, there is a commonly shared sentiment that helping hands-on with a project that yields tangible results is more rewarding than getting involved in long-term public policy advocacy. Second, people often volunteer in arenas that are somewhat close to home and therefore are less interested in seeing the bigger picture underlying those problems. Third, and this brings us back to the question of the role of NGOs in advocacy, citizens have internalized the idea that legitimacy for speaking in public is tied to "speaking for yourself."

Political talk about broader issues therefore tends to take place in "backstage" contexts, whereas public talk in "frontstage" environments shrinks to the narration of personal experience. Media feed into the evaporation of frontstage politics by granting legitimacy of voice more often to those directly affected than to those who speak on broader public concerns or who want to speak for those who are affected (see the later discussion).

For the United States, there is additional evidence that people refrain from discussing politics in order to avoid conflict and preserve social harmony (i.e., Mutz 2006: 107ff.). Thus, public talk shrinks to instances of personal stories, and the civic alphabet of publicly speaking *for others* gets decimated. NGOs could attempt to nurture a connection between volunteering and public voice, but, as Eliasoph shows, public voice must be trained and the contestation it might involve must be accepted as part of the social fabric of societies. Some recent interventions have therefore suggested "learning from the 'not-so-nice' volunteers" (Cravens 2004: 1) how to combine proximity and hands-on experience with repertoires of public contestation and voice.

I do not want to cast all volunteer activity as nonpolitical; in fact, some NGOs have developed much expertise in the deployment of volunteers for public advocacy. Student actions against sweatshop labor on campuses, petition campaigns to protest the Iraq War, and the Copenhagen protest during the COP15 meetings would not have happened without volunteer corps giving their time to public advocacy. However, the evolution of a civic culture in which personalized civic engagement meets professionalized NGOs often results in the orchestration of public involvement through highly managed activities by NGOs that offer concerned citizens easy roles to play in acting out their causes. A visible trend to professionalize public advocacy has put collective public voice and action into the hands of a few well-trained activists while appealing to broader constituencies for quick and easy means of support, such as a signature, a donation, or a fleeting appearance in a flash mob. The image of the Greenpeace protesters on the Brent Spar, or the Robin Hood tree climbers, or the PETA activists rescuing animals from test labs convey actions of highly professionalized activists. Greenpeace, for example, gives intensive training to professional activists before they enter a contested public situation. PETA, while encouraging volunteers to produce self-organized public events, only gently nudges its audience into a more contested repertoire. Its Action Center states in the rubric for grassroots activism a number of activities such as "set up an information table" and "ask your library to order animal-friendly books." The activity with the most public contestation potential is introduced in a peculiar manner. It reads, "Plan a demonstration. Organizing a demonstration is a great way to help animals, and it's not as scary or difficult as it may sound. In fact, demonstrations can involve as little as passing out leaflets and holding posters."[24] I am not quoting this to elicit smiles. This quote, I submit, may reflect the distance that many early 21st-century volunteers in the global North feel from active voice and contestation in public spaces. The volunteer citizen, in this light, needs assurance by an outspoken public advocacy NGO that taking a stance publicly is not so dangerous after all and can in fact be considered acceptable behavior. Yet seen from a different perspective, the individual volunteer in need of these kinds of assurances might be a successful fit for neoliberal states.

In sum, for the most part, NGOs in the global North operate within volunteer cultures that disincentivize public advocacy. A 2008 survey of a representative sample of U.S.-based nonprofits in four policy areas by the Johns Hopkins University Center for Civil Society Studies found that, although nearly three-quarters of nonprofits engage in some form of public advocacy during the year, less than 2 percent of these organizations' budget is devoted to these activities and most "rely on the least demanding forms of engagement (e.g., signing a correspondence to a government official endorsing or opposing a particular piece of legislation or budget proposal)" (Salamon and Lessans Gellner 2008: 2). Advocacy is concentrated "in a narrow band of organizational players – chiefly the executive director. Most organizations report that clients or patrons are 'rarely' or 'never' involved in their lobbying or advocacy" (2), thus leaving volunteers to perform almost exclusively service-oriented tasks. Even public-advocacy-oriented NGOs like PETA have established a three-tiered system of activation in which volunteers play only a limited role. On the first tier operate a small number of professionalized and well-trained activists who stage and publicize its messages; a second tier of volunteers is encouraged to practice occasional outreach that is tailored to be consonant with their lifestyles; and a third tier of "checkbook advocates" is enlisted to provide the funding for public advocacy. Thus the volunteer orientation of late modern citizenship is not conducive to generating engaged publics. NGOs have learned to turn a vice into a virtue: By focusing on institutional advocacy, NGOs might not have extensive need

---

[24] PETA Action Center at http://www.peta.org/actioncenter/act.asp (accessed June 13, 2010).

for an activated base of citizens and thus might avoid citizen engagement altogether.

TRADITIONAL NEWS MEDIA

A fourth factor that has significant influence on NGOs' public advocacy is access to and representation in established news media. Although the relationship between NGOs and the news media is changing considerably as new communication technologies facilitate direct communication and targeted outreach to constituents, donors, and interested publics (see Chapters 6 and 7), coverage by print media and TV has long been considered indispensable for successful public advocacy. Even as their dependency on established media is waning, NGOs still acknowledge the capacity of just one positive or negative news story in a major newspaper or international news outlet to make or break a campaign (Cottle and Nolan 2009). Thus, at the same time as NGOs explore new civic spaces on Facebook, Second Life, or other Internet-based working platforms, a prime indicator for successful mobilization remains coverage in established news outlets.

The study of NGO representation in traditional media, however, is still in its infancy; empirical analyses are few and far between (i.e., Hale 2007; Cottle and Nolan 2009).[25] Yet some observations are supported by several studies and seem to be gaining increasing salience. One, NGOs have long had a difficult time getting into established media, and if they do, they had to make large investments in order to get even minimal coverage. Two, with many traditional news outlets having downsized the number of reporters who can cover an issue or an area with in-depth knowledge, NGOs have increasingly become their own news source, which media outlets take as welcome (and cheap) replacements that compensate for their own downsized independent reporting. Three, the predilection of media for personalized stories affects the ways NGOs tailor their public image and their advocacy; they sideline broader political messages in favor of direct and personalized accounts of how someone is personally affected by an issue. Let us consider each of these observations separately.

---

[25] For an excellent introduction to the recent debates on NGOs and the media, see the discussion papers from the 2009/2010 Harvard Nieman Lab Series on "NGOs and the News. Exploring a Changing Communication Landscape," at http://www.niemanlab .org/ngo (accessed February 17, 2012).

NGOs Are Marginalized in the News

The marginalization of NGOs in established media is becoming more evident in different arenas from the global to the local level.[26] A report by Steve Ross for the Fritz Institute and the Reuters Foundation in 2004, analyzing media coverage of humanitarian relief efforts, found that endemic problems both of journalists and of NGOs contribute to overall thin coverage of global relief issues in general and of NGOs in particular (Ross 2004). As for national-level NGOs, my own exploratory study on media exposure of five large national urban/housing and five national women's advocacy NGOs in four U.S. national newspapers in 2004 (Lang 2009) showed that, during this one-year period, the five women's NGOs were mentioned overall only 16 times in these four papers, and the five urban development NGOs were included in a mere 49 articles across four papers.[27] In more than two-thirds of these articles, the NGO was referenced only once, suggesting only a fleeting interest by the reporter in the NGOs' contribution to a specific issue. Of the 49 articles on urban development in which an NGO was mentioned, there was only a single mention in 35 articles; 11 of the 16 articles that cited a women's NGO only mentioned it once. Although we had assumed that national NGOs in these two arenas would be prominent in promoting "debate on issues pertinent to the concerns and agendas of their constituents" (Minkoff 2001: 191), our findings present evidence that the context of reporting was service-related in almost half of the cases. These articles reported on the "good deeds" of NGOs overall much more than on their public advocacy. Of the 10 organizations, 4 were never mentioned in any newspaper during the year. Not surprisingly, it was prominent NGOs such as Habitat for Humanity and the Feminist Majority that received the vast majority of coverage. A similar preference for a small number of

---

[26] One exception to this limited media exposure of NGOs seems to be the abortion debate in the United States. Ferree, Gamson, Gerhards, and Rucht find in comparing U.S. and German abortion discourse that in the United States, the NGO and activist sector provides 43 percent of media speakers in major news outlets. In Germany, by contrast, these groups only represent 19 percent of the speakers, whereas government has a much larger discursive footprint (Ferree et al. 2002: 90). One might speculate that the abortion issue embodies a very specific and long-standing polarized civil society cleavage in the United States that lends itself to media reports where NGOs become speakers for polarized constituencies.

[27] For their assistance with coding and analysis I would like to thank Aylan Lee, Lindsay Schrupp, and Zach Hansen. These are the same national NGOs whose financial situation in 2004 we explored in Chapter 3. Most increased their income substantially during the period from 1998 to 2005. The combined LexisNexis and ProQuest analysis included the *New York Times, Washington Post, Los Angeles Times,* and *USA Today.*

already well-established NGOs seems to exist in local newspaper coverage. When sociologists Ronald Jacobs and Daniel Glass (2002) evaluated the media footprint of a random sample of 750 New York–based nonprofits over eight years in the three major New York newspapers, the distribution of the more than 9,000 articles that cited NGOs was highly skewed. On one end of the spectrum, almost one-third of the NGOs were never mentioned throughout the eight years. On the other end, about 2 percent of the NGOs appeared in more than 100 news articles each; "median publicity was two news articles over the eight year period, suggesting that news publicity is a relatively rare event for most organizations" (Jacobs and Glass 2002: 240).

Looking beyond the United States, a similar lack of NGO voice has been found in the coverage of European issues provided by national quality newspapers across Europe. Hans-Jörg Trenz showed for EU countries that media coverage on European governance largely fails to mention NGOs. Although topical articles on Europe account for between 40 and 50 percent of news coverage in the six countries of his sample,[28] the vast majority of the articles identify national governments and the European Commission as agenda setters. Trenz noted,

The remarkable absence of non-institutional, non-statal actors – be it on the transnational, national or local level – is striking. . . . There is a clear media bias towards institutional and governmental actors and not towards civil society. Although NGOs and civic associations have become progressively included in European governance and quite often play a decisive role in EU policy deliberation and decision-making, this activity is not documented in news coverage. (Trenz 2004: 301)

Although there is evidence for NGOs being overall scarce interlocutors in the established news media, there is less consensus on the reasons for this marginalization. Is it self-inflicted by the lack of professional media relations of NGOs? Or do many NGOs perceive "no news as good news" and carry on their work well outside the spotlight of traditional media? Or do the media actively index the news according to the perceived importance of speakers, and governments as well as established interest groups rank higher in reputation than the NGO sector? To some degree, I submit, all three rationales are at work. Many medium-sized and small NGOs lack any press training. If they have professional PR experts, they are in the headquarters and not in the field. Yet it is the

---

[28] Data on news coverage are based on quality news outlets in Italy, Great Britain, France, Germany, Austria, and Spain (Trenz 2004: 296). The sample included 4,225 articles from the year 2000.

field from which journalists want to draw personalized stories. NGOs also are acutely aware that donors tend to be hesitant to fund press operations. On the other side of the mismatch, media concentration has led to fewer experts in specific fields of NGO activity, resulting in increasingly inexperienced journalists who take on complex matters and cover several beats simultaneously (Ross 2004: 5). As a consequence, NGO members cannot rely on either journalists bringing expertise into a conversation or taking the time to learn. The result is decontextualized reporting, in which the background of conflicts is often distorted or omitted. The serious news media "are still more prone to focus on a descriptive 'who, what, where and when' rather than on a causative 'why'" (Darley 2000: 152).

To capture media attention, NGO advocacy must be meticulously prepared and professionally arranged. These peak moments of publicness are the work of well-versed PR strategists who focus their energy on creating lasting images that will rally citizens around a cause while at the same time "branding" the NGO (i.e., Fenton 2009). Greenpeace has been singled out frequently as being the role model for crafting such iconic images in the minds of journalists and the public; doing so takes planning, ample finances, creative energy, boldness, and a set of potent lawyers in the background. Greenpeace does not rely on the media finding its events: It takes the media to its events. For example, while the organization was engaged in an anti-whaling mission in Russia, the Greenpeace ship Sirius took eight members of the press into the port of Leningrad. Photographs of iconic Greenpeace moments, like the arrest of seal campaigner Pat Moore by Canadian authorities while he was holding a baby seal in his hands, galvanize the public into support and mobilization for the various Greenpeace causes (Brown and May 1991: 65). Yet, once the mind clears out images such as Greenpeace speedboats circling the Brent Spar or Habitat for Humanity rebuilding houses in New Orleans after Hurricane Katrina, consumers of traditional media will be hard pressed to identify a large NGO footprint in the news.

In fact, medium-sized and small NGOs have either substantial difficulty getting news coverage or have given up on getting into established media. Moreover, such coverage might not even be necessary, because service and program work might run smoothly without public scrutiny. The sense that "no news is good news" is therefore quite familiar to many NGO operatives.[29] Donors, moreover, still "lack . . . appreciation

---

[29] See for example interviews in Chapter 5.

for the benefits of good press relations" (Ross 2004: 3), and therefore PR personnel are often not accepted as a "fundable" part of grants or donations. Finally, and this in particular hampers coverage of political advocacy of NGOs, news media "indexing" (Bennett 1990) means that an issue is put on the news agenda only if there is valorized input from government representatives. An NGO simply advocating a position would therefore not entice media outlets to cover it, unless it would "express opinions already emerging in official circles" (106). Because NGOs frequently address issues and voice opinions in areas that are neglected by government, indexing in effect deletes much NGO activity from the news cycle.

NGOs Become Their Own News Source

Actually creating somewhat of an opening into traditional media markets, NGOs are increasingly becoming their own news source and in this capacity enter symbiotic relationships with established media (Cooper 2009). Ross reports in his study on media–NGO relations in the humanitarian relief field that established media ostensibly lack the resources to finance crisis coverage and that journalists overall lack "specialist knowledge" such as local or regional history of conflicts that is needed to contextualize an issue (Ross 2004: 4). Cooper describes how the British mainstream media have come under increasing pressure to downsize and in particular decrease the size and number of their foreign bureaus (Cooper 2009). As the economy of news limits established media's reporting, some NGOs willingly step in to compensate, creating "free" filmed reports and articles that often find their way one-to-one into established news outlets. Cooper cites the example of the cyclone hitting Myanmar in 2008, when the material provided by Merlin, a UK-based medical relief agency, fed the opening story of the BBC newscast; in fact, 80 percent of the material used in the BBC report came straight from the NGO. The head of communications in a large international NGO notes that NGOs can benefit from the bind that media journalists are in:

Journalists are now expected to write copy for the newspaper and write copy for the website and maybe to blog and maybe actually to produce podcasts now as well. So what we are looking at is how we can make the journalist's job as easy as possible. They will take exactly what you give them. I think that has changed from before, when you gave a journalist a press release or an idea of a story that would then be worked up. I think now we see much more of our stuff appearing verbatim. (quoted in Fenton 2009: 7)

In effect, Cooper argues, autonomous journalists and photographers are increasingly looking to NGOs to finance their work, citing photographer Marcus Bleasdale's comment: "In 2003 I made calls to 20 magazines and newspapers saying I wanted to go to Darfur. Yet I made one call to Human Rights Watch, sorted a day rate, expenses and five days later I was in the field" (quoted in Cooper 2009: 9). Even though NGO resources are overall not conducive to funding news reports, large NGOs can and are willing to do so.

How NGOs Deal with Personalization of the News

Getting coverage of NGOs is also made difficult by how the media present issues in general and conflict in particular. Traditional media rely on personalized narratives to present issues and are interested in the voice of conflicting parties. Focusing on the directly affected parties in disputes will often eliminate coverage of those involved behind the frontlines. Moreover, the voice of those directly affected is generally individualized and personalized, rather than put in the context of an organizational affiliation. Local and regional NGOs or social movements in the global South might try to enlist those in the North to help them frame issues in a way that resonates with the vocabulary and values of the global North. "The marketing of rebellion" through a few well-positioned northern NGOs has contributed, for example, to the Mexican Zapatista movement's and the Nigerian Ogoni movement's goals being transmitted in human rights terms throughout the world (Bob 2005).

In the global North, successful marketing of one's organization and the ability to tailor media messages are the prerogative of a relatively few well-to-do NGOs. PR professionals, a well-developed information infrastructure, and money are considered essential to provide media visibility for the nonprofit sector (Jacobs and Glass 2002: 238). Bennett and colleagues compared coverage of meetings of the World Economic Forum (WEF) and the World Social Forum (WSF) in U.S. media and found that the WEF, comprising high-status elite organizations and individuals and supported by more than 1,000 corporate sponsors, was far more prominently featured in the media than the much larger, but global activist and less elite-oriented WSF (Bennett et al. 2004). Some NGOs try to serve the personalized and elite-driven media logic by designing personalized and attention-catching strategies such as bringing celebrities into the story they would like to communicate. When Angelina Jolie visits a children's NGO in Haiti or Brad Pitt inspects NGO housing projects after Hurricane Katrina, they bring immediate media attention to a specific cause. Cottle and Nolan (2009: 8) cite the Australian Communications Manager of Médecins Sans Frontières, who said, "I think some media outlets just won't run some stories . . . then perhaps you get a Cate Blanchett or someone to go in there and advocate on behalf of it. So if it's a female genital mutilation or something that some outlets are going to cringe at, you do it through a celebrity possibly." Andrew Webster, the author of the first comprehensive study on celebrity diplomacy, sees NGOs as responsible for part of the hype around celebrity NGO relationships. In a 2009 discussion at the Annenberg School of Journalism, he asked the audience whether it "could name more than one or two heads of NGOs. These people are faceless, even odorless in some sense – at least in the context of the media" (Norman Lear Center 2009: 11). This facelessness can in part be compensated for by either putting a face to one's constituents – and thus giving up some definition of power over the issue – or by packaging a narrative into a high-power event, thereby buying into the media's hunger for sensationalism. Both these strategies require substantial communication management tools that only few NGOs have.

In sum, and despite the opportunities that new technologies afford,[30] there is still a compelling rationale for NGOs to pursue traditional media to raise awareness of an issue, collect donations, and gather public support for policies. Yet NGOs' traditional media footprint is minimal compared to their numbers and to their activities in civil society. The NGOs' lack of professional media relations and interest in working under the radar of the news and thereby at least not making *bad* news, as well as the media's indexing of potential stories according to what government credentials a story has, contribute to this thinned-out representation of NGOs in established news sources. Ironically, the crisis of journalism helps bring NGO narratives into the newsrooms, with more news outlets relying on reporters from outside and in effect requiring NGOs to be their own news source. To make their voice heard, NGOs, particularly large ones, might also adapt to the proclivities of personalized and celebrity-oriented reporting. Yet the vast majority of NGOs are not well represented in traditional media and thus are constrained in their public voice and ability to generate larger publics.

CONCLUSION

We have identified four sets of conditions that present challenges to public advocacy for NGOs. The first challenge is the legal regulatory

---

[30] Effects of web 2.0 technology on NGOs' public profile are discussed in Chapter 7.

environment in which what is considered public, but nonpolitical, as opposed to public and political, is a massive gray zone that tends to subtly silence NGO voice. Charity regulations in most countries, even though they might not directly repress NGO political advocacy, are prone to disincentivize it through unclear definitions and enforcement regulations. A movement to clarify and thereby relax stipulations around political activity for NGOs is only in its infancy. The Labor government under Gordon Brown in the UK and recently the Canadian government have undertaken efforts to provide NGOs with more reliable knowledge about their rights to public political advocacy while also signaling that promoting public political advocacy is not negatively sanctioned in institutional governance contexts.

A second challenge to public NGO advocacy concerns recent attempts to limit NGO accountability either to internal issues of management and transparency or to external donor relations. If NGO legitimacy is reduced to a matter of transparent management and finances, the substantive publicness of NGOs evaporates. Within this narrow accountability discourse, incentives for NGOs to gain legitimacy through active engagement in the public sphere and through publicness become muted. Along the same lines, we found that perceiving NGOs as firms that draw legitimacy from merely functional sources has a similar effect: The analogy shifts NGO identity away from their roots in civil society and from their capacity to foster and aggregate citizen voices. It would be only rational if the nongovernmental sector would feel compelled by these limited forms of accountability to focus even more on internal aspects of their operations at the expense of public engagement. Instead, we have put forward four modes of public accountability that tie an NGO not just to its internal operation or to donors and immediate constituents but also to larger publics. These four modes are transparency, debate, engagement, and activation. In this perspective, NGO legitimacy rests on generating publics. The sector's voice might be less constrained if it could envision a central source of accountability to be partaking in aggregating and organizing citizen input.

A third constraint that challenges NGOs' advocacy in the public sphere and the fostering of public accountability is the dominance of depoliticized civic engagement practices. The increasing pull to professionalize, to work with a core of reliable staff, and occasionally to engage volunteers to organize an outreach activity is not conducive to NGOs' ability to incubate and work with subpublics. It produces inward orientation and disconnect with constituencies.

The final constraint to NGO advocacy is the lack of a footprint in the established media. Only large and resourceful NGOs seem able to attract substantial media attention, and many small NGOs have given up on even trying to make it into established news outlets. Even though there are signs that the downsizing of traditional media might provide opportunities for NGOs to become their own news source, this applies primarily to topics whose relevance the news outlets have already established. In other words, active news sourcing by NGOs does not necessarily imply changes in agenda setting.

This is not to argue that constraints on NGO public advocacy are all fueled externally. NGO staff themselves might not even see the need to work in and with their publics. They might see the publics that NGOs confront as polarizing or ideologically opposing the mission of the organization. An NGO working on teenage health issues might prefer not to engage publics in socially conservative milieus. As an interviewee in the previously introduced Harwood study explained, "Many of the people who work in the social sector don't like the public" (Harwood 2009: 5). Or NGO staff might see these publics as uninformed and needy, leading NGOs to enter "therapeutic relations" of dominance with their constituencies (McFalls 2007: 9). Mostly, however, NGO leaders in the global North might share the sense of an increasingly elusive public, captured in the statement: "How do you engage people when you can't make physical contact? . . . People work two jobs, they don't go to their neighborhood schools, they pull into their garage after work." Another interviewee added, "I can't prove that (engagement) is a good return on investment," which was seconded by a third NGO leader who argued, "We lack examples about how this might play out. We encourage our chapters to get involved with the community, but we can't tell them what the benefits will be" (Harwood 2009: 18). The conclusion often drawn by NGOs when confronting the issues raised in this chapter is that it might be easier to stay focused on implementing a specific program or working in institutional governance arenas rather than to invest the time, effort, and resources in "trying to find a public that may never materialize" (Harwood 2009: 17).

Some NGOs try to approach their lack of publicness in a purely functional manner. The solution at hand is to outsource public outreach by employing "grassroots lobbying firms" that help generate support via engineering public participation for specific causes (Walker 2009). The public here becomes something that needs to be "managed" rather than cultivated, "targeted" rather than actively engaged and incorporated. Other NGOs are content with enticing from their constituents the occasional "checkbook advocacy" (Skocpol 1999a), responding to the observation that citizens are overall less committed to a specific cause and therefore in principle not continuously involved (Jenkins 2006).

Outsourcing or simply monetizing the occasional interaction with constituencies, however, might not be sufficient to strengthen the public advocacy dimension of NGO work. If indeed the nongovernmental sector is to become a central hub for democratic voice in civil society, other pathways need to be considered. Some NGOs embrace new technologies that provide the means to engage publics with relatively few resources and might increase the level of interactivity between an organization and its constituents. Using new media might be the easiest way to engage with broader publics and synergize advocacy. NGOs might also consider joining advocacy coalitions in which their own contribution carries weight within a much larger assembly of voices. This again might alleviate resource scarcity for some organizations; for others it might help diffuse direct responsibility for more politically outspoken or controversial messages. However, these attempts to incubate publics need to take place within a political environment that is, if not outright supportive, at least not opposed to civil society operating as a public sphere. What role NGOs can play in civil society "depends crucially on the larger political setting" (Foley and Edwards 1996: 48). I established earlier that governments, to some degree, rely on the NGO sector to represent citizens. In turn, NGOs could ask more of government and governance institutions to increase the limited public sphere footprint of NGOs.

In the short term, debates about modifying the ban on political activity for charities seem to be inevitable. Crafting regulations that would increase the opportunity for small and resource-poor NGOs to practice more public advocacy would need to be part of these debates. Moreover, NGOs could ask their governments to be less strict about funding public advocacy when contracting with them to provide service. Even though advocacy tends to have more support in politics and business than activism and contestation, governments and foundations as well as many private donors do not like to fund it (Blueprint 2002). Governments place strict scrutiny on what kinds and how much advocacy can be pursued, and for foundations and private donors, the focus on results-based programs tends to sideline advocacy efforts. If governments combined contracts or grants with a stronger emphasis on public outreach and engagement, it would incentivize NGOs to see their organizations more as public advocates.

What would be the motivation for governments to incentivize NGO advocacy? For one, state actors increasingly realize that, with NGOs forming a circle of assumed publics around their institutions, the legitimacy problems of policy making do not necessarily disappear, but may, in fact, increase. If governments claim NGOs to be their publics and these NGOs in turn rarely engage with their constituencies, the democratic line of public accountability is broken. Second, because of the weakness of established political parties, there is a need to alter how coalitions are being fostered and how public opinion is being formed. New alliances between parties and NGOs might be possible if legal restrictions were changed and parties realized that they need civic partners to renew their ties with civil society. Such alliances have been suggested for the global South as a means to undo the consequential positioning of civil society actors against, or independent of, the state. The question instead is how civil society actors can enhance state practices by more closely aligning with political parties (Carothers 2002a: 19).

Another reason why governments might need to be part of the solution to enhance NGOs' formation of publics is that civil society actors need resources that provide some balance to privatized sponsorship. Civil societies that rely for the most part on private donors tend to reproduce existing inequalities. In Western countries, a vast amount of private donations goes to middle-class causes. Those in poverty and on the margins of society have neither a strong voice, nor a strong lobby, nor the resources to craft either. Producing more equal voice in civil society requires government involvement. Even though "the revolution will not be funded" (Incite 2007), as one activist project famously quipped, generating public voice and citizen agency cannot be done without the support of governments. Thus, government funding and public advocacy can, under certain conditions, be complementary features of civil society.

In sum, governments and international governance institutions are in a prime position either to incentivize NGOs to practice public advocacy or to dampen such efforts. The next two chapters present case studies on how government–NGO relations might help or hinder public advocacy.

5

Urban Development Advocacy in the United States and Germany

> The city may be described as a structure specially equipped to store and transmit the goods of civilization.
>
> Lewis Mumford 1961: 30

> As the optimum unit for democracy in the 21st century, the city has a greater claim, I think, than any other alternative.
>
> Robert J. Dahl 1967: 964

It is a damp evening in late spring of 2005 when I make my way from the Bremen central train station out to the neighborhood of Tenever. Bremen, a proud Hanseatic city of 700,000 in Germany's northwest, has long struggled with perceptions of Tenever as the "sore wound" at the outskirts of an otherwise well-integrated local polity. After a 20-minute tram ride I change to a bus, and the first signs of the 1970s building euphoria peek out in the distance: an ensemble of about three dozen 15- to 20-story concrete buildings in tight formation, zigzagging their way along a highway. Here, within about three square miles live approximately 6,000 people from 88 countries, of whom 70 percent are migrants and 33 percent receive welfare benefits. And here, under the most unlikely conditions, strong public engagement flourishes. The Tenever public and its advocacy power are known throughout the city and beyond. I am visiting because I want to know *why* and *how* this happened.

After navigating through a maze of buildings, I enter a large open space buzzing with voices, located on the ground floor of a public services building. I am visiting the monthly Citizen Forum in which neighborhood

groups, NGOs, business owners, building managers, and city representatives discuss urban development issues, sign up for projects, and try to
reach solutions. About 200 people are in the room. Behind me sit five
men in their sixties, conversing in Russian. To my right settle seven cool-
looking teenagers sporting skateboards and ball caps of Werder Bremen,
the local soccer club. Many people know each other; they sip tea from
plastic cups that is served at the entrance.

The meeting is called to order by Joachim Barloschky, the long-
standing head of the Project Group that coordinates Tenever initiatives
by NGOs and citizen groups. "Barlo," as everybody calls him, is an ener-
getic presence in his fifties. He runs a tight ship: On the agenda are more
than 20 items, ranging from complaints against the building management about nonfunctioning elevators to an NGO's appeal to refurbish
the local preschool. The Russians behind me announce that they have
just incorporated as a charity in order to convert an empty apartment
into a public community sauna. The cool-looking teenagers are here to
make their plea for conversion of an empty space between two buildings
into a skate park.

Four observations strike me. One, the more institutionalized actors
in the room, such as city social workers, building managers, and the
local police, are there to listen, not to drive the agenda. They answer
questions and engage where needed, but do not structure or dominate
the debate. Two, NGO representatives speak, but they do not speak for
a clientele; instead, they suggest ways to do things that are then pushed
back and forth in the discussion. Three, the stakes are high, because there
is money involved. The Tenever Citizen Forum has a yearly budget of
about 300,000 Euros[1] to support NGOs and groups with good ideas that
get buy-in from the community. So how many people will be served by
the Russians' sauna? Is it, at this point, more important than the skate
park? The teenagers have prepared a good presentation on their cause,
and the Russians ultimately accept the fact that the teenagers' request
serves a larger need. Instead they will start by building one small sauna
room in a basement and will seek approval for a larger project from the
Citizen Forum after the idea catches on. My last observation is that all
decisions are made by consensus. If there is anybody in the room who

---

[1] In 2012: 325,000 Euros; data from sign-up list for 2012 projects at http://www.bremen-
tenever.de/Stadtteilgruppe%20Bremen-Tenever_Tenever%20Aktuell_o_ak_1047_Antr%
E4ge%20f%FCr%20182.%20Stadtteilgruppe.html.

absolutely cannot live with a decision, it will be deferred. At about 10:30 pm, I walk toward the bus station with a buzzing head and a sense of what might make Tenever special: I may have witnessed a public at work.

This chapter focuses on the dynamics of NGOs and advocacy in urban public spheres and, in particular, on the role of government in shaping NGO voice. Cities and urban environments, as noted in the opening quotes by Lewis Mumford and Robert Dahl, embody the democratic promise of a public place between home and work in which practices of citizenship are learned. Theories of democracy have argued that it is in the spatial radius of the local where initiation into public advocacy takes place and that local political communication and participation options are a prerequisite for any kind of sustained civic engagement (see Barber 1984; Phillips 1996). Even though participation in local elections is often lower than on the national level, participation rates in other forms of engagement, such as attending neighborhood meetings and petitioning, are higher. And even though new communication technology allows individuals to express themselves in quick, multiple, and delocalized acts of advocacy, studies claim that meaningful participation over time still involves face-to-face encounters and that these are primarily organized at the local level (see for Great Britain, Parry et al. 1992; for the United States, Berry, Portney, and Thomson 1993; and for Germany, Roth 1994). The local public sphere provides the most accessible and organized political arena in which opinions can be transformed into political action through participation in political organizations, issue-specific networking of NGOs, or neighborhood initiatives. If social and political capital is acquired primarily through socialization processes in the immediate life world (Bourdieu 1984; Putnam 2001), then the urban public sphere should be an ideal space in which to investigate engagement practices of NGOs and government's role in incentivizing NGOs to organize outreach and public advocacy.

Just as local interest group politics cannot be easily compared with national interest group politics (Berry 2010), the local public sphere has distinct properties that it does not necessarily share with national or global publics (Lang 2004) and that influence NGOization and advocacy:

(1) We can assume that there is more shared knowledge about the common public space than in larger contexts. We can think of this as the *cognitive property* of local publics.

(2) The experience of being part of a locality with some degree of common cultural, social and political practices, at least among

subpublics, produces identification and allegiances, however fragile. We will call this the *affective property*.

(3) The local level allows for more face-to-face interactions and inter-
personal communication opportunities than larger publics. This
will be called the *interactive property*.

(4) The local sphere enables easier participation in public affairs by
offering closer proximity to and manageable scale of venues. This
is the *participatory and public advocacy property* of local publics.

(5) Access to political institutions is facilitated by proximity. We call
this the *institutional advocacy property* of local publics.

While avoiding any glorification of local democracy, we can assume
that local publics' distinctive cognitive, affective, interactive, participatory, and advocacy properties should enhance the capacity of NGOs to
serve as catalysts for public advocacy. The degree to which each of these
properties shapes the local public sphere varies. Cognitive and affective
dimensions, for example, might look quite differently in New York City
than in Boise, Idaho, and at times affective identification with a sub-
group in a city might actually entail contestation and conflict with others.
Larger cities allow for fewer face-to-face contacts among citizens than
a New England town with 300 inhabitants. In addition, some cities put
more weight on developing participatory dimensions of governance than
others. These differences notwithstanding, these five distinctive properties
point to a relatively stable cluster of qualities of the local as opposed to
the national public sphere.

Measurements of the quality of local democracy use different methods, ranging from the thick descriptive and analytical narratives following in the footsteps of Robert Dahl's depiction of New Haven in *Who
Governs?* (1961) and Jane Mansbridge's participatory analytics in New
England towns (Mansbridge 1983), to more quantitative measurements
of urban democracy such as in Robert Putnam's Community Benchmark
Index (Putnam 2002). Some analysts focus on urban social movements
(i.e., Mayer 2003; Brenner, Marcuse, and Mayer 2009), whereas others
concentrate on urban economic inequality (Sellers 2002) or on the inter-
sections of global and local democratic renewal (i.e., Allahwala and Keil
2005).

Kantor and Savitch, in their provocative article, "How to Study Comparative Urban Development Politics" (Kantor and Savitch 2005), have
scolded the field for producing "not much" and ultimately "not very comparative" analyses, marred by problems such as conceptual parochialism

and subsequent overstretch. Safeguarding against conceptual overstretch in this chapter, I submit, is best done by establishing that the following cases are meant as illustrations of NGO–government interaction in urban governance and do not attempt to paint a detailed picture of urban development politics or urban democracy at large. Each of the cases presented here is painted with a broad brush in an attempt to distill some distinct features of NGO advocacy in different urban development arenas. The focus is on two, albeit important, features of democratic renewal: the role of NGOs in contributing to public advocacy in urban development and the role of local government in strengthening or weakening NGO voice.

NGOs[2] and civic groups have been identified as central actors in the reshaping of governance under the auspices of empowerment and citizen participation (Berry, Portney, and Thomson 1993; Coaffee and Healey 2003). Yet after two decades of experimentation, both empowerment and citizen participation have lost some of their cache and credibility. What often is subsumed under these terms in contemporary urban governance arenas are underconceptualized patchwork attempts to gauge citizen will formation. Although empowerment and citizen participation initiatives might suggest active involvement, most stop short of either actually risking public debate or producing material effects (Mayer 2003). The specific question this raises in our context is this: Under what conditions do NGOs and civic groups actually develop public voice and the power to alter established political or administrative structures? In a broader context, this chapter seeks evidence of whether institutionalization of advocacy also applies to the local public and which specific properties of the local might enhance the public advocacy capacity of NGOs. Hence, the cases presented here illustrate the interaction of NGOs and local governments, with a focus on the dynamics that we developed in Chapter 2: identifying conditions under which NGOs do or do not operate as (1) central communicative actors within mostly non-mass-mediated subpublics that

---

[2] It should be noted that some scholars and practitioners call these "community-based organizations." However, because some of my cases include larger organizations with local community chapters, I refer to them with the umbrella term "NGOs." In addition to these NGOs, every city harbors groups that have less routinized and more informal interaction patterns and are less professionalized in their means of action. I refer to these groups as "citizen initiatives" or "citizen groups." However, often, the distinction between NGOs and these citizen groups gets blurred because the groups increasingly have to behave like NGOs to become powerful actors in local publics or subpublics. For pragmatic reasons, citizen groups often cooperate with NGOs to advance their agendas. Therefore, as elaborated earlier, even citizen groups are not exempt from the pull to NGOize.

(2) provide an organizational context for citizen voice and thus organize the "publicness" of civic concerns by (3) directing advocacy at different levels of the political or economic system via (4) discursive and nondiscursive means of expression and in that process foster public accountability.

Germany and the United States offer interesting starting points for such an inquiry because they exhibit quite differently structured civil society properties. In Germany, a number of well established state-supported NGOs have been the main carriers of an organizationally strong, yet also stagnant civic sector for most of the 20th century (Anheier and Toepler 2003; Enquête-Kommission 2002). In the United States, by contrast, the state historically has encouraged, but not actively funded the multilayered and ubiquitous civic landscape that today has a wide array of organizational diversity with many different funding sources (Skocpol 1999a and b). Although these differences in civil society organization could lead to the conclusion that the polyarchic structure of American governance produces a stronger NGO voice in urban development, this inquiry does not support this state-centered vs. pluralist argument. Instead, the analysis suggests that strong predictors for whether local NGOs practice public outreach and thus develop public accountability in urban development are their respective governance conditions and, in particular, the scope and quality of NGO interaction with government – an interaction that seems to cut across broad system types such as the corporatist-pluralist one. The following cases illustrate that these governance conditions are critical to how much NGOs contribute to generating and sustaining strong publics.

URBAN NGO ADVOCACY: CASES AND DATA

The cases presented here draw from fieldwork in three cities in the United States (San Diego, Oakland, and Seattle)[3] and three cities in Germany (Leipzig, Berlin, and Bremen), each with different populations and civil society properties. Case selection was based on inventories and measures of social capital (see Chapter 1, fn. 18) and on the city's nonprofit density footprint. A cautionary note is in order: Nonprofit density in Germany and the United States do not compare directly, because German registrar

[3] Initial research for this chapter was sponsored by a grant from the German-American Fulbright Commission and by the German Federal Parliament Enquête Commission on Civic Engagement. At the University of Washington data collection was cleared through Human Subjects Certificate of Exemption #07–5942-X/C.

TABLE 5.1. *Civil Society Properties of the Six Cities*

City	Population[a]	Social Capital Index[b]	Nonprofit Density per 1,000 Inhabitants	Nonprofit Density German Charities Total[c]
Seattle	595,000	High	2.4	N/A
Oakland	404,000	Medium	2.6	N/A
San Diego	1,279,000	Low	1.7	N/A
Bremen	640,000	High	1.7[d]	5.8
Berlin	3,404,000	Medium	2.5	5.9
Leipzig	506,000	Low	2.5	6.0

[a] Population figures for the United States from U.S. Census projections for 2008/9; for Germany, from Statistisches Bundesamt Wiesbaden.

[b] Social Capital Index for U.S. cities from Robert Putnam's Community Benchmark Survey 2004; for German cities from Bertelsmann Foundation and expert interviews.

[c] Available *absolute* data for the two countries are *not* comparable. The German charity registrar does not differentiate charities using the same categories as the IRS. German charity density overall is much higher because it includes certain social, business, professional, political, and social welfare nonprofits that do not have 501(c)(3) status in the United States. Data for Seattle and San Diego are from the Corporation for National and Community Service at http://www.Volunteering.America.gov; for Oakland, measurements with data are from the National Council on Civil Society at http://nccs.dataweb.urban.org. For Germany, data are from Vereinsstatistik (2008) and http://www.handelsregister.de.

[d] If business, professional, and political organizations were included, Bremen would score at 3.54: 25.3 percent of all its nonprofits fall under this category versus only 12 percent of Leipzig's nonprofits.

data include charities that would *not* fall in the 501(c)(3) category. Thus Table 5.1 should not be used for cross-country comparison, but solely for inner-country comparison.

Data from the Johns Hopkins Comparative Nonprofit Sector Project give Germany overall a much lower Civil Society Organization Index score than the United States. This rating system puts the United States in third place, following the Netherlands and Belgium in terms of capacity, sustainability, and impact of the sector. Germany is in 11th place (Anheier and Salamon 2006: 102).

Table 5.1 indicates that in both the United States and Germany there is no significant correlation between high social capital and nonprofit density. In fact, in the United States, the city with the highest social capital has lower NGO density than the city with the medium level of social capital. In Germany, the highest social capital city scores lower on NGO density than the medium and low social capital cities, which are tied in NGO density. We can thus stipulate that the density of NGOs of local civil societies is not dependent on the level of social capital. We can further assume that

NGOization – the process by which associations professionalize, institutionalize, and bureaucratize – occurs just as much in cities with low levels of trust and community building as in cities with high levels. Overall, in both countries, the number of registered charities, as well as the size of their workforce, rose substantially in the past two decades. In Germany, the sector almost doubled from 286,000 associations after unification in 1990 to 554,000 associations in 2008.[4] Its workforce expanded from 3.9 percent of the economically active population of West Germany in 1990 to 5.9 percent in unified Germany in 2005.[5] The data for the United States, as presented in Chapter 1, corroborate this increase in professionally employed NGO staff.

One of the policy fields in which citizens tend to have a high stake, and therefore public advocacy tends to be strong, is urban development. Struggles about urban private and public space are directly linked to social exclusion and the power of public voice (Haus 2005). Therefore capacity-building, especially to enable involvement of marginalized groups, is often a key part of urban development and provides for interesting case material.

I began the process of case selection during my first interviews, conducted between 2000–2. I asked stakeholders from NGOs, government, and the media what they saw as the most central conflicts in urban development and then selected the cases that they mentioned most often. These cases served as empirical material for exploring two questions: First, how do local urban development NGOs act in their capacity as advocates in the public sphere? To put it differently, how does the NGOization of urban publics broaden, channel, or restrict public communication and participation? Second, what role do local governments play in whether these NGOs become catalysts or proxies for urban democracy? In all, I conducted 60 interviews in these six cities between 2000 and 2007.[6]

I studied the self-perception of NGOs and government actors in regard to activating citizens and encouraging public involvement, as well as policies, actual interactions, and policy results in the selected cases. Semi-structured interviews, analysis of government and NGO documents, and participant observation provided the empirical base for illustrating why NGOs in some cities become catalysts for public voice, whereas

---

[4] Data from Vereinsstatistik (2008) and Anheier and Seibel (2001: 74).
[5] Data from the Johns Hopkins Comparative Nonprofit Sector Project (cited in Anheier and Salamon 2006 and online at http://www.ccss.jhu.edu).
[6] See Appendix 1 for details of the interview procedures.

in other urban contexts they tend to become proxies for participatory governance.[7]

The cities show cross-national similarities in terms of the strength of NGO capacity to enable and carry public advocacy. The majority of both San Diego and Leipzig urban development NGOs have not acquired strong institutional or public advocacy capacity. Most NGOs are weak, whereas a few strong players have become part of a tightly *governed public sphere* that presents itself as fairly exclusive. In the middle we find Berlin and Oakland, where attempts to manage diverse urban development constituencies have led to an outsourced but government-*managed public sphere*. NGOs have some autonomy, but are ultimately restricted in public advocacy by the cities' governance practices that remain fairly closed to public input. In effect, NGOs operate with more deference to government than public constituencies. On the other end of the spectrum, in Seattle and Bremen, both NGOs and their constituents have stronger institutional and public voice. In both cities, I submit, the local government operates at the center of a *networked public sphere* that during the time of this investigation operated fairly inclusively and actively pursued input from citizens through multiple venues. Hence, in both Seattle and Bremen, fostering public accountability of NGOs is a stronger part of the local governance culture than in the other cities. In the following sections, we examine in detail the properties of a governed, managed, and networked public sphere and their implications for NGO advocacy and accountability. The cases illustrate the larger questions of governance processes in relation to the NGO sector.[8]

THE GOVERNED PUBLIC SPHERE

San Diego, the border city on the Pacific Ocean and Mexico that reinvented itself from a military hub in the postwar era, via a detour as *Time* magazine's "Bust Town"[9] of 1962 to a more diversified manufacturing economy, has to some degree remained a military town. Military

---

[7] Because the study has an exploratory design and does not include control cases in the strict sense, the results should be considered tentative. Nonetheless, the evidence collected during fieldwork is persuasive and thus warrants further research.

[8] For a more systematic discussion of the levels and dimensions of urban governance processes see Coaffee and Healey (2003).

[9] *Time* magazine, August 17, 1962 portrays San Diego as a town that "had brashly bet heavily on the aircraft industry and cleaned up for nearly 15 years," but was now "in missile-age trouble."

expenditures still make up about 20 percent of the city region's gross product, and more than 300,000 military retirees live on pensions in the region.[10] As a hub for West Coast tourism and conferences, San Diego also relies on a large service sector economy that is fueled by low- or minimum-wage workers. Many workers commute from San Diego's Mexican "alter ego" in Tijuana on a daily basis through the busiest border crossing in the world. In 2004, 48.2 million people walked or drove into the United States at the San Ysidro crossing between San Diego and Tijuana, or roughly 132,000 people a day.[11]

As in many other cities across the United States, urban development decisions in the past decades were largely driven by the need to increase revenue, attract investors, and redevelop the downtown; in San Diego a large baseball stadium was part of this development process. Yet while debates over urban investments made headline news, they also exposed a puzzling problem: San Diego had no visible footprint of public advocacy organizations in the urban development arena. Given that housing prices in the San Diego region had roughly tripled over the past 30 years and downtown revitalization meant displacement for substantial pockets of low-income housing, vibrant NGO advocacy around issues of affordable housing in the city could have been expected. Instead, I found a city suffering serious blight with a civil society unable to articulate its grievances (SD-7-ND).[12] As one of my interlocutors put it succinctly, "the bottom line here is, there is not much (NGO activism) here" (SD-9-DC). One explanation that was given was that neither retirees nor service workers are "naturally" strong mobilizers. Yet I did in fact discover outspoken individuals advocating for affordable housing. I found them at San Diego University and at University of California-San Diego, among engaged women and men in downtown condominiums and in neighborhood councils. What these citizens shared was frustration that their critique had not coalesced into advocacy organizations. It seemed as though advocacy efforts had been absorbed and monopolized by two public nonprofit corporations – the Centre City Development Corporation (CCDC) and the Southeastern Economic Development Corporation (SEDC) – both established by the San Diego City Council between 1975

---

[10] Greater San Diego Chamber of Commerce. *Economic Bulletin* (1994) Vol. 42, No. 7, pp. 2–3.

[11] Data from Research and Integrative Technology Administration at http://www.bts.gov/data_and_statistics (accessed November 24, 2009).

[12] All interview citations of this chapter are documented in Appendix 1.

and 1981 to develop downtown and redevelop 15 other project areas.[13] It was these two nonprofits that ran urban development projects, and it was only via these two highly professionalized and institutionalized nonprofits that any affordable housing issue in their redevelopment areas could be addressed successfully.

On paper, both CCDC and SEDC had established citizen participation processes, in which some of the local housing activists I met were or had been participating. When I visited CCDC offices, where 39 staff workers overlooked the city's downtown, I was introduced to an elaborate theory about citizen empowerment; a few weeks later, I observed it during a meeting of CCDC's Project Area Committee (PAC).[14] California redevelopment law, I learned, requires a PAC if redevelopment displaces low-income housing. The PAC consisted of 28 elected members representing residential homeowners and tenants, as well as business owners and NGOs. It was supposed to be the communication link between citizens, the development corporation, and the city government. A CCDC member described to me the process of assessing the community impact of new developments: "The PAC, they are going to listen to people's concerns. They are going to look at parking, architecture, art, impact." I asked whether the PAC could block a project. The answer was no: "The PAC's voice is heard. [But] if it is good for the economic benefit of downtown, the CCDC moves it forward, no matter what... this is what CCDC is there for. The citizen's group is there to make us see how a development could impact the citizens... but they are an *advisory* group, not more" (SD-1-CB). I asked what other venues for advocacy PAC members might have. My interlocutor hesitated and then said, "PAC members can appear as individuals before the City Council." Yet she made clear that, if they do appear before the City Council, they speak as individuals, not as representatives of a citizen advocacy group.

I arranged to meet with one former and one present PAC member. Both are affluent women who live in beautiful downtown condominiums. One is a long-standing activist who manages an online community discussion list for urban development issues; the other had started an initiative to make the PAC more responsive to, and proactive in, integrating broader participation into the process. Both had witnessed how incensed local

---

[13] The City of San Diego, *Redevelopment Agency Annual Report* 1999. Available at http://www.sandiego.gov/redevelopment-agency/overview.shtml#reports (accessed April 3, 2004). For an overview on the role of city development corporations in revitalizing urban neighborhoods in the United States, see Kirkpatrick (2007).

[14] Their title has since been changed to the Centre City Advisory Committee.

communities had become at events when CCDC took the public stage, and they took it on themselves to establish better relationships with their publics. "We need to do more as far as public relations goes; we need to let our constituents know what we represent," one of the women said (SD-8-JS). Because there were no funds in CCDC's budget for outreach activities, this member approached CCDC, requesting funds to print posters announcing a community outreach meeting she was planning. CCDC agreed to print the posters, but at the time of our interview, which was just a week before the meeting, the posters had not yet been delivered. Both women felt ambivalent about their role as intermediaries advocating for community interests, describing the PAC as being a resource-deprived appendix of CCDC.

Community activists shared the perception of a closed governance structure in which only a few major NGOs participated. I spent time in a neighborhood that tried to obtain funds from SEDC, the other major development corporation, to redevelop a rundown shopping area that had become a hub for drug use. Again, I heard similar complaints about the symbolic politics of participation in the city. SEDC had a PAC that is "just an advisory committee that has no power at all. Even if they say 'no,' and SEDC wants it to happen, it will happen. That's a problem" (SD-6-SM), explained one of the activists driving the shopping area revitalization idea. "What can you do?" I asked her. She described a two-tiered strategy: Younger people would use e-mail to bombard the City Council, and older community members would go from door to door and collect signatures on a petition supporting the project. "Is going to SEDC meetings an option?" She shook her head in frustration, saying, "One time we had about 200 to 300 people there, and we had our little bit of time that we could speak, two or three minutes. The last time we were there at one of their meetings, the police got called. It is an intimidation thing.... They did not do anything, they were just there in case things got out of control. But I don't know. You have the right to raise your voice and speak your mind" (SD-6-CM). By contrast, this group invited SEDC to its community forums, and the nonprofit at first sent a representative, but that individual stopped attending.

In sum, organizing public voice in San Diego is difficult. Even "the labor movement here is San Diegoized a little bit," chuckled one of my interviewees, making creative use of the institutionalizing feature of NGOization. "Compared to other places, there are very few advocacy organizations, very few political organizations" (SD-9-DC). The government is closed and seen as not responsive to citizen needs, working only with a few hand-picked NGOs that dominate the civic terrain and absorb most public advocacy attempts. It has not encouraged its incorporated NGOs to develop public accountability by practicing meaningful outreach. The community development corporations' outreach to constituents was thus little more than symbolic politics.

Organizing public advocacy in Leipzig turned out to be equally problematic, albeit for somewhat different reasons. The city is hailed as the birthplace of the East German revolution that brought down the Wall in 1989. So-called "Monday Demonstrations" started in Leipzig in September and then spread throughout the former East Germany (GDR). The largest demonstration, with about 70,000 citizens, took place on October 9, 1989, and is credited with marking the beginning of the end of the GDR regime. Ten years later, the city was involved in a variety of dialogues between government, NGOs, and citizens about fostering civic engagement. The city won second place in the CIVITAS competition of 1999, a contest funded by the Bertelsmann Foundation to improve citizen engagement in German cities. A unit was established as part of the mayor's office whose task it was to provide information on the level of citizen participation in town, as well as to take up citizen complaints and handle them effectively. In the urban development arena, several projects were commissioned with local planning bureaus to assess the needs of citizens in urban problem zones. The city also became active in the Bertelsmann Foundation's CIVITAS network to strengthen local democracy and adopted a local Agenda 21 process[15] whose aim was to bring government, NGOs, citizens, and other stakeholders together to develop and implement sustainable city practices. Yet what looked like an inclusive and citizen-oriented governance culture turned out on closer inspection to be, as in San Diego, a restricted public communication sphere that did not promote the public advocacy function of NGOs.

At the core of the Agenda 21 process in Leipzig were efforts to bring local actors together, ranging from two neighborhood development initiatives in blighted areas to the establishment of an office of civic engagement and the development of a local Democracy Balance Sheet. The basis for this Democracy Balance Sheet was a large survey in which 2,000

---

[15] Local Agenda 21 processes are the result of an action plan drafted at the 1992 UN Conference on Environment and Development in Rio de Janeiro, in which 180 countries signed on to promote sustainable development. More than 1,000 cities and communalities worldwide have signed on to Agenda 21.

citizens were asked for input about their living conditions, their perceptions of Leipzig's sustainability issues, and challenges that needed government and civil society attention.[16] Coordinated by the Leipzig Office
for Civic Engagement, also called the City Office, this Balance Sheet was
to provide a road map for government investment and increased cooperation with local NGOs in addressing citizens' needs. The City Office
invited a small number of the city's 3,700 NGOs to participate in drafting
and evaluating the Balance Sheet (LEI-1-RK).

Since its creation in 1999, the City Office had been run by an urban
planner and a part-time assistant. The planner, a soft-spoken, guarded
man in his mid-thirties, was hired despite interventions from some local
NGO members who regarded him, to cite one of the harsher comments,
as a "weak puppet of the mayor" who "in these five years has never put
his foot down for our causes in government" (LEI-7-PF). On paper, the
City Office's record looked impressive. It conducted a needs assessment
regarding the relationships between citizens and the local bureaucracy
and presented the results to municipal department heads and the City
Council. It selected a set of projects to increase citizen engagement and
identified several urban culture and development NGOs as partners for
these projects; these NGOs also regularly participated in meetings that
the City Office convened every two months to discuss civic engagement
in Leipzig.

However, the record looked less impressive on the output side. Interviews with NGOs revealed frustration about the process and the city's
commitment to working with the results of the survey. Most of the
projects that were selected by the City Office as strategic responses to
the Democracy Balance Sheet and as model projects of civic engagement
had already been in place long before, sponsored by NGOs and without
government endorsement. NGO representatives felt that the local government, through its civic engagement initiative, had become a free rider
on their territory, without any added value of government engagement or
any additional funding. The NGO actors called the bimonthly meetings
"mostly a waste of time" and "superfluous," because "everything that
costs additional money is off the table there" (LEI-5-IH). They described
government agencies as largely closed to communication with local
NGOs, the exception being again the two neighborhood development

---

[16] The survey had a return rate of only 23.4 percent and thus cannot be called representative. Oversampled were older Leipzigers; immigrants and citizens with less than high
school diplomas were underrepresented (Stadt Leipzig 2005).

initiatives and the Agenda 21 bureau, which had close contractual relationships with the local government. Whenever citizen participation
needed to be organized in development projects, a single private planning contractor came into play. He drafted the surveys, performed evaluations, and, on the whole, seemed to be the government's sole link to
urban development participation. This contractor defined his role largely
in a technocratic manner. He saw himself as a service provider with
the tools to facilitate specific, one-time-only citizen input in an urban
development project. The notion that he might help citizens gain public voice and acquire means to sustain advocacy seemed foreign to him
(LEI-9-RE). His government-contracted services produced the occasional
one-time civic input mostly in survey form, but did not generate aggregated and sustainable forms of civic participation. Neighborhood NGOs'
opinions were solicited only infrequently.

By 2008, and after three more years of stagnant implementation of a
few showcase projects, several members of the Democracy Balance Sheet
initiative left the process under protest. Their claim was stark: Nothing
had been done to give local NGOs and their constituents influence in local
government during the past ten years. The public engagement processes,
they claimed, had turned into a farce. Citizens and their associations, edi-
torialized the Leipziger digital newspaper, "feel excluded and hoaxed."[17]
Positive change in the city, concluded the paper, could only happen "if
citizens come together according to the example of 1989: with self organized demonstrations and self organized, not government-led meetings."
This sentiment was echoed by some of the representatives of the participating NGOs, who claimed, "We don't need institutionalized steering, we need transparency from the government.... There should be all
3,700 NGOs in town involved.... We are being used as poster children"
(LEI-5-IH).

Thus the local government of Leipzig, while publicly displaying a focus
on civic engagement, has in effect, through its mode of institutionalization, restricted public communication venues and disabled the public
advocacy function of the majority of NGOs. By generating a smokescreen
of citizen activation it effectively counteracted the demands by NGOs for
more open government, more communication, and more resources for
civic engagement projects. A few selected accommodating NGOs and a
private firm were representing the public in government; beyond that, the
NGO sector had to find its own resources and communication means to

[17] *Leipziger Internetzeitung*, March 28, 2009.

practice and encourage advocacy in the city. Both San Diego and Leipzig thus had developed governance structures that, although differing in their language regarding participatory empowerment, in fact govern the public sphere effectively through either a tightly controlled semi-institutionalized set of quasi-NGOs or a city agency. Both cities selected partners that control public engagement according to how it fits the cities' agendas. Both practice disempowering symbolic politics of engagement that include a small slice of the NGO sector and marginalize critical NGOs.

THE MANAGED PUBLIC SPHERE

The two cities with medium levels of social capital in our sample, Berlin and Oakland, are similar in that both have outsourced a considerable amount of civic engagement activities in the urban development sector. In Oakland, large urban NGO intermediaries have taken on the government-sponsored role of training smaller NGOs in participatory and empowerment strategies. In that city, relatively independent NGO intermediaries have traditionally been the links between citizens, smaller groups, and the local state. In Berlin, the city outsourced much of its civic engagement by creating and funding intermediaries, in particular hot spots of urban blight. In both cases, these intermediaries establish, train, and channel existing initiatives and encourage citizen activation. Yet here the similarities end.

The Berlin government, after identifying 15 city quarters with special social and economic needs, established so-called neighborhood-management (Quartiersmanagement) projects in 1999 by contracting with urban development NGOs after a competitive selection process. Using a mix of federal, state, and EU funding, these urban development NGOs were given the responsibility to mobilize existing nonprofit and for-profit resources to stabilize the neighborhood and generate citizen engagement. Neighborhood-management NGOs contracted with the city and had only limited funds (15,000 Euros per neighborhood) to support NGO or citizen-led initiatives. On top of this base funding, each of the neighborhoods received 250,000 Euros for two years in 2001 and 2002 to invest in new projects. These projects were selected from an application pool by newly installed neighborhood councils, in which citizens were to hold at least 50 percent of the seats, with institutional actors and NGOs holding the remaining seats. This windfall funding was not repeated and was largely used to repair infrastructure such as playgrounds and parks and to install dog litterbags (Eick 2005).

For the most part, in Berlin the neighborhood-management process relies on synergizing already existing NGO activities by drawing them into the institutionalized venue for providing information and advocacy. The main agenda that all neighborhood-managements share is a focus on jobs, crime and public space. Small NGOs complain that it is almost impossible to be heard if an organization is not part of the neighborhood-management process or has a different agenda. They find it much more difficult to interact with city officials, because all matters are now channeled through the neighborhood managers, who in the early phase of the program did not come from the neighborhood and tended to be distrusted by established citizen groups (BER-5-FW). The neighborhood-management NGOs have been installed as intermediaries: They manage public communication and citizen engagement in the neighborhood, while at the same time serving at the political level as aggregates of that citizen engagement (BER-8-KH).

Neighborhood managers are well aware of the potential for funding streams to dry up if too many contested public issues surface. They are success oriented and, just as in other donor–client relationships in which the donor does not encourage dissent or public voice, tend to avoid risky projects that might fail. They select interventions that are in line with the neoliberal restructuring of a financially stressed city, while at the same time ignoring suggestions of many other long-standing associations and NGOs in the quarter (Fritsche 2003: 185). Moreover, critics point out that their management of the neighborhood is not always benign. They have been identified as offering low-wage work and acting as the extended arm of the police by financing security services (Fritsche 2003), thereby contributing to the "poor policing the poor" (Eick 2003).

As opposed to Bremen, where a similar funding mix is used to support urban development projects in neighborhoods like Tenever, the neighborhood-management NGOs in Berlin are bound by contracts that in effect make them beholden to government. Critics claim that the funds go mostly into revitalization of building stock and much less into generating civic or social capital (Schnur 2008). In addition, neighborhood-management NGOs are stigmatized as operating only in "troubled neighborhoods" (BER-6-SK). The managers' need to focus on short-term effects leads to problems of trust within their neighborhoods. Local sub-publics thus perceive quarter neighborhood-management NGOs as an extension of government (BER-3-MT; also Fritsche 2008). Even though these NGOs were mandated to be the public voice of the "troubled neighborhood," they seem to shy away from public accountability. "Going public," as they seem to have realized, does not help as much in the next funding cycle as listing examples of the seemingly vibrant associational democracy under their umbrella. In fact, the neighborhood-management scheme results in the highly institutionalized advocacy of a few NGOs, largely at the expense of a broader mobilization of citizens. The local government legitimizes neighborhood-management NGOs not on the basis of public accountability, but on the basis of their ability to manage problem areas and mute dissent.

Whereas Berlin has outsourced civic engagement to institutionalized intermediaries under government control, Oakland has outsourced civic engagement to large NGO intermediaries without keeping control. As a result, according to a government official, Oakland city agencies have in recent years lost their capacity to manage civil society (OAK-9-MB). When a new mayor and city manager were elected in 1998, their primary task was to regain what was labeled "direct contact with citizens." The new city management announced that their sponsorship of large NGO intermediaries had resulted in a loss of government input into local community affairs; now they were confronted with "fiefdoms of intermediary NGOs" (OAK-9-MB) that prevented citizen activation by predefining and then supporting only particular interests in the community. Thus, eliminating these NGO fiefdoms was one of the prime tasks of the new government (OAK-6-GN/KK), and they did so by deliberately excluding these intermediaries from funding streams and discussions on civic engagement projects. Smaller NGOs in the urban development arena were pressured not to contract anymore with these larger NGOs (OAK-7-US). The intermediaries, who had traditionally understood their mission as "being consultants for community change" (ibid.), were taken by surprise and saw their power as facilitators threatened. At the same time, they voiced frustration with "the change efforts where we were closely allied and sometimes almost inside the bureaucracies trying to work on change with them and trying to find champions within the institutions and support them (and)...then being frustrated with not seeing much change" (OAK-7-US). One representative admitted, "Right now we're having a running battle with the city administration...about the role of the nonprofit sector. I think that they are very comfortable with nonprofits in the service provision role; they are a lot less comfortable with nonprofits doing advocacy and especially the intermediary community in Oakland" (ibid.). The NGO representative cited an example of these frictions that occurred regarding an urban development program administered through Oakland schools, and his comments are worth quoting at length:

Central to us was a notion that these weren't just afterschool programs, but engines for neighborhood change and therefore they had to have a strong component of community organizing and community governance. We wrote that into the proposals, we raised money to give to the sites to develop community centers, and as we looked at a citywide governance structure for this initiative; every time we started out with agencies at the table, every time a site was authorized by the group, they got two seats at the table: one for a resident and one for a lead agency. And so sites started building and we had three sites, and the table was even in terms of CBOs, lead agency, and folks from the neighborhood. They came to the table and [the City Official in charge] came to a few meetings and basically said we lacked direction, we didn't have good outcomes da da da, all sorts of excuses, and basically pulled away from that table, and set out an alternative table, through another project, where the county health services agency director [The City Official himself], the superintendent of schools, and the East Bay Community Foundation were in control of it. At one point I went over and said, "Something is going on. I want to know, have we done something wrong?" But I've had this really chilly reception all through the school district after years of having real open access and them seeking out our advice is now just a stone wall, and I said I want to know what is going on, and he said, "It is me. I think you are doing things that you should not be doing, you are playing roles that you should not be playing, and you are not accountable and you are doing things that basically government should be doing." And we had a prolonged argument about why we were there because government wasn't doing it and resisted doing it and even when they tried, tended to mess it up. So, anyway, that went on, and it really impacted the work we were doing in the [project] because he refused to designate any additional sites even though we had raised money for them.

He goes back over to the city... mad, and he takes it back and again all through city agencies we get a stone wall. In places where we had access and good relationships, people are afraid to deal with us. About a month ago... I went over to talk to him and said, "What is going on?" And basically his reasoning has become much more sophisticated at this point: "Basically, intermediaries have stopped progress in Oakland" is his assessment. You have many of the relationships with constituencies that government should have, and our basic approach is: "Remove the intermediaries government."

And I went through a list of every major project we were doing and said: "Well, is there any role you can see for an intermediary?" And he said, "I can't think of any." So I went down a list of our major projects and said, "Is that an appropriate role for an intermediary in your judgment?" And he said "no" to all of them. (OAK-7-US)

When I interviewed the government official in charge of the demise of Oakland intermediaries, he shared an alternative perception of that same process:

About 16 years ago, the government turned to the activist community, the CBO community, the civic engagement community, and literally turned over huge chunks of city government to those groups with very little oversight.... I personally do not highly value intermediary organizations, because government ought to be willing, able, and capable of dealing directly with the community. That we don't need an intermediary to have that happen, and often the intermediary brings their own agenda, especially with long-standing intermediaries like we have in this town.... As opposed to doing community organizing to organize citizens to do things, they now organize citizens to become lobbyists for government to do things. And the partnership of doing things *with* government has changed to organizing to be concerned with the power of government.... And building community capacity to solve their own problems is very difficult work. To organize community to come and advocate government to do things differently is much easier work. (OAK-9-GM)

The clear message from this city official who serves as liaison to the intermediaries is that the role of community-based NGOs is *not* to organize citizen voice, particularly voice that could be critical of the state. "I see CBOs as a provider community vs. an advocacy community or an intermediary community," argued the Oakland city official (OAK-9-GM). Local NGOs are to organize citizens "to do" something; that is, to help out as volunteers and thereby compensate for the lack of state funds and intervention in problem zones. Yet those citizens are not entitled to collectively put demands onto government. In other words, they should get things done and in the process be accountable to the government funders; strengthening public accountability to constituents is not part of Oakland officials' vision for the nongovernmental sector.

This limited role is similar to what the Berlin government demands of its intermediary neighborhood-management NGOs. As different as these two case studies are, both governments' attempts to manage the NGOized urban development public via intermediaries led to clientelistic relationships with the local government. In Berlin, that relationship is tightly controlled through the locally run funding structure and strong government input in the kinds of projects that are sponsored. The neighborhood-management NGOs are institutionally weak advocates themselves and are therefore badly positioned to promote citizen advocacy. In Oakland, much stronger NGO intermediaries that had diversified their funding sources and could challenge local government accountability still needed government access to be effective in their neighborhoods and issue areas. When the city government decided that the intermediaries had become too strong and too independent a voice, it took nothing more than a high-ranking official to put a stop to a long tradition of institutional advocacy and access to local government. Doors were shut down from one day to the next. Yet, at least during the time of this field research, Oakland

city officials did not present their own initiatives on how to organize
civic engagement processes without the facilitation of these large NGOs.
Ultimately, both cases indicate that NGO advocacy, within a tightly government managed communication sphere, is at risk of creating clientelistic
and precarious NGO–government relations and publics that constrain the
nongovernmental sector's potential to incubate broader public advocacy.

THE NETWORKED PUBLIC SPHERE

Bremen is a city in northern Germany with around 660,000 inhabitants.
It has one of the highest levels of public debt nationwide and the highest
ratio of public employees as a percentage of the general population. Yet
it is a city that has been called in a recent survey by German Manager
Magazin one of the "most dynamic cities" in the country.[18] Bremen's government has long practiced a dual urban development approach: Responsibility for high-stake prestige projects is kept within the confines of city
parliamentary committees and the urban development department, but
most other urban development decisions are made on the neighborhood
level. A well-networked NGO environment in the neighborhoods represents diverse, often contradictory interests that are mediated in institutionalized planning processes organized either by the local government or
by neighborhood groups. One feature of this networked NGOized urban
development public that is immediately apparent is its communicative
density. The NGO representatives interviewed for this study, when asked
whether they knew where to go in the city and whom to talk to about
any number of issues involving urban development, claimed consistently
that there was a "politics of open doors" (BRE-11-JH), that they knew
personally the people in charge (BRE-10-BH) or someone near them, and
that they rarely encountered a communicative breakdown either between
groups or with the city. As one activist put it, "When you walk across
one of the markets Saturday morning, you're likely to run into the mayor,
someone from the urban planning committee and at least three other city
people that you needed to talk to" (BRE-6-KW). Bremen's political communication culture has an eye-to-eye quality in which NGOs and other
actors in the public sphere for the most part do not recall experiencing

---

[18] *Manager Magazin* August, 2005. Bremen is also number 1 for attracting high-tech
industry and number 16 among German cities in work-life balance (cited in BAW Institut
für regionale Wirtschaftsförderung 2005: 4).

strong hierarchies, closed doors, or arcane decision making (BRE-4-HG). City officials present Bremen's dense communication circuits and their neighborhood focus as a democratic resource that has historically enhanced Bremen's reputation and just needs to be fed with what John Dryzek calls a modernized "institutional software" (1996: 104) to keep it vibrant (BRE-2-FH). Political institutions thus do not just see themselves as providing "institutional hardware" but also as part of the software of "associated and supportive discourse" (Dryzek 1996: 104) in the city. Subpublics are encouraged and equipped to communicate with political and economic actors, and these actors turn to NGOized subpublics to engage with citizen concerns in planning processes. Even though Bremen's NGOs are quite disillusioned with the ability of the local media to represent their causes, they have found alternative outlets in the sublocal free weeklies and in government-sponsored, web-based communication forums.

As described in the beginning of this chapter, Bremen has a number of troubled neighborhoods. Among them, Tenever had attracted the city's attention as early as the late 1980s when its state-subsidized apartment units were serving increasingly as an arrival point for immigrants from Southern Europe, Africa, and later Eastern Europe and Russia. The percentage of German renters declined. Social tensions between Germans and migrants, as well as among immigrant groups, flared and unemployment rose. In the early 1990s, the investor who owned a large part of the neighborhood abandoned the buildings and left them to the city. The revitalization program, "Living in Neighborhoods," was created, and instead of focusing mainly on the building stock of the quarter, it practices an integrated approach of job creation, economic revitalization,[19] and the establishment of communicative ties between Tenever's diverse subpopulations. The city commissioned two full-time staff into the neighborhood to work with the existing neighborhood initiative Stadtteilgruppe, providing it with professional support and building citizen engagement. This staff is on the city's payroll, but Tenever's citizens lobbied successfully to hire a Tenever activist/social worker and an urban planner, both of whom had long lived in the neighborhood and were perceived as committed activists rather than as public officials. That their institutional

---

[19] Mixed funding sources from different city departments are used to sustain, among other programs, a family center, a child care facility, a youth job creation program, and a youth center.

position within the Stadtteilgruppe NGO and their institutional position within the city have conflicted so little over the years is primarily due to the fact that, as one of them claims, "the city never forced me to execute something; they listen to me as a spokesperson for the neighborhood" (BRE-3-JB) and Tenever citizens know that he is a well-connected, effective, and publicly outspoken advocate for them.

A central piece of the city's efforts to engage Tenever's citizens is the WIN (Wohnen in Nachbarschaften; Living in Neighborhoods) initiative, a citywide program established in 1998 to invest in urban development in blighted areas of Bremen. Tenever receives about 300,000 Euros per year for grassroots projects and jointly decided tasks to improve the neighborhood.[20] How these funds are used is decided in the meetings described at the outset of this chapter. The most striking feature of this decision-making process – for any outsider, but maybe more so for the social scientist – is that everybody in the room, not just people with institutional affiliations, has veto power. If one person objects to funds going toward a specific goal, the money will not be allocated to that particular cause, and discussion will be renewed at a later time. What in larger political arenas often results in gridlock works well in this local communicative space. Citizens engage with each other's issues and devise strategies to convince others of the relevance and legitimacy of their projects. The Stadtteilgruppe NGO serves as convener and mediator of this public communication event. Local government enables it by attending as one participant among many, taking up issues in a nondefensive way, and providing funds to address community claims without predetermining how this money is to be spent. Interviews in the neighborhood echoed two themes: (1) the importance of establishing not only discourse but also decision-making spaces with financial impact and (2) the role of government as coming not "from the outside" but instead working on a daily, accessible basis on the inside of the neighborhood (BRE-7-TK; BRE-8-FH; BRE-4-HG). The Stadtteilgruppe NGO functions as a communication hub not only for citizens and between citizens and local public officials; it also handles contacts with journalists, groups of activists, and politicians from other European cities who come to town to observe how Bremen has successfully enabled NGOs and citizens in Tenever to function as catalysts for public communication and civic engagement.

---

[20] Several other neighborhoods receive comparable funds.

This tight sublocal public has not collapsed, even under stress. After building consensus within the quarter, the city government decided in 2002 to downsize living space in the Tenever neighborhood by demolishing about one-third of the apartments (Gesellschaft für Stadtentwicklung 2007). In response, the Stadtteilgruppe met for several months with city officials, builders, and the city-owned housing company in charge of the restructuring of the neighborhood. It kept citizens and NGOs informed and involved every step of the way. To date, more than 900 apartments have been razed and more are to be torn down (24). Citizens have negotiated new parks, new infrastructure, and a commitment from the city to strengthen the local economy. The Tenever networked public sphere thus has at its core an intermediary NGO that sees itself and is considered by the local state as the mediator in a network of NGOs and citizen initiatives, rather than merely as a part of the government's intervention squad.

Seattle, in the United States, has a very similar profile as Bremen; it has around 540,000 inhabitants, a large public sector by U.S. standards, innovative industries, and a medical research and computer technology hub. Seattle is a self-declared city of neighborhoods, with an established institutional structure of district councils and neighborhood councils made up of local activists and small neighborhood-oriented NGOs. It was one of the first cities in the United States to have a Department of Neighborhoods with the directive to "advocate for the community's ability to have a voice in positions. So to that extent we are advocates, in that we give tools to a community so that it has a stronger voice politically, to therefore being able to advocate on their behalf with regard to their specific issues" (SEA-8-BC). City government, in 1995, introduced one of the first comprehensive Neighborhood Planning Program (NPP) in any U.S. city. The program set forth broad goals, including improving the quality of life in Seattle, managing growth for the next two decades, involving neighborhoods in urban planning, and creating a civic environment based on fostering community.[21] It placed most of the responsibility and resources for neighborhood planning development in the hands of neighborhoods, with the result that 20,000 citizens, in 38 neighborhoods, have become engaged in the process (Diers 2004). The Seattle government provided resources by dispatching city planners to the neighborhoods for extended periods to help organize and move forward the planning process. After

---

[21] Available at http://www.seattle.gov/neighborhoods/npi. For a critical overview of the NPP see Ceraso (1999).

four years of work in 1999, the process produced detailed and citizen-needs-driven road maps for Seattle's future.

Seattle's Department of Neighborhoods was put in charge of neighborhood planning. Its director Jim Diers had a background in organizing and, when given this responsibility, he declared, "As a former community organizer, I hated neighborhood planning. Planning was too often the city's substitute for action. Plans came out of City Hall with only token involvement of the community" (Diers 2004: 128). Therefore, when his office was charged with administering the planning process, he hired organizers, not planners, to give substance to the road maps. The citywide Neighborhood Council, comprising representatives from the District Councils, which in turn were made up of Neighborhood Council representatives, was put in charge of implementing the road maps, with resources and staff provided by Diers's department. Even though the neighborhood planning process was never as inclusive as suggested when civic engagement awards rained down on Seattle, it did foster public advocacy and public accountability by NGOs in their respective neighborhoods: It provided institutionalized spaces for public exchange and organized deliberation; it distributed resources of between 150,000 and 200,000 USD each to 38 neighborhoods (SEA-7-CW), thus raising the stakes and public legitimacy of the process; it encouraged NGOs with different issue agendas to weigh their interests against and with each other; and it provided institutional communicative space to interact with government and business on a regular basis. Thus, even though the process was far from pristine (Ceraso 1999), it provided Seattle groups and NGOs with the means to network and established a yardstick of government-sponsored outreach against which city governance has been measured since. It enabled the NGO sector in particular to network and establish itself as a catalyst of citizen voices in the process.[22]

The process that historically made Seattle NGOs a stronger public force than in other cities worked with similar incentives as in Bremen: The local government gave seed money to citizen initiatives with few strings attached. It had open and frequent communication with citizens

---

[22] A complementary element in Seattle's networked public sphere is the city's support for a variety of neighborhood engagement activities. A Neighborhood Matching Fund, in which about $3.5 million is distributed annually, helps get small NGO-led or citizen projects off the ground. The city provides funding "in exchange for the community's match of an equal value in cash, volunteer labor, or donated goods and services in support of citizen-initiated projects" (Diers 2004: 55).

and NGOs, which in turn perceived city officials as generally open to input and dialogue. The city also fostered a communication infrastructure that helped NGOs network among themselves. Finally, decision-making processes were discussed publicly and critically in the two free city weeklies where NGOs could get heard more easily than in the established daily newspaper. As a result, in Bremen and in Seattle, thresholds for participation appear to be overall lower than in the other cities, the actively NGOized local public has resources to communicate and network, and existing NGOs are thereby encouraged to serve as catalysts for public voice.

At the same time, because networked publics are the product of specific conditions, their character can be altered by a change in environment. They often depend on the involvement of professional engagement experts in government, progressive political constellations, or favorable economic conditions. Thus, they are susceptible to implosion if certain promoters leave their positions or exogenous conditions change. The Seattle case indicates how fast and easily a broadly networked public sphere can become subject to political challenges and reactivate older insider and clientelistic relationships between selected NGOs and local government. When Mayor Greg Nickels took office in 2001, he fired Jim Diers, the director of the Department of Neighborhoods. The number of staff in charge of implementing neighborhood plans was cut from six to three, and the Neighborhood Matching Fund program was cut by 20 percent.[23] Under Nickel's reign, many neighborhood plans were modified or put aside to make room for the imperative of growth-related development. The city's strategy changed from giving the neighborhoods resources to organize their own deliberation processes to driving a growth agenda into the neighborhoods. Access to City Hall and government employees became more difficult (SEA-S-JF). By the time Nickels was voted out of office in 2009, the networked urban development public had all but imploded. A few, very well-connected urban development nonprofits had carved out dominant stakes in the city's governance arena while other NGOs became more marginal to public communication in the urban development field. Neighborhood-focused communication processes across a broad spectrum of groups had given way to institutional advocacy by a few central NGO "players" – and this structure was strengthened by the Mayor's Office with financial incentives. As one

---

[23] Quoted from an article in the *Seattle Times* by Bob Young, August, 2003, titled "Community Leaders Lose Influence at City Hall."

NGO representative put it, there now were "grassroots advocacy groups that represent marginalized groups like our own at the low end of the spectrum...and then as you go up the scale there are more affluent communities, and they have the resources to play these games far more effectively than us; they can hire attorneys and have surrogates who have the time to play these games" (SEA-2-JF). Seattle's urban development arena had moved from having a relatively stable networked public, in which public advocacy was an engrained part of NGO activity, to a more hierarchical insider/outsider structure in which institutional advocacy prevailed and which was managed by government.

CONCLUSION

Local governments increasingly rely on NGOs not only as experts in policy drafting and implementation but also to provide and organize citizen input (DeFilippis 2001; Andrews and Edwards 2005; Haus et al. 2005; Klausen and Sweeting 2005; Walker and McCarthy 2010). The key to whether an urban community develops a culture of public advocacy can be found in the very properties of the relationship between state and non-state actors. It is the way governments establish their role vis-à-vis citizens and their organizations that either enables or disincentivizes public voice. All six local governments showed strong rhetoric regarding their communication with NGOs and its generally positive effects on encouraging citizen participation, yet in practice they had developed a broad range of interaction patterns with their respective nongovernmental sectors. Bremen and Seattle have received national and international recognition for actively encouraging and networking their civic sector and for exploring innovative participatory venues. The governments of Leipzig and San Diego, however, govern their civic landscape very carefully. Communication with NGOs and citizens appears to be primarily geared toward creating an investor-friendly public image and maximizing economic effects. Although government actors within urban planning departments, mayor's offices, and neighborhood or community departments interviewed for this study – with the exception of Oakland – reported increases in contacts with NGOs and more intense collaborations to reach communities and engage citizens in public affairs and debates, the kinds of interactions varied quite extensively.

The governments of both San Diego and Leipzig operate with a combination of neglect and dominance in organizing public communication in the urban development sector. The hegemony of community development corporations in San Diego has resulted in market-based actors dominating communication with both government and larger communities.[24] In Leizpig, the lack of government-sponsored incentives to reach beyond selective NGOs results in a polarized civil society in which inclusion in governance seems to be engineered solely through governments. At the margins, one encounters a small number of activists over and over again, often acting alone as critical commentators on different urban development projects. Close up, San Diego's and Leizpig's NGOized urban development publics are highly institutionalized and operate as proxies for nonincorporated citizens. A few dominant NGOs, in concord with government, monopolize civic voice and make it difficult for others to engage with urban development issues.

Oakland and Berlin overall have established more inclusive, but government-managed communication cultures. There citizen engagement is channeled through large intermediary NGOs, with governments preserving their prerogative as to who gets to have voice. Thus, although civic engagement has been, in effect, outsourced, government remains the most powerful agenda setter. NGO intermediaries operate within a heavily government-dominated governance arena that limits chances to conduct effective advocacy by creating dependencies and exclusionary circles of knowledge and insisting on NGO service performance over civic engagement. The situation in Oakland, moreover, showed how quickly government can marginalize NGO intermediaries that are too committed to organizing public advocacy.

Government is also crucial for the kind of networked public sphere that NGOs in Seattle and Bremen have historically promoted. In those cities, substantial funds have been awarded to self-organizing neighborhoods to build capacity that in turn connects citizens to NGOs and empowers public over institutional advocacy. In both these cities, governance processes have in the past channeled urban development initiatives that were inclusive in their outreach to different constituencies and provided incentives to NGOs to be pubic advocates for their constituencies. The cities have encouraged NGOs to act as conveners and facilitators in public venues, thereby promoting NGO public accountability while at the same time strengthening citizen voice and public advocacy. Both Seattle and Bremen provide examples of governments that facilitate public engagement by opening up and flattening hierarchies in their communication processes

---

[24] For a similar argument regarding the role of community development corporations in Oakland, see Kirkpatrick (2007).

and providing resources for the civic sector that enable structured communication about civic affairs in neighborhood-oriented smaller scale spaces. Advocacy capacities of NGOs hence do depend on institutional design; that is, on whether networked, managed, or restricted communication cultures are established and sustained within local governance.

By contrast, those cities that only practice the "democratization of the irrelevant"[25] are particularly subject to contestation and change. San Diego went through a major civic meltdown in 2005. Misappropriation of finances and conflict of interest issues forced the president of CCDC and some of her staff out of office. The wife of a legendary San Diego surfer almost upset the establishment by running on an "enough is enough" agenda in a mayoral race against the two major Republican incumbents, which she called "Mr. Status" and "Mr. Quo." The city's employer's pension fund was found to have accrued a deficit of at least $1.2 billon (Broder 2005). Three members of the City Council were indicted on corruption charges. It was "the death rattle of the old regime," as Steven Erie, political scientist at UCSD, called it (ibid.). By 2010, the activists who wanted to redevelop the shopping area had created their own NGO. CCDC fought for survival because its mandate had expired.

In 2006, after many years of highly individualized politics, a group of young journalists created a nonprofit Internet site, VoiceofSanDiego.org, that has become a beacon of investigative journalism in the city. They chastise the closed communication circuits in the city and offer alternative ways to open up government.[26] In Leipzig, five major NGOs have recently left the government-run project Democracy Balance Sheet under protest and have asked the city to be more inclusive in who gets invited to the project table.

Thus, when cities manage their public spheres so tightly as to in effect exclude NGOs from most governance arenas, democratizing pressures from below are likely to develop. However, government willingness to hear the noisy communication of various publics is also needed to enable the process to evolve toward more coordinated public involvement that rises above the much heard rhetoric of individual civic engagement. In Chapter 1, I argued that NGOs might gain voice under two mutually exclusive conditions: if they are kept out of governance arenas or if they

---

[25] *Frankfurter Rundschau*, "Die Politik drängt das Ehrenamt an den Rand," September 21, 2007.
[26] The *New York Times* reported on the project in 2008. Richard Perez-Pena, "Web Sites that Dig for News Rise as Watchdogs," September 17, 2008.

are actively supported in their role as catalysts of the claim-making of their constituencies. The cases presented here, in which different approaches of local governments in urban development governance clearly correspond with different public advocacy capacities of NGOs, provide evidence for this incentivizing role of government.

6

Transnational Women's NGO Networks
in the European Union

During the past two decades, NGOs have had particular impact on governance contexts beyond the nation-state (i.e., Keck and Sikkink 1998; Kaldor 2003a; Kaldor 2003b; Steffek and Hahn 2011). Because transnational governance arenas lack an identifiable *demos* and thus traditional modes of legitimacy, NGOs and their networks have advanced to become stand-ins for citizen voice in international negotiations – in the process not only gaining policy influence but also fueling debates about their accountability and representativeness. In the European Union, there is widespread agreement among academics, political actors, and feminist activists that the EU gender equality architecture of the last decade is the result of successful mobilization of women in member states (Woodward and Hubert 2007).[1] With mass media discourse on gender across Europe being infrequent and marginal, the issue of who speaks for European women and who advocates for gender equality gains particular relevance. Standing out as potential enablers and communicators of EU gender equality issues are European women's NGOs and their transnational advocacy networks (TANs[2]). They are widely credited as having

---

[1] An earlier version of this chapter has been published in Social Politics 16 (2009). The empirical analysis was supported by grants from the Center for West European Studies, the European Union Center for Excellence, and the Nancy Bell Evans Center on Nonprofits and Philanthropy at the University of Washington. Interviews were cleared through HSR #07-5469-X/C. I am indebted to research assistants Elizabeth Zherka, Elisabeth Lyons, Gillian Frackelton, David Nash-Mendez, and Chris Schulz. Details on methodology are found in Appendices 2–4.

[2] I use the term "transnational advocacy network" (TAN) with a more narrow focus than do Keck and Sikkink in their seminal study in 1998. Keck and Sikkink include as TANs all actors "who are bound together by shared values, a common discourse, and

been central in bringing about changes in European gender equality legislation (Woodward 2004; Zippel 2006; Montoya 2008).

This chapter focuses on how women's transnational advocacy networks in the EU communicate gender issues, and, more specifically, what kinds of advocacy repertoires they employ to reach their goals. I start by exploring how institutions within the European Union conceptualize the role of the nongovernmental sector and, in particular, its capacity to contribute to a European public sphere. I then introduce five European transnational women's NGO networks and assess their communication and advocacy strategies. The focus here is on whether and how these networks mobilize when faced with a controversial EU policy such as gender mainstreaming. To make that case, a brief detour is necessary, explaining what gender mainstreaming is and how women's NGOs in the EU are implicated in the strategy. Interviews, website analysis, and the mapping of networks provide the data for the gender mainstreaming advocacy case. In the second part of this chapter I assess more broadly what means of communication are used by women's TANs in Europe, whom they target with their communication strategies, and to what degree they network among each other to gain broader public visibility. Taking up the framework developed in Chapter 2 on measuring the strength of an associational public, I focus on the density of the TANs' communicative ties, the modes of communication they employ, and the targets of their communication.

STRONG PUBLICS AND ADVOCACY IN THE EU

Scholars, politicians, and civil society groups agree, in principle, that the legitimacy of the European Union rests on generating strong publics (Habermas 1996; Eriksen and Fossum 2002; Nanz 2006; Fossum and Schlesinger 2007; Koopmans and Statham 2010; Risse 2010). Yet what defines strong European publics is contested. Recent scholarship has built

---

dense exchanges of information and services" (Keck and Sikkink 1998: 2). They therefore include both institutional and noninstitutional actors such as "(1) international and domestic nongovernmental research and advocacy organizations, (2) local social movements, (3) foundations, (4) the media, (5) churches, trade unions, consumer organizations, and intellectuals, (6) parts of regional and international intergovernmental organizations, and (7) parts of the executive and/or parliamentary branches of governments" (2).

In contrast, the TANs I refer to in this chapter are all networks of NGOs; thus they do not include political institutions such as parliaments and political executives or the media.

on Nancy Fraser's (1992) distinction between strong and weak publics, the former being publics "whose discourse encompasses both opinion formation and decision-making" and the latter being publics "whose deliberative practice consists exclusively in opinion formation and does not also encompass decision making" (134). Hence, in Fraser's account, weaker publics can strive to become part of stronger publics, whereas strong publics are not necessarily located in the core institutions of political systems. Strong publics, moreover, are those that best bridge the gap between multiple venues of opinion formation and decision making. By contrast, Eriksen and Fossum (2002: 401–5) define strong publics as "institutionalized bodies of deliberation and decision-making" situated in the center of political systems; in contrast, civil society publics are weak publics fostered by civic activity but excluded from decision-making processes. Departing from Fraser's distinction, they re-institutionalize the strong public within the confines of established political institutions. In fact, the institutionalized deliberations of the European Parliament, the process leading to the Charter of Fundamental Rights in 2000, and the meetings of the European Convention in 2002–3 would all fall under the rubric of a "strong public" (Eriksen 2007: 37). All three processes share a location within the political system of the EU, are broadly based on the principles of citizen inclusion and empowerment, and foster rational exchanges of argument. Even though Eriksen and Fossum acknowledge that the Charter Convention and the Constitutional Treaty Convention gave very little space to statements by NGOs and TANs and that a preselection process was employed to decide which NGOs and TANs to grant face-to-face interaction with the Convention members, they highlight the formal openness of processes in which civil society actors can engage in public deliberation in a circumscribed space and time. They thus place less emphasis on the fact that civil society participation in the Charter and Constitutional Convention was highly scripted, reduced to consultative rather than participatory interactions, and favored well-organized Brussels-based NGO networks (Cammaerts 2006). For Eriksen and Fossum strong publics are institutionalized decision-making publics that *in principle* allow for civil society access.

On the other side of this debate over strong publics are academics and activists who use Fraser's distinction less categorically and instead employ a more process-oriented model of a European public sphere. These accounts tend to emphasize permeability between weaker and stronger publics and specifically the opportunities for access that institutionalized publics provide to non-institutionalized actors. The verdict on the ability of the European public sphere to allow for such access is still out, yet research cautions against optimism. For Michael Greven, access to and the repertoire of advocacy on the Brussels stage are both severely limited. The "political space and the communication that constitute the EU are semipublic" at best, because "very few citizens are involved on this level" (Greven 2000: 51; see also Warleigh 2001). Institutions serve as gate-keepers barring strong public input. Moreover, activists face logistical challenges when trying to rely on traditional mobilization repertoire (i.e., protests, demonstrations, sit-ins, boycotts, or acts of civil disobedience) in transnational European arenas. Movements, NGOs, and TANs need to rely on "professional support and expertise to be effective" (Greven 2000: 51). The specific governance culture within the EU provides specific access points, and these in turn shape the advocacy repertoire of activists. There is also evidence that institutionalized semi-publics prevent the emergence of stronger civil-society–based publics. Thomas Risse argues that mostly EU-level executive branches and national governments populate Europe's public, whereas "societal actors . . . have a minimal presence in the emerging Europeanized public spheres" (Risse 2010: 161). Likewise, Ruud Koopmans and Paul Statham show that NGOs have very little input in Europeanized media debates (Koopmans and Statham 2010), suggesting that the permeability between institutionalized and non-institutionalized public spheres is low.

Process-oriented accounts emphasize the potential of actors to use insider and outsider mobilization repertoires simultaneously (Rucht 2001), thus effectively delocalizing strong publics from their institutional confines. A strong public can develop in European civil society if and when it employs a mix of mobilization strategies that target larger audiences, as well as institutional actors. One of the obvious examples of a successful combination of insider lobbying and bargaining in combination with public mobilization and contentious media-savvy strategies are EU farmers' protests (Imig and Tarrow 2001). Even though advocates in different policy sectors face different challenges, they all navigate between effective institutional lobbying and public outreach. Strong publics in this theoretical conception are not per se institutional publics, but rather publics that are able to combine and bridge institutional and public advocacy. It is this conception of strong publics that is used here.

THE EUROPEAN UNION AND NGOS

The institutions of the European Union have, in recent years, increased their efforts to define and institutionalize the role of NGOs and transnational networks within EU governance. In 2000, the European

Commission published a discussion paper, *The Commission and Non-Governmental Organizations: Building a Stronger Partnership*, that extended the earlier EU focus on NGOs in the social policy arena to address civic actors across all relevant policy sectors (European Commission 2000). Cooperation between the EU executive and the nongovernmental sector is encouraged, because "belonging to an association provides an opportunity for citizens to participate actively in new ways other than or in addition to involvement in political parties or trade unions. Increasingly NGOs are recognized as a significant component of civil society and as providing valuable support for a democratic system of government" (4).

Although the Commission report states that "the decision making process in the EU is first and foremost legitimized by the elected representatives of the European people," it emphasizes the specific contribution that the nongovernmental sector can make, namely to foster a "more participatory democracy both within the European Union and beyond" (European Commission 2000: 4). NGOs are perceived as stakeholders for disenfranchised and marginalized populations, because they have the ability "to reach the poorest and most disadvantaged and to provide a voice for those not sufficiently heard through other channels" (ibid. 5). Furthermore, the Commission values the expertise of NGOs in negotiations and decision-making processes and acknowledges their capacity to manage and monitor projects financed by the EU. Finally, by encouraging cooperation among national NGOs and stimulating the formation of European NGO networks, the Commission hopes to foster the formation of a "European public opinion." Overall, the report conveys that NGOs and, more specifically, transnational networks of NGOs are perceived as prima facie expressions of civil society (ibid.).

In 2003, the Commission established minimum standards for consultation and dialogue, specifically addressing which stakeholders and NGOs should be consulted at what time and by which process (EU Commission 2002a). In 2005, it launched the European Transparency Initiative and opened a public consultation process on its standards online (Greenwood and Halpin 2007), followed in 2008 by an, albeit voluntary, joint "Transparency Register" for civil society organizations interacting with Parliament or the Commission. Even though these documents and initiatives convey the institutions' interest in setting standards for their interactions with civil society, both the Initiative and the Register skirt central questions regarding representativeness and accountability. Whereas the Commission and Parliament are clear about their expectation that

NGOs and their networks serve as transmitters and translators of EU policies in their respective fields of operation (Greenwood and Halpin 2007: 192) and thus are accountable to the EU in their public presentation of European matters, they are much less clear about how to increase public accountability of NGOs in regard to their constituencies. To some degree, Commission and Parliament take internal democratic procedures as a proxy for public accountability. Yet there is persistent concern that mere adherence to instrumental accountability is no adequate measure of an NGO's legitimacy to speak for constituency interests. In sum, NGOs operating on the level of European institutions at this point struggle with how to 'prove' representativeness and accountability. Particularly since a "one-size-fits-all" solution for assessing accountability of civil society actors might prove to be not just impractical but in fact counterproductive (see Greenwood and Halpin 2007: 190), each NGO and each transnational network in the EU are in need of showing how they engage with constituents.

EUROPEAN WOMEN'S TRANSNATIONAL ADVOCACY NETWORKS

Women in Europe have organized across borders long before the inception of the European Community in 1957. Cooperation and joint mobilization among women's organizations were part of the fabric of the first women's movement in the late 19th century and can be traced to the second women's movement starting in the 1970s. Yet there are certain characteristics that make women's TANs of the late 1980s and since unique and potentially very powerful.

First, they responded to new institutional configurations. With the rights-based take-off phase of the EU in the 1980s, fueled by the first equality ruling of the European Court of Justice in the 1970s (Cichowski 2007: 203), social actors gained recognition and became empowered to act as advocates for the rights of European citizens. Women's rights advocates acquired some degree of institutional legitimacy to mobilize for the right to equal pay, a nondiscriminatory (work) environment, and equal access to all parts of the labor market.

Second, women's rights activists saw new strategic opportunities. Women's TANs began to use the transnational institutions of the EU to target national policies, thus relying on Keck and Sikkink's *boomerang effect* (1998: 13). At the same time, European institutions increasingly relied on expertise from civil society actors, and thus the EU actively encouraged the development of women's TANs (Hoskyns 1996; Mazey

1998). EU governance began to offer not only an occasional opening for NGO participation but also provided regular institutional space (i.e., through Commission-sponsored consultations and parallel NGO conferences) that in turn encouraged networking among women's NGOs (Cichowski 2002: 2; Pudrovska and Ferree 2004: 5). In addition to granting organizational space and opportunities for networking, the EU also started to fund transnational networking activities, which then became highly attractive for NGOs. Major funding sources such as programs within the European Structural Fund or the European Fund for Regional Development today contain provisions for transnational cooperation and exchange of "best practices" among similar projects in the EU member states. Hence, networking among NGOs has been made an institutional priority within the EU, which in turn helps organize transnational civic practices.

Third, new means of communication made transnational cooperation and mobilization easier and potentially more effective than ever before. E-mail alerts and web-based campaigns as well as internal communication networks allow for faster dissemination of information and mobilization across European women's NGOs.

These three innovations – institutional scale, strategy, and communication – define the specific political opportunity structure for women's TANs on the stages of Europe. The EU has redefined *goals* of women's advocates by creating institutional means for supranational leverage. It has redefined *strategies* by opening up institutional spaces for access of NGOs and networks and thus invited institutional advocacy. At the same time, innovation in communication has led to a whole array of cheap public advocacy *means* for NGOs. Women's TANs in Europe thus face an enhanced political opportunity structure for both institutional and public advocacy. This chapter assesses whether and how they make use of this opportunity.

Transnational women's networks are perceived to be highly active, visible, and overall successful actors in the European Union (Cichowski 2002; Woodward 2004; Zippel 2006; Montoya 2008). The most prominent and largest network is the *European Women's Lobby* (EWL), founded in 1990 as an umbrella organization for European women's groups. In the mid-1990s, the EWL began to experience a dramatic increase in membership (Woodward and Hubert 2007), growing to about 2,700 affiliates in 2000 (Helfferich and Kolb 2001: 143) and to more than 4,000 affiliates after the large accession round of 2004 (EWL 2005c).

Since its inception, EWL has become "the favoured dialogue partner with the European Institutions" (Woodward and Hubert 2007: 7; see Helfferich and Kolb 2001). It is "almost exclusively dependent" on yearly grants by the European Parliament, from which it receives about 80 percent to 85 percent of its budget (Helfferich and Kolb 2001: 148; EWL 2007a). According to its former president Barbara Helfferich, EWL's mission has three components: (1) working on noncontroversial issues shared by all affiliated organizations; (2) providing information, expertise, and funding to national and local groups; and (3) encouraging communication between members and the *EWL* bureau in Brussels (Helfferich and Kolb 2001: 150). It is apparent that public advocacy is not a central part of its mission. Instead, its "survival and effectiveness depend on "friendly individuals" inside the Parliament and the Commission (148).

No other European transnational women's network comes close to having EWL's institutional influence, transnational membership base, or yearly funding from the European Union.[3] Yet it has been criticized for operating according to the principle of the smallest common denominator and thus sidelining controversial issues such as sexual reproduction and minority rights (Fuchs 2006; Lang 2009a). As alternative networking spaces, a number of smaller transnational women's networks in Europe have gained prominence in the past decade. Four of these groups are included in this analysis, representing the largest constituencies in the fields of violence against women, development, and environmental protection with a focus on Central and Eastern European countries (see Table 6.1).

The women's network *WAVE* (Women Against Violence in Europe) is a coalition of European women's organizations that was founded in 1994 in the context of the UN Women's Conference in Beijing. WAVE represents more than 4,000 women's organizations and communicates with them via 81 so-called focal points across Europe. These focal points are women's NGOs in charge of disseminating information and serving as coordination links to the central office in Vienna. WAVE and its members receive substantial funding through the EU DAPHNE program that is geared toward combating violence against women and children.

---

[3] In 2003, EWL received 820,000 Euros from EU funding. The KARAT network, by contrast, had no income from the EU in 2003 and 2004. In 2005, KARAT received 34,000 Euros from the EU (KARAT, e-mail interview, 2006).

TABLE 6.1. *Transnational Women's Networks in Europe*

	Founded	Mission	Members	Funding	Projects	Strategies
EWL European Women's Lobby	1990	Fostering coordination of women's NGOs on the EU level	Delegates from 4000 women's NGOs on national and EU level	Ca. 80% EU, 20% membership fees and other resources	Women's empowerment and gender equality–no feminist rhetoric	Monitoring, networking, and institutional lobbying
KARAT Coalition of CEE/CIS Women's NGOs	1995	Network of women in Eastern and Central Europe and the Commonwealth of Independent States	Warsaw based association with 65 NGOs and individual members	International and national public authorities and NGOs	Promoting gender equality in CEE/CIS states	Monitoring the implementation of international agreements, lobbying, projects
WAVE Women Against Violence Europe	1994	Network of women's NGOs combating violence against women/children	4000 women's NGOs across Europe	International and national public authorities and private donations	Strengthening human rights of women and children, feminist analysis	Information exchange, influence policies, promote feminist analysis

WECF Women in Europe for our Common Future	1992	Stimulates cooperation between women in NGOs in environment, health, sustainable development	Network of 80 women environment organizations in 33 European and Central Asian countries	Foundations, private donors, and public/institutional sponsors	Gender sensitive environmental policy and gender impact assessments – no feminist rhetoric	Institutional lobbying
WIDE Network Women in Development Europe	1985	Network of development NGOs, monitors and influences global economic and development policy and practice	National platform in 9 EU member states, individual members and associations	National governments, foundations, and EU; membership fees of platform	Promoting gender equality through feminist analysis	Information exchange, networking

WECF, Women in Europe for a Common Future, is a network of 80 environmental women's organizations in 37 European and bordering Asian countries that was founded in 1994. It promotes advocacy and capacity-building to address environmental issues with a gendered lens and to foster cooperation among European NGOs.

WIDE, Women in Development Europe, is a network that was founded in 1985 and has in recent years focused its advocacy on monitoring trade relationships and capacity-building in Central and Eastern European (CEE) countries. WIDE is made up of 13 national and regional platforms that serve as communicative hubs between state or regional and EU-level members.

Women's organizations from CEE countries have joined in the *KARAT* coalition. KARAT was founded in 1997, in the aftermath of the Beijing UN Women's Conference (Fuchs 2006; Marksova-Tominova 2006; Aigner 2007). It comprises about 30 women's organizations. It seeks influence at the UN, as well as on the EU level, and puts special emphasis on fighting against the inward orientation of "fortress Europe" proponents in EU member states.

WOMEN'S TANS AND GENDER MAINSTREAMING

In this section I explore TAN advocacy in regard to gender mainstreaming, which is widely perceived as the most encompassing and potentially transformative strategy that the EU has introduced in regard to gender equality (Rees 1999, 2005; Squires 2005; Verloo 2005). It is considered to be the third leg of equality policy, in addition to antidiscrimination and affirmative action policies. The Council of Europe defines gender mainstreaming as "the (re)organization, improvement, development and evaluation of policy processes so that a gender equality perspective is incorporated in all policies at all levels and at all stages, by the actors normally involved in policy-making" (Council of Europe 1998: 15). Gender mainstreaming has thus shifted public and institutional focus from special programs that advance the status of women toward demanding gender sensitivity across all policy arenas within the European Union. It is conceptualized as a process that engenders governance, increases public awareness of gender inequalities, and commits more actors to the goal of gender equality (Lombardo 2005; Verloo 2005, 2007; Rees 2005).

Transnational women's networks have been crucial in the lobbying efforts for gender mainstreaming, succeeding with demands for its integration first into the Platform of Action of the Fourth World Conference on Women in Beijing in 1995 (True and Mintrom 2001). Institutional-ized women's lobbies of EU member states were instrumental in pushing the UN agenda onto the European stage, claiming that the EU's tradi-tional programs targeting women was by itself not sufficient to advance gender justice and parity (Pollack and Hafner-Burton 2000). Today, gen-der mainstreaming has been incorporated into the Amsterdam Treaty, as well as into the Treaty of Lisbon, as the major strategy for fighting gender inequality.

Yet even though its radical and transformative potential is widely acknowledged, gender mainstreaming is a globally contested strategy in policy arenas ranging from the transnational to the local level. Stephen Lewis, the UN Special Envoy for AIDS in Africa, calls it a "cul de sac for women" (Lewis 2006a: 2) and argues "there is not a single assess-ment of gender mainstreaming that I have read – and there have been many assessments, commissioned by donors, compiled by the UN itself, done by NGOs – that is fundamentally positive. Every single one of them ranges from the negative to an unabashed indictment" (Lewis 2006b). On the national and regional level, governments' framing and implementa-tion of gender mainstreaming have been uneven and produced mixed results (Behning and Sauer 2005). In Central, Eastern, and Southern European countries the strategy tends to be applied primarily in pol-icy fields where additional resources and major reorganization can be avoided (see, for example, Einhorn 2006; Krizsan and Zentai 2006, for Hungary; Guadagnini and Dona 2007, for Italy; Sauer 2007, for Austria; Lang 2007, for Germany). In Northern and Western Europe, some governments similarly downsize the transformative potential of gender mainstreaming by draining governance bodies of gender expertise (for example, see Outshoorn and Oldersma 2007, for the Netherlands) or avoiding additional spending (Holli and Kantola 2007, for Finland).

Hence, the strategy has fueled a string of debates in EU gender pol-icy circles[4] and is considered to be an "essentially contested concept and practice" (Walby 2002; also Kuhl 2003). Judith Squires, among others, suggested that "mainstreaming might be most likely to be a truly trans-formative strategy when technocratic expertise, social movement partic-ipation, and transnational networks are in place" (Squires 2005: 371), pointing to the need for parallel insider and outsider advocacy to carry the strategy into the mainstream of European politics and economy.

---

[4] For example special issues of *Social Politics* 12(3) 2005, of the *International Feminist Journal of Politics* 7(4) 2005, as well as of *Feminist Legal Studies* 10(3–4) 2002.

European Women's NGOs and their networks are implicated in gender mainstreaming in several ways. One of the founding documents of the European gender mainstreaming strategy, the previously cited 1998 report by the Council of Europe, explicitly relates gender mainstreaming to a shift in actors – "passing matters related to gender equality from the hands of the specialists of the equality units to a greater number of people, including external actors" (Verloo 2005: 351). Women's NGOs are conceptualized as one of these external actors, as groups that can help support the strategy with their knowledge and can create the political will to keep gender mainstreaming on the public agenda (ibid.). Thus, on the one hand, feminist advocates and NGOs are involved in gender mainstreaming as coaches, policy advisors, and implementation experts (Gender Mainstreaming Experts International 2008). On the other hand, European women's NGOs and their networks are called on to be public advocates for the strategy. They are seen as actors with responsibility for contributing to public debates because they have firsthand and comparative insight into the impact that the strategy has on the national level (Mazey 2002).

In addition to being outside experts that offer training, publicly promote, and monitor gender mainstreaming, some women's NGOs are more directly involved in implementing the strategy by being partners in EU-funded programs. Gender mainstreaming is a requirement in all programs of the European Structural Funds, and cooperation of national or regional governance bodies with civil society actors is one of the program's pillars (Braithwaite 2000). In the recent round of the Community Initiative Program EQUAL, a program initiative that specifically operates on the premises of social inclusion, transnationality, empowerment, and with a bottom-up approach, about 2,000 NGOs across the EU participated with projects, many of them women's NGOs (EAPN 2007). EQUAL, while being a driving force for gender mainstreaming, has also encouraged and strengthened partnerships with women's NGOs (EQUAL European Thematic Group 4 2005; EQUAL Policy Brief 2005). Feminist NGOs are affected by gender mainstreaming because showing a strong mainstreaming component increases funding chances (Kuhl 2003). Some women's NGOs thus seem well positioned to contribute to and analyze implementation from within partnerships. In sum, women's NGOs across Europe are facing demands to monitor gender mainstreaming, to train gender experts, and to practice and implement gender mainstreaming when they participate in EU-funded projects.

Different "hats" that women's NGOs wear in regard to gender main-streaming might, however, present challenges. Engaging in implementation and monitoring at the same time might pose a potential conflict of interest, as might receiving funds for building institutional expertise while doing public advocacy that might challenge institutional commitment. How do European women's NGOs navigate these different identities and differing demands? One way to deflect constraints that a single NGO might experience is to make use of transnational organizational leverage. Women's TANs are well positioned to politicize issues that might be "too close to home" for some NGOs. We can thus assume women's TANs have sufficient incentive to use transnational NGO networking capacity to build expertise, monitor, and practice advocacy regarding gender mainstreaming. Yet how exactly do European transnational women's networks try to influence gender mainstreaming discourse?

Probing the networks' influence in the EU gender mainstreaming debate, I have compiled three sets of data. The first set consists of 12 interviews with directors/board representatives and members of the networks. The interviews were structured (1) to address the networks' position on gender mainstreaming with a focus on attempts to influence frames, policies, or practices and (2) to examine the networks' overall propensity to engage in public advocacy campaigns, including the availability of resources for advocacy. I conducted the interviews between 2005 and 2008 at two nodes of the networks – with representatives of the central network structure and with NGO representatives of organizations that are network members. Through e-mail or phone calls, I asked the TAN and member organizations to refer me to an executive board/executive office member knowledgeable in the area of gender mainstreaming and campaign advocacy. I then conducted three interviews by phone and nine in person in five EU member states. The interviews were between 45 minutes and 120 minutes long and semi-structured. Eight interviews were taped and transcribed; for four I only took notes.

The second set of data analyzes the networks' web presence to investigate how the networks address the issue of gender mainstreaming in their websphere and how they launch and sustain advocacy campaigns via the web. The web has developed into a fast and low-cost communication tool for information, networking, and strategic action among civic groups (Castells and Cardoso 2006). Because all the TANs span multiple European cultures and languages, their websites serve as a central and widely accessible focal point for joint discursive frames and collective action. Whether and how these networks engage with gender mainstreaming on their websites provides evidence of priorities, frames, and public outreach.

The third set of data consists of network maps generated by the Issue Crawler software developed by Richard Rogers from the University of Amsterdam. Issue Crawler maps links among websites and thus provides heuristic evidence of networking activities such as joint agendas, projects, or mere informational exchange relationships. This network tool assesses relative networking strength and gauges the capacity to engage in joint public advocacy (see Appendix 4).

Network Representatives' Positions on Gender Mainstreaming

Interviews with network representatives highlighted their positions on gender mainstreaming, which may be best summarized in the contention that "it's something that seems quite positive, but that can work against women" (WECF 2005; this and the following references to the five TAN in this chapter refer to Appendix 2). Concerns crystallized around three themes: (1) Network representatives argued that gender mainstreaming is being increasingly functionalized on EU stages in order to bypass concerns regarding lingering inequalities of women, (2) they stipulated that gender mainstreaming reduces a radical democratization agenda to one of economic questions within an "added value" discourse, and (3) they contended that mainstreaming "buried women's issues in the state" (EWL 2007a) by infusing state and suprastate actions with the language of gender-conscious behavior, while neglecting communication and dissemination into civil society.

Functional Reduction. The functional approach to gender mainstreaming turns the gender equality agenda into a merely *"technical"* matter (WIDE 2007a). Gender mainstreaming opens the door to a kind of functional checkbox equality in which projects are measured by how well they serve both sexes. At times it is employed to include men in program activities and thus gloss over the focus on women's empowerment: "In the practical program implementation we had a lot of fights [with EU agencies], because they claimed that now that we use gender mainstreaming we have to find ways to integrate men into projects" (EWL 2007a). At other times, it is used to marginalize or exclude more women-centered approaches to gender equality. "The fact that gender mainstreaming is a strategy that is integrated into the Amsterdam Treaty, as well as into national legislation, has made it easier to operate with the term. The problem is that we always have to add: 'But this does not replace women's empowerment activities'" (WECF 2005). Whereas gender mainstreaming now serves as a door opener, "the flip side is that advocating affirmative action programs for women now closes every door. We have no chance with this term anymore; we in fact *have to* use the language of gender mainstreaming. If one refers to traditional women's equality language, one encounters a lot of rejection, not from all, but from many [within the EU]. One hits walls immediately now" (WECF 2005). The fact that the majority of programs now have a gender mainstreaming component underscores the problem. It tends, in effect, to produce a "writing out" (Jenson 2008) of women's policies from public documents and programs. These comments from the representatives support Jenson's point:

- "It means that everybody uses the terms [gender mainstreaming and women's policies] synonymously" (WECF 2005).
- "Gender mainstreaming has been invented for us in order not to have to use the word 'women' anymore" (EWL 2005a).
- "The gender mainstreaming frame glosses over existing inequalities" (WAVE 2005).
- "If women's equality is mentioned, that is good. But with gender mainstreaming, women's issues are omitted" (KARAT 2005).
- "It is somehow not demanding a deep reflection on discrimination" (WIDE 2007a).
- "What is being lost [with the gender mainstreaming frame] is that we focus on prevention of new inequalities" (EWL 2007b).

The networks in question thus are apprehensive about the functional reduction of gender mainstreaming to either always include men or sideline an explicit women's equality agenda; this reduction risks losing sight of existing inequalities. As a result, they use the term cautiously, realizing that at any given point in negotiations with political institutions they have to be prepared to add layers of interpretation. The only positive effect mentioned is the creation of a new labor market segment for gender experts: "As an effect of gender mainstreaming, women from our network can utilize their knowledge as gender experts and trainers" (WAVE 2005).

Economic Reduction. A WECF representative points to other possibly problematic effects of gender mainstreaming strategies:

Gender mainstreaming... invites reactions that I find strange. The reactions are that we have to prove consistently that gender mainstreaming produces some added value for politics. This is an argument that many women and gender experts have signed on to – and I find this problematic. Maybe we can measure political improvements in some individual cases, but why should adding a gender perspective for example improve environmental policies or climate protection? I think that this is one of the traps that gender mainstreaming has produced. (WECF 2005)

This spokeswoman suggests that the gender mainstreaming discourse might feed well into policy evaluation's larger economic turn: If quantitative evidence for the added value of including gender is demanded, then arguments about the basic democratic virtues of descriptive representation and the need for a radical restructuring of masculinist governance become sidelined. Gender mainstreaming thus inadvertently might serve to reframe the "traditional" emancipatory focus of the second wave women's movements by inviting "added value" arguments.

Bureaucratic Reduction. A third set of reservations voiced by network representatives concerns the explicitly top-down implementation of gender equality that the mainstreaming strategy entails. Networks take issue with the state-centered debates that the strategy produces and the lack of substantive input from civil society actors. As a result, women's network representatives speak of increasing resistance to use the strategy. The *WECF* representative argued,

I see an emerging wave of radicalization among the women's organizations that have supported gender mainstreaming – that are also financed to support it, like WECF – but that raise the question frequently: Is this really what we wanted? Don't we have to adapt too much within the frame of gender mainstreaming? Because more progressive positions are simply not listened to anymore, and that in turn produces separation, because those that are too radical in their positions are not listened to at all anymore – only those that swim on the wave of gender mainstreaming. And that is in part buried in the concept itself, that its critical edges are ground down. (WECF 2005)

Although some governance institutions use mainstreaming to deradicalize feminist demands, other bureaucracies are reluctant to do so or profess ignorance when it comes to implementing it. "In the beginning we were very enthusiastic. But the problem is that it [gender mainstreaming] is completely misunderstood on the national level. Governments are not interested" (KARAT 2005). To one network representative, it looks as though gender mainstreaming has been "buried in the state"

(EWL 2005b), as though adaptation to state and suprastate EU-level prerogatives organized around "femocratic" goals turns the strategy into a
compulsory but hollow exercise for TANs in their dealings with state
institutions.

In sum, the interviews suggest that European women's TANs are critical of gender mainstreaming. The main constraints that the interviewees
observed are the functional, economic, and bureaucratic reduction of a
feminist equality agenda. As a result the strategy does not seem to provide
an adequate set of tools for their gender equality work. Some articulate
dissatisfaction with the strategy as a top-down set of tools; others prioritize the lack of definitional clarity and their inability to communicate the
strategy to broader public constituencies. The policy itself is considered
to be a potential liability, if not always combined in a two-tier system
with specific women's equality measures. Based on their extensive criticism, we would expect the five women's networks to exhibit strong public
advocacy against or, at the very least, for a modification of the gender
mainstreaming agenda.

Networks' Web-Based Engagement with Gender Mainstreaming

Because generating public discussion is one of the central goals of TANs
(Keck and Sikkink 1998:19), criticism of gender mainstreaming should be
reflected in their public presentation. The web is considered to be the most
important networking and mobilization arena for transnational alliances
(Bennett 2004). It not only enables rapid and horizontal dissemination of
information but also offers the potential for interactive opinion formation and low-cost mobilization of voice for campaigning. The following
section examines how networks engage with the strategy publicly by analyzing web-based data on gender mainstreaming. We assessed networks'
engagement with the gender mainstreaming strategy through an analysis
of web content between March and April 2006. All five websites were
coded three levels deep for any mention of gender mainstreaming.[5] In a
second step, we employed context analysis to assess informative, positive,
and negative framing of the strategy (see Appendix 3).

The central finding of the web content analysis is that, in their official
public presentation, the five women's networks do not use nor address

---

[5] The levels refer to (1) the initial website of the main URL, (2) all sites that are clickable
from the initial URL, and (3) all sites that are clickable from this second set of sites. We
assume that importance of an issue will be reflected by posting it on these first three levels
of a site as opposed to deeper within the websphere of a TAN.

TABLE 6.2. *Referencing Gender Mainstreaming on TAN Websites*

	1st Level 5 Pages	2nd Level 64 Pages	3rd Level 236 Pages	No Reference –All Levels
EWL	no	no	no	38
KARAT	no	2 (I)	9 (7=A; 2=I)	92
WAVE	no	no	no	29
WECF	no	no	2 (I)	99
WIDE	no	3 (2=I; 1=C)	5 (1=I; 3=A; 1=C)	16

Notes: I = informative referencing; A = affirmative referencing; C = critical referencing.

gender mainstreaming, but instead make overwhelming use of the traditional frame of gender equality (see Table 6.2). Only three of the five
networks mention gender mainstreaming at all within the analyzed three
levels of web content. On the first level, the respective networks' home
pages, no website mentions gender mainstreaming. On the second level,
which comprises 64 pages taken from all networks together, we find five
references to gender mainstreaming, of which four are informative and
one is critical. On the third level, from a total of 236 pages, 16 references
to mainstreaming appear. Of these 16 references, 5 are informative, 10
are affirmative, and 1 takes a critical stance on gender mainstreaming.

The East European KARAT coalition has by far the most active engagement with gender mainstreaming, with two references on the second level
and nine on the third level. Seven of these references assess gender mainstreaming positively, and two are informative; none are critical of the
strategy. Two organizations, WAVE and EWL, do not mention gender
mainstreaming at all on any of the analyzed three website levels. The only
network that is critical of the strategy on the analyzed three depth levels
is WIDE. On the third level, we find a summary of gender mainstreaming
in development and trade policies of three EU member countries (Great
Britain, Belgium, and Austria) that articulates in detail how "gender mainstreaming policies evaporate in the move from policy to practice" (WIDE
2005). This assessment reflects the critical position in its representatives'
interviews, but does not actively address the question of political voice
and agency.

In sum, the TANs overwhelmingly appear to either ignore or subvert
the gender mainstreaming language. This reluctance to actively engage
with the central EU equality strategy is particularly glaring in the case of
EWL. The European Women's Lobby was established to serve as a link
between the women's civic sector and the institutions of the EU. Sonia

Mazey argued in 2002 that "mainstreaming places new demands upon the limited resources of the EWL and raises difficult strategic issues" (Mazey 2002: 228), pointing to the central position that EWL holds in regard to disseminating the concept and monitoring the strategy. Yet empirical evidence from its websphere suggests that four years later, EWL had publicly sidelined the issue: It only engaged with gender mainstreaming on the fourth and fifth sublevels of its website, hence voicing criticism in a space that is at the margins of its websphere. Placing an issue on the fourth depth level will not command the attention of site visitors to the degree necessary to spread a viral message throughout the network and organize public voice.

Rather than using their capacity to initiate debate around the EU's dominant gender equality tool, the TANs all shared a pragmatic strategy: They seemed to have learned to work around gender mainstreaming. The EWL spokeswoman explained, "We just don't use the expression 'gender mainstreaming' without also using 'specifically targeted programs' for women – it is like automated thinking by a computer" (EWL 2007c). In effect, the web analysis exposes a rather pervasive abandonment of the term "gender mainstreaming." Representatives from the networks shared this insistence on a more viable counterframe that focuses on women's equality measures. One might interpret the emphasis on women's equality language as an implicit attempt to reframe the discussion. Yet this does not explain the lack of an orchestrated and prominently placed public debate about a strategy that seemed to harbor much controversy. The web analysis suggests a two-tiered explanation for why the TANs did not orchestrate such a debate. The first tier, discussed in the following section, examines networks' overall lack of focus on, and capacity for, public advocacy. Institutional advocacy absorbs much labor at the expense of broader public outreach and advocacy. The second tier addresses a key condition for women's networks' ability to pressure for broader policy changes beyond their specific issue focus: their ability to network not just internally, but *among* each other. I address this point in the last section of this chapter.

PUBLIC ADVOCACY: MOBILIZING ONE'S OWN CONSTITUENCY

Public advocacy, as established in Chapter 1, takes place when issues are brought to the attention of broader constituencies whose engagement and support are being solicited. It implies practicing outreach and, in the case of European women's TANs, generating publics that can debate controversial issues such as gender mainstreaming. Outreach may be organized directly by the network or via its member organizations; tools may be as diverse as attracting media exposure, launching viral campaigns, or staging local protest activities to expose the ambiguities of gender mainstreaming. Yet even mobilizing one's own issue network is a time- and resource-intensive endeavor. In 2002, Women in Europe for a Common Future formed an intranetwork group for gender mainstreaming. Yet the WECF leader who chaired this group cautioned against high expectations regarding its mobilization potential. It was formed, she reported, with funding from the EU. It met once a year, providing a venue for information sharing regarding gender mainstreaming issues. Tasks like policy evaluation and extended public advocacy would exceed its capabilities: "Meeting once a year is too little to really work on questions like 'what is gender mainstreaming, what does it mean for our work, and what kind of instruments are there around?'" (WECF 2005).

In general, network success seems to depend less on public mobilization and more on traditional lobbying strategies like finding the right door opener to EU institutional settings. One could argue that in the "tough competition" for access to EU units and finances (KARAT 2005) the mobilization of feminist publics might be helpful. However, as several interviewees pointed out, having an office in Brussels is more effective than activating broader constituencies. Limited resources require that a decision be made between a "lobby focus" and "public outreach," and networks tend to choose the former (WIDE 2007a).

Compounding this trend, EU institutions do not facilitate public outreach of women's NGOs and TANs. As the largest "donor agency" in Europe, the vast majority of its outreach funds in the gender equality arena go to institutional political actors. The Commission establishes its financial commitments in terms of framework programs that span several years. From 2001 to 2006, the EU financed the fifth Community Action Program for the implementation of gender equality with a total of 50 million Euros.[6] Its main objectives relating to gender equality included raising awareness, improving analysis and evaluation, and developing the "capacity of players to promote gender equality" (European Commission 2001). Yet the majority of these funds did not go to women's NGOs. In fact, women's NGOs rank fifth after a host of institutional

---

[6] The Council decided in 2004 to extend the fifth framework into 2006 to accommodate the accession of the 10 new member states. The budget was increased to 61.5 million Euros.

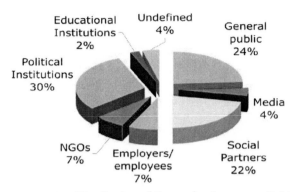

FIGURE 6.1. Distribution of Grants for Awareness Raising under Fifth EU Community Program for Gender Equality (2001–2006). *Source*: European Commission 2008; working document SEC (2008) 2365.

actors: (1) member states, (2) local and regional authorities, (3) other institutionalized bodies promoting gender equality, and (4) social partners. As the final report on the fifth Community Action Program showed, in the category "raising awareness," only 7 percent of these funds went to NGOs (see Fig. 6.1), and in the category "transnational cooperation" they received only 25 percent (European Commission 2008). The majority of funds for raising awareness about gender were made available to government actors (30 percent), the general public (24 percent), and social partners (i.e., business and large welfare associations [22 percent]).

This distribution of funds indicates how government actors define and structure specific project missions, and when NGOs participate, they have to adapt to predefined goals set within institutional politics. This bias toward institutional funding has continued in the following program cycle called "Progress" (from 2007–12). "Progress" reserved a total of 433 billion Euros in spending for sustainable development goals and projects, including research programs, education, social, and labor market policy initiatives. Within these parameters, "Progress" merged several key programs of the Social Agenda of the EU to reach synergy effects and to mainstream gender equality. Funding for the program component that includes activities related to gender equality has stayed about the same as in the fifth Community Action Program; the program design and the kinds of activities it promotes continue to cater to institutional actors such as governments, universities, and labor unions (Progress 2007). In effect, although women's NGOs and their TANs receive just enough funds to make seeking institutional insider status worthwhile, EU institutions show little initiative to support NGO outreach activities and attempts to organize stronger women's publics across Europe.

Lack of public outreach is also the result of an inability to identify the subjects of possible mobilization. One interviewee pointedly asked, "Who are these publics, anyway?" – voicing a more general skepticism regarding the potential for women's mobilization in the aftermath of the turn to identity politics (EWL 2007a). A WIDE representative echoed this observation by arguing that the network "doesn't really have the kind of membership it can mobilize;" she added, "I think that's something we should certainly build – more capacity to actually get our voice out there and be heard" (WIDE 2007a). Network members showed some reluctance to identify the publics that their network might speak to, help generate, or stabilize. Instead, network identity appeared to be based almost exclusively on gaining institutional influence. Lack of available resources also contributed to TANs' lack of focus on public advocacy. Yet at the same time network representatives also voiced discomfort with the inward orientation of their organization and saw a need to increase ties with constituencies and into the wider public sphere. The construction of stronger public accountability was, if not at the center, certainly on the agenda of the networks.

Mobilizing Gender: Characteristics of Successful Advocacy

As noted in the introduction to this chapter, the rise of the European Union as a norm entrepreneur for gender equality is widely attributed to the successful mobilization of women's NGOs and their networks since the 1980s. Women's networks pushed for pay equity and for antidiscrimination legislation, fought against sexual harassment, and struggled for the inclusion of gender equality principles into the main treaties of the emerging EU. These successes are not in dispute; what is of interest here is how they came about. What kind of strategies did transnational women's advocates employ to reach their goals in successful advocacy campaigns of the past? Who was targeted and what means of communication were used? To investigate these questions in more detail, this section examines three case studies of several conflicts over policies, focusing not on the policy results but on who was mobilized and which strategies were employed. The three cases are the successful incorporation of sexual harassment into the 2002 Equal Treatment Directive, the introduction of gender mainstreaming into the Treaty of Amsterdam, and the partially successful attempt to include gender equality as a main frame into the Charter of Human Rights attached to the EU Constitution draft in 2002.

Sexual Harassment in the Equal Treatment Directive. It was a "gender equality TAN" that successfully raised the issue of sexual harassment in the EU in the 1980s and then pushed for its incorporation into the revised Equal Treatment Directive of 2002 (Zippel 2004, 2006). During a time when national governments remained largely unresponsive to the issue of sexual harassment, a network of policy insiders within the EU, as well as transnational NGOs, helped push the issue into the EU employment agenda.

In terms of its members, the "gender equality TAN" that Kathrin Zippel identifies consisted of only a few "small, single-issue, nationally based women's organizations" (Zippel 2004: 63). In her assessment, more important TAN members than these women's NGOs were "friendly policy makers within EU institutions and unions, legal experts, and researchers" (ibid.). Thus the gender equality TAN had less of an NGO base and was more an expert and insider advocacy coalition geared toward directly engaging with the institutional policy-making process. Its members, such as academics and other researchers, solicited funding from the EU to generate, discuss, and disseminate this expert knowledge. The sexual harassment TAN relied on the power of networking, committed principled actors across borders, and a few small single-issue organizations. Having "multiple access routes to policy making arenas" (Zippel 2004: 63) was key. Zippel cites three factors for the success of the campaign: (1) the policy expertise created by the TAN, (2) the political opportunity structure within the EU, and (3) a "ping-pong effect" in which the TAN and national and supranational institutions engaged together to advance specific issues.

This campaign exemplifies an insider-driven institutional advocacy culture that operates smoothly without having to rely on the "traditional" mobilization mechanisms of social movements. The advocacy that was practiced was confined to the administrative offices of Brussels and prepared in expert circles. It did not rely on public advocacy for its success: "[T]here [were] neither coordinated protests nor lobbying activities from advocates for sexual harassment policy. Few press releases or position papers were issued. Neither women's groups nor labour organizations coordinated campaigns, protests, or widespread lobbying efforts in the late 1990s" (Zippel 2004: 78). The mobilization of broader publics was not part of the campaign success.

Gender Equality in the Amsterdam Treaty. One of the most crucial advances toward gender equality in the European Union was made with the Amsterdam Treaty of 1997. According to Barbara Helfferich, then president of EWL, a successful

> co-ordinated lobbying campaign spearheaded by the European Women's Lobby resulted in legal milestones for gender equality, introducing the gender main-streaming principle and provisions to fight discrimination outside of the employment sector.... [It] included a variety of different strategies and activities, from informational and educational efforts to lobbying actions and activities on the European as well as on the national levels, plus the *occasional protest mobilization.* (Helfferich and Kolb 2001: 144; emphasis added)

What enabled the campaign to be successful, according to Helfferich and Kolb, was EWL's coordination of multilevel action, combined with a favorable political opportunity structure. It coordinated activities at both the supranational and national levels, bringing together those actors under the umbrella of EWL. A window for reform, initiated by the new Scandinavian member states Sweden and Finland, in conjunction with Denmark and Greece, provided a gender-friendly environment for the campaign. EWL's main target was the limitation of the gender equality principle to the workplace, as laid out in Article 119 in the Treaty of Rome. During the initial debates on treaty revision in 1996, the EU decided to convene an expert group with the evocative name, the "Group of Wise Men." EWL responded with the appointment of a shadow group called the "Wise Women's Group." Creating this group of legally versed feminists was essential to match the level of expertise from insiders, particularly because at that time the European Union was still not a site for mobilization efforts for most national women's organizations. Educating these national and local organizations about the issues at stake was therefore another crucial advocacy component.

Even though institutional forms of lobbying clearly had priority, EWL in this specific successful campaign also tried to attract media attention. It initiated an EU-wide petition for signatures in support of EWL's position on the treaty provision. Within six weeks, member organizations collected 40,000 signatures, which were handed to a member of the treaty negotiations team during a public rally in Brussels (Helfferich and Kolb 2001: 157). Thus this campaign combined institutional and public advocacy, albeit with a strong bias toward gaining institutional leverage. Yet the occasional mobilization of constituents was a successful pressure tactic. At the same time, it made broader publics aware of the work of EWL.

The multilevel coordination strategy that EWL employed to strengthen its legitimacy and institutional advocacy succeeded: EWL's gender mainstreaming position was incorporated into the Amsterdam Treaty. The campaign employed a strategic mix of targeted mobilization that helped bring gender issues into the European public arena, broad expert involvement, media attention, and mobilization of uncommitted citizens. However, as in the previous case study of the sexual harassment campaign, institutional advocacy was at the center of this TAN's strategy. Its "Wise Women's Group" possessed the necessary knowledge of the legal framework of the EU. To be effective in Brussels demanded a strategy that "combined expert advice with the widest possible consultation with affiliated organizations, in order to propose clear textual amendments to the existing treaty of the Union" (Helfferich and Kolb 2001: 153). Even though a public advocacy repertoire was employed, it remained marginal to the success of the campaign and was more a secondary dimension than a key part of EWL's strategy.

Gender Equality in the Constitution for Europe. EWL launched another powerful campaign around the 2002 Constitutional Convention. Early in the constitution-drafting process, EWL criticized the gender imbalance found in the convention's governing body, the Presidium, which included only two women despite earlier interventions in support of equal representation of women (EWL 2002a). In January and February 2002, EWL asked its members to sign a petition in which the organization demanded that women's rights and interests be fully taken into account and parity democracy be practiced in the convention. Moreover, EWL participated in the forum set up by the Treaty Secretariat and wrote several letters of concern directly to the convention president Valerie Giscard D'Estaing. These letters were posted on its website. A central concern for the European Women's Lobby was to ensure the anchoring of gender equality in Articles 21 and 23 of the Charter for Human Rights. By failing to introduce gender equality as an overarching value in the first sentence of the Charter and not using the language of gender mainstreaming to indicate its relevance in all policy arenas, the Constitutional Convention, and the Charter text in particular, had shrunk the equality agenda to the employment sector and failed to address structural discrimination. EWL also criticized the masculine language in the draft version of the Preamble and demanded gender-neutral language throughout the document as well as a gender-inclusive approach in general (EWL 2003). Despite its interventions, EWL was not satisfied with the final version of the Convention text (EWL 2005).

EWL's demands were a radical call for gender parity and mainstreaming in all aspects of the Charter and the Treaty. The advocacy repertoire it used was again largely geared toward providing expert input. Its advocacy effort relied first and foremost on institutional lobbying. EWL articulated its positions within the forums that were granted to the Civil Society Contact Group and used direct correspondence with the Presidium as a means to influence the Charter drafting process. Only at one point was a feminist public mobilized, and even then using the classic instrument of letter/postcard writing. It did not use other forms of public communication (i.e., press events staged on the same day in European capitals, publicly visible protests, or symbolic actions). Even more than during the Amsterdam Treaty campaign, the internal logic of a predefined space assigned to civil society actors absorbed the advocacy power of EWL. This is not to diminish the partial success of the campaign and the surely difficult task of pulling the resources and experts together to wage it. Yet it indicates that institutional advocacy regularly trumps public advocacy in the campaigns of women's transnational networks in the EU.

At the same time, this "institutional influence" does seldom take on a "public" character, in that the participation of European women's TANs is only rarely acknowledged in official documents. Emanuela Lombardo and Petra Meier have studied the frames of gender concepts in EU documents over time. They reach the conclusion that even though women's TANs provide expert memoranda and reports in policy arenas, it is not common practice to give them a voice in official documents. This disappearance of a feminist activist voice from official publications is not only a result of negligence, and its consequences are more than cosmetic. Lombardo and Meier (2008) establish a relation between the depth of a gender frame in a policy arena and the extent to which gender experts and feminist activists speak or are spoken of in official policy documents (119). They also show that it is in only one frame – that of the "domestic violence" discourse – where feminist activists and their networks, EWL and WAVE in particular, are visible in public policy documents. In the discourse on gender inequality in politics, by contrast, "feminist NGOs such as the *EWL* (. . .) are rarely mentioned in official documents" (118).

Thus, institutional advocacy by these TANs, as successful as it might be in the realm of policy, does not guarantee visibility even in the institutional publicity of documents. Women's TANs for the most part find their advocacy relegated to the discursive contexts of EU-sponsored meetings

TABLE 6.3. *European Transnational Women's Networks: Information and Advocacy Focus*

	Links to Local/Regional Membership Associations	EU Lobby Focus	Regional Advocacy Focus	Public Campaign/ Media Focus	Internet Based Campaigns
EWL	yes	yes	no	yes	no
KARAT	yes	yes	yes	no	no
WAVE	yes	yes	yes	yes	no
WECF	yes	no	yes	no	no
WIDE	no	yes	no	no	no

Note: Material accessed November 2005 and September 2006.

and conferences. Their actual input is neither recorded in official documents nor generally registered by gender publics or a wider audience across Europe.

The Public Advocacy Profile of European Women's TANs

If institutional advocacy is the default modus operandi for these TANs, then how do they engage with broader publics beyond their member organizations? An increasingly important indicator for TANs' public outreach and advocacy is their web presence. It is through the use of this relatively low-cost but high-profile tool that interested citizens find issues and connect to causes. Networks increasingly are using web-based modes of mobilization (Bimber 2003) that "reduce the costs of participating" (Della Porta and Tarrow 2004: 12) for both network organizers and interested citizens. People consult websites if they are contemplating joining a network or a specific campaign. Journalists who research issues and activities turn to web-based information from NGOs and their interlinked partners. And governments are getting clues about civic activism from the web (Rogers 2004). We can therefore consider the Internet websites of these networks to be a crucial element of their public advocacy. Table 6.3 assesses several dimensions of these five TANs' web presence.[7]

Four of the networks – EWL, KARAT, WAVE and WECF – provide links to their local and regional membership associations, but do not showcase the aggregated weight of member NGOs and individual members. Whereas four TANs exhibit a strong EU lobby focus and three

[7] For details of the coding protocol, see Appendix 3.

a regional advocacy focus, only two – KARAT and WAVE – combine institutional EU lobbying with a regional or local advocacy focus. EWL is involved in some policy matters between the supranational and the national levels and asks for direct member input in its General Assemblies. Yet there is no evidence of top-down outreach from the national umbrella groups to mobilize regional constituencies. The websites of only two networks, EWL and WAVE, were designed to attract media attention for their campaigns. On several occasions, EWL asked visitors to its site to write letters to members of Parliament or the Commission or to pressure national politicians regarding a specific gender issue. In most cases, it provided letter templates or postcards designed to be printed. At the time, none of the networks enabled any online campaign activity, such as visitors being able to sign a petition online or click to be connected to groups in their vicinity for mobilization activities. Overall, the five networks at the time of this study made only limited use of new information technology to reach out and engage their constituencies (see also Klein 1999; Bennett 2003).

The reasons cited in interviews for their overall thin efforts to practice more, and in particular more interactive, public outreach primarily echoed the theme of resource poverty. Public advocacy is something that these TANs would like to do more of, but they lack personnel and resources. Skepticism about the nature of feminist publics today also adds to the focus on institutional advocacy, but at the same time mirrors the disconnect between TANs and their constituents. Another answer, albeit less prominent, was that TANs do not engage in extensive public advocacy simply because they do not need to do so. Insisting on a role as intermediaries, some representatives of TANs pointed toward national and regional members as much more competent and effective organizers of public outreach and advocacy. Yet there are at least two reasons why this line of thought is wanting. First, because EU institutions formally understand and treat Brussels-based TANs as representatives of larger European publics, TAN legitimacy rests to some degree on evidence that they actually perform this aggregate function. Institutional decision makers need some substantiation that TANs are serving as a voice for an EU issue public. Second, because TANs themselves lay claim to an identity as speaking for European constituents, a lack of a visible aggregate function over time turns into a public and inner-organizational image problem.

A somewhat different explanation for the lack of public advocacy, though not voiced in interviews, might be that it is not only resource intensive but also potentially high risk. Institutional and public advocacy are not always compatible; for example, when public advocacy virally spirals out of a TAN's control or becomes too confrontational. TANs risk reputational costs if public advocacy efforts they have initiated turn against their institutional interlocutors. Institutional advocacy is more manageable. A WIDE representative suggests that

the debate about inside/outside is always going on. Some people think, we, including me here, spend too much time engaging policy makers, sitting down at the table, talking to them. Other people are kind of living in an alternative universe and they're not engaging at all [institutionally], so what impact do they have? So you need both if you're going to keep your autonomy, keep your independent voice, but you must strategically engage. (WIDE 2007)

NETWORKING WITHIN AND AMONG EUROPEAN WOMEN'S TANS

Advocacy is more effective if one cooperates with others. As Beate Kohler-Koch has observed, how fast ideas and attempted policy changes travel, and whether they reach national policy contexts, depends not only on specific *properties* of one network but "also on the interface structure of related networks" (Kohler-Koch 1998: 9). Interfaces between networks can be conceptualized as communicative relays that drive joint frames and action. Do European women's TANs have such communicative relays? Do they cooperate with each other to coordinate advocacy efforts and maximize their influence? This last section contributes to our understanding of network strength by providing a web-based assessment of the ties among transnational women's networks. General network density, which is defined in detail later, cannot explain all aspects of networking among women's TANs in Europe. However, it can provide heuristic evidence about the structure and scope of network interfaces and cooperation.

Tetyana Pudrovska and Myra Marx Ferree have shown that the European Women's Lobby is considerably less networked with other transnational women's networks than are other women's TANs (Pudrovska and Ferree 2004). The authors attribute this lack of virtual global networking to the EWL's "intra-EU focus" (2). However, I found that, even within the European Union, the EWL does not reach out extensively beyond its member organizations – in fact, this finding applies to four of the five networks studied here, with the exception of KARAT.

The following network maps were generated using Issue Crawler, a software program that visualizes web-based networking; for example,

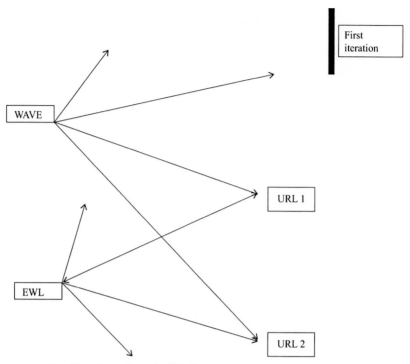

FIGURE 6.2. How Issue Crawler Works.

among groups, organizations, and institutions (see Fig. 6.2).[8] The crawls, which pick up links between actors, can be manipulated in three ways: (1) the depth of sites within the web presence of an organization; (2) the number of starting points; that is, site origins; and (3) the iterations; that is, how far the network analysis stretches into a network sphere. Actors appear on the network map if they are co-linked; that is, if at least two other actors in the network sphere link to them. Network diagrams also show the direction of main linkages (the arrows), the relative strength of a linked actor (size of the dot), and its broadly defined institutional form (URL suffixes such as .gov, .org, or national suffixes are shown in different shades of gray here). The destination URL marks the actor that is at the center of linkages, and we see who links to it and to whom it links.

Our initial attempts to correlate two networks and obtain network maps had only limited success. The only crawls rendered were between

---

[8] See http://govcom.org.

TABLE 6.4. *Networking among Networks, 2005*

	EWL	KARAT	WAVE	WECF	WIDE
EWL	N/a	Network	No network	No network	No network
KARAT	Network	N/a	No network	Network	Network
WAVE	No network	No network	N/a	No network	No network
WECF	No network	Network	No network	N/a	No network
WIDE	No network	Network	No network	No network	N/a

KARAT and WIDE, KARAT and EWL, and KARAT and WECF (see Table 6.4). All other correlated websites did not show networks two levels deep, indicating that they were not actively connecting to other networks on the first two levels of their websites and that other networks did not connect to them.

When we put all five networks as starting points into a crawl of two depth levels and two iterations, the resulting thin network map depicts WECF Germany networking with the transnational WECF network, and KARAT networking with WIDE (eurosur.org). The fact that EWL (womenlobby.org) is not present on this map indicates that it has far fewer overall links than WECF and KARAT. EWL might link out, but only very few actors link back to it (see Fig. 6.3).

This finding does not imply that these TANs do not network at all *within* their respective issue arenas; in fact we find somewhat stronger networking attempts among member NGOs within a network. An example is WECF and all its links that extend into a rather strong network of ecologically oriented actors (see Fig. 6.4).

The fact that WECF, as the starting point, disappears from these network linkages suggests that even though it is reaching out, the other actors are not linking back to WECF. A similar picture is generated when we crawl EWL and its internal links. KARAT's networks tend to be stronger, with the organization receiving many more co-links and therefore staying present in the networks that it initiates.

Map 3 (see Fig. 6.5) captures the centrality of issue focus for European women's networks, which comes partly at the expense of networking among each other. It maps network linkages of EWL and WECF, going three levels deep into their respective webspheres.

In this map, *wecf.org* and its German member *wecf. de* form a distinct environmentally focused network. The WECF TAN connects to the second distinct cluster of NGOs that centers around the United Nations through its German affiliate only. EWL (*womenlobby.org*) stays

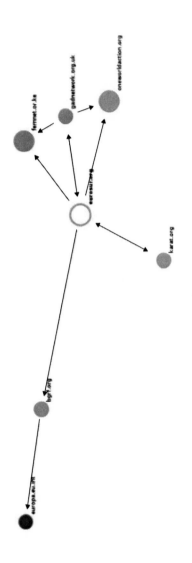

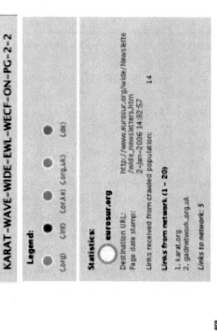

FIGURE 6.3. KARAT-WAVE-WIDE-EWL-WECF-On-Pg-2-2, 2006.

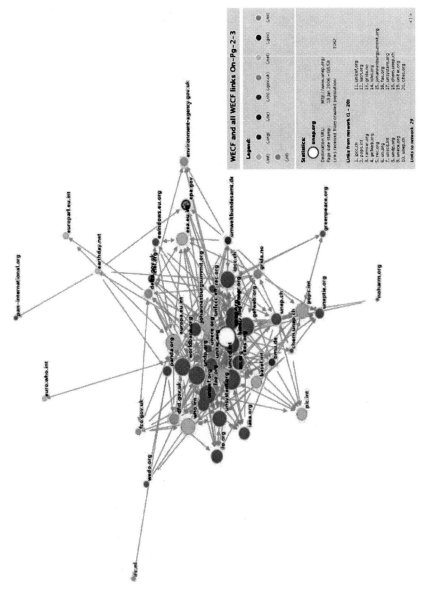

FIGURE 6.4. WECF and All WECF Links On-Pg-2-3, 2006.

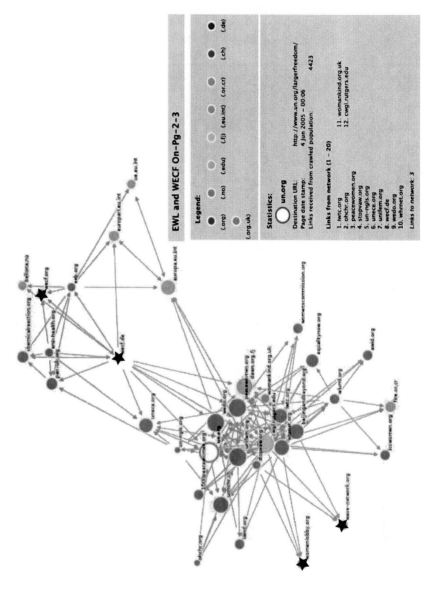

FIGURE 6.5. EWL and WECF On-Pg-2-3, 2005.

somewhat on the margin of the UN centered network cluster, which also includes WAVE. Staying on the margins, as EWL does, indicates that it links less and is being linked to less than more centrally clustered organizations. The arrows pointing one-way also show a bias of linkages to EWL that it does not return. WECF clearly puts more emphasis on connecting to its issue-related transnational connections than EWL. In sum, the Issue Crawler maps visualize a lack of communication and interaction among our five transnational women's networks – communication that would be key not only to joint policy interventions of overarching concern such as gender mainstreaming but also to the initiation of broader public outreach and activism for their respective agendas. The fact that they so rarely link to each other underscores their representatives' comments that cooperation among networks is for the most part limited and systematically only sought by WIDE and KARAT. Relating the lack of networking to gender mainstreaming, a representative of WECF argues that what is missing is a "joint evaluation and monitoring by women's networks that asks: how does it [gender mainstreaming] affect networks and how can networks affect the gender mainstreaming strategy – that has not happened so far" (WECF 2005). Both a KARAT and a WECF representative point to EWL as being best positioned to organize public voice in regard to gender mainstreaming (WECF 2005; KARAT 2008). However, EWL's organizational structure is based on national coordination platforms and thus privileges vertical integration of members over horizontal networking with issue-specific women's TANs. Overall, the Issue Crawler evidence suggests that at this point only limited networking capacity exists for joint evaluation and mobilization for women's issues among European women's TANs.

CONCLUSION

This chapter has pursued two lines of argument. Our starting point was the gender mainstreaming debate and its assessment as a problematic strategy to advance gender equality by all five networks. First, we investigated why the explicit criticism of gender mainstreaming, voiced in the interviews, does not translate into stronger public advocacy. Although the networks cited resource poverty as a primary reason, we explored the tensions between expert identity and possible mission and strategy drift through engaging publics, the precarious status as interlocutors, and possible negative sanctions by institutions as additional explanations for lack of public engagement, outreach, and advocacy. Second, we analyzed web-based evidence of public advocacy of the five TANs beyond the gender mainstreaming issue. In principle, the organizations have a broad range of web-based and low-cost mobilization tools at their disposal. Yet their overall approach to communicating with constituencies has a more "informational" than "activating or advocacy-oriented" quality. In particular, they underutilize interactive repertoires of the web, and hence discursive engagement of broader constituencies seems weak. The TANs also do not network extensively with each other. Thus, women's TANs in this study forfeit publicness for policy engagement.

The five TANs take issue with the mainstreaming strategy, yet tend to forego public debate and instead attempt to tacitly reframe discourse by employing strong women's equality language. Thus, density of communication on the issue is low. Material as well as institutional rationales seem to guide the networks' decisions to prioritize counterframing over engaging publics. On the material side, capacity needs to be built to secure network infrastructure and its personnel. Grant writing, pursuing project cooperation, and managing human resources are considered by all networks as central to survival and occupy considerable work time. Because much labor goes into developing specialized expertise, broader questions regarding overall EU gender equality strategies necessarily take backstage. Lack of resources for mobilization and public advocacy seems to be a possible fallout from this precarious institutionalization of women's TANs. With influence depending to a large degree on internal organizational capacity (Della Porta and Tarrow 2004), the kinds of internal capacities that a network develops will determine the strategies with which it will try to influence an issue.

Yet resources are not the only rationale at work. As our analysis showed, there are other explanations why networks focus on institutional advocacy. First, the three successful TAN interventions presented in this chapter share what Liebert (2002: 255) calls "knowledge-based communication strategies," relying primarily or solely on expert discourses. Although these knowledge-based communication strategies might bring about policy change, they might also sideline public engagement. For policy successes to be visible to broader publics, expert communication needs to be translated into broader (local or national) public debates. If this translation is not pursued insistently, there is a disconnect between institutional advancements in gender policies and public marginalization of gender issues in Europe. Institutional actors such as policy makers, members of Parliament, and administrators value TAN expertise not just for its substance but also because it adds legitimacy to European policy-making processes. The former president of EWL states that "informal friendly contacts have led to formal and more important lobbying interactions, strengthening not only the role of *EWL* but that of agencies trying to advance equality as well" (Helfferich and Kolb 2001: 148). At the same time, engagement with wider arenas of constituents might produce mission and strategy drift that might endanger the relationship between experts and EU institutions.

Second, women's strategic choices are rooted in the kind of institutional settings and practices they confront (Ferree and Mueller 2003). The European Union has provided considerable openings for civil society actors, and women's TANs have become experienced interlocutors and institutional advocates in Brussels. Advances in gender equality have been largely dependent on the creation of "velvet triangles" (Woodward 2004); that is, on the cooperation of political institutions, femocrats within institutions, and feminist activists in civil society. As part of the feminist activist cluster, TANs have taken on the role of being intermediaries between political institutions, femocrats, and activists. They depend on others to organize Europeanized feminist publics. By definition, they experience "several degrees of separation" from grassroots women's groups and local and regional organizations – from those that might best be able to mobilize large numbers of citizens and use (local) public space for protests and civic action repertoires. National platforms tend to reserve exclusive rights to communicate with local members, thus making it difficult for Brussels-based TANs to do so. Moreover, EWL officials point to the difficulties of constructing joint positions among a wide variety of members with different cultural, economic, and social backgrounds. Transnational interest formation, then, becomes primarily a problem of reducing complexities and settling sometimes on lower common denominators than originally envisioned. Therefore the preference for institutional advocacy might also be driven by the need to reduce complexities and avoid conflicts. Framing positions institutionally might be easier than organizing public outreach into such diverse constituencies. In effect, modes of communication signal an inward orientation and institutional focus.

Third, public advocacy might produce stronger identity conflicts for TANs in regard to how institutional actors view them. There is concern among TANs that public outreach, including possibly confrontational public strategies, could "undermine" the position of NGOs and networks "that have gained recognition as 'serious', 'responsible', and 'calculable' players" (Rucht 2001: 136). The institutional habitus of the EU thus might discourage public advocacy. Along the same line, scarce resources and EU funding might contribute to a focus on institutional communication and advocacy. Helfferich and Kolb point to the "ties that bind" problem in the context of the National Council of German Women. The fact that it "receives yearly funding from the German government," they argue, "made it harder for the group to take positions independent of the German government" (Helfferich and Kolb 2001: 149). The same co-optation logic could be applied to EWL in a European context. Communication is thus targeted to convince political actors in institutional contexts rather than to mobilize constituencies.

In sum, validation of expert status, lack of proximity to constituents, adherence to institutional habitus, and scarce funding all disincentivize public advocacy. The danger of practicing transnational advocacy merely as lobbying and as mobilization of institutional capital is that constituencies across Europe might not know about, or might not identify with, the ideas and issues for which women's TANs stand. Moreover, the literature on European civil society generally points to problems of accountability and democratic legitimacy if civic actors are highly incorporated and do not manage to keep communication channels open with broader constituencies (Warleigh 2001). In this line of reasoning, if the constituencies for European women's TANs are not adequately integrated in deliberation and interaction, neither NGO actions nor policy outcomes are adequately legitimized. To be clear, if this study finds public outreach strategies that would mobilize broader constituencies and network linkages that could advance overarching women's policy goals to be less developed, this does not imply lack of policy success. Yet it might imply that on matters of overall importance in European gender governance, such as the future of the gender mainstreaming strategy, women's TANs at this point in time lack incentive and capacity to organize and facilitate EU-wide public debate. In terms of their legitimacy vis-à-vis political institutions and European citizens, they have yet to establish public engagement processes that in turn provide legitimacy.

7

NGOs' Inclusion in Governance and
Public Accountability

> Democracy is... a kind of society, not merely a mechanism of choosing
> and authorizing governments.
>
> C. B. MacPherson, 1973: 51

NGOs face mounting and, to some degree, contradictory expectations.
We want them to be uncorrupted experts, unbureaucratic social intervention agents, accountable citizen representatives, and knowledgeable interlocutors of political institutions. Ideally, they are "the engine for ideas
and aspirations of what sort of society we might become, how we might
choose to live together and alternative directions for us to consider and
debate. As well, they provide places for learning the democratic process,
they build a sense of community and they help the average citizen wanting to speak to government about an issue" (Staples 2008: 15). Although
not all NGOs can and or even want to fulfill all aspects of this glorified
organizational profile, this book has made a case for treating NGOs as
public actors and for holding them accountable to their publics. In particular, it is NGOs' function of organizing publicness by making issues
public and of organizing publics by stimulating citizen voice that has
fueled our investigation. With the lingering crisis of political parties and
the demise of aggregate functions of traditional media, NGOs find themselves occupying a central position in organizing meaning in civil society.
Given that NGOs' outreach and engagement practices might define civil
societies of the 21st century, we explored the conditions under which they
do that job and how well they actually do it. The observation that all too
often NGOs serve as stand-ins, or proxies, for publics without substantially acting on their public engagement capacity led to an analysis of

the configurations that actually enable NGOs to develop stronger public accountability. Refuting the liberal credo that government should minimize its footprint in civil society – a credo that neoliberal politics itself consequently undermines – this book has shown that states and their civic spaces are intertwined and that therefore governance conditions are key to how NGOs engage with their environment. We have established that specific governance cultures can incentivize NGOs to practice public advocacy and in the process generate stronger public accountability through communicating and interacting with constituencies. Legal frameworks, funding arrangements, and the different properties of networked, managed, or restricted communication cultures can promote or weaken NGOs' publicness and their ability to be catalysts for organized citizen voice.

Raising concerns in public, however, has its costs, and NGOs face a number of obstacles as public advocates. Institutional advocacy tends to be more predictable, more immediately gratifying, and reputation-enhancing. Working with publics, by contrast, means engaging in a field of much less calculable civic dynamics with inherently unpredictable outcomes. Legal limits to public advocacy and economic pulls to synchronize NGO activity with donor expectations compound the problem. The money trail for NGOs leads to governance contexts dominated by political institutions, business corporations, and foundations with specific agendas. Few funders provide grants for NGOs to do public advocacy and outreach with the goal of establishing stronger publics. Each one of these factors carries weight; in combination, they provide the backdrop against which we understand NGOs' focus on organizational reproduction and institutional advocacy. Again, not all NGOs fit this profile; some do have a strong commitment to outreach and to public advocacy. Thus, trying to avoid overgeneralizations, this book highlighted the *configurations* that enable NGOs to employ stronger public voice and organize publics. It has addressed the pull-and-push factors at work when NGOs want to develop stronger public accountabilities.

Before we revisit the argument, a final disclaimer is in order: This investigation may weaken the overly enthusiastic assertion that NGOs "breed new ideas, advocate, protest, and mobilize public support" or that they necessarily deepen democracy by "disrupting hierarchies" and spreading "power among more people and groups" (Mathews 1997: 52). On the flip side, however, the cautionary narrative provided in this book is not part of the choir of NGO-bashing that seems to be pervasive these days, primarily in the neoconservative circles inside the Washington beltway. The voices of this choir are most often ideologically motivated and have little interest in strengthening civil society's capacity for public debate. For these voices, destroying the NGO "halo" (Steinberg 2009) is about silencing what are perceived to be overly critical progressive government and business watchdogs. Some academic voices have joined this choir, claiming that NGOs are merely ineffectual "troublemakers" (Cohen 2006: 4) or unelected and therefore undemocratic "stand-ins" for citizens (Anderson 2003). The analysis offered in this book finds that NGOs are best able to shield their operations against such claims by attempting to be normatively legitimized by their publics. Public accountability involves attending to the four tasks of providing transparency, organizing debate, engaging constituents, and encouraging activism. Ultimately, public accountability will legitimize an NGO more effectively than attempts to increase internal transparency, professionalize management, or draft new performance measurements.

This chapter proceeds by summarizing the central argument of the book with an emphasis on factors that might strengthen public accountability of NGOs. It first reassesses NGOization, focusing on how it incentivizes or disincentivizes NGOs' ability to actively seek communication and interaction with constituencies. The second part of the chapter addresses the effects of two factors that in the coming years will starkly alter NGO advocacy and engagement: new media and the increasing transnationalization of advocacy. Finally, we revisit the role of governance structures in shaping NGOs' ability to create public accountability and thereby act as catalysts of the public sphere.

NGOIZATION REVISITED

NGOization is best understood as a sensitizing concept without direct normative underpinnings. It signifies the process by which social movements professionalize, bureaucratize, and institutionalize. As such, it is neither good nor bad; it holds both opportunities and costs. Not all civil society groups put on the legal and organizational cloak of an NGO, but many do so and with good reasons. Groups need a legal status and tax-related incorporation to qualify as charities and thus for tax-exempt status. Activists want to turn their commitment into a profession. Donors and governments confer predictability and pay a regular salary. Thus, to professionalize, institutionalize, and bureaucratize is rational to stabilize the organization. Yet this very process tends to turn down the volume of public advocacy. With professionalization often comes a focus on assessment, education of policy makers, and strategic planning (Harwood 2009: 15). Publicness appears, if at all, in the guise of fundraising drives and occasional campaigns to which citizens can sign on. More resource-ful organizations have all but given up on fostering publics and instead rely on litigation as a means of public advocacy and as an alternative to mobilization (McCann 1994; Barzilai 2003: 134ff.). NGOs have learned to strategically manage publics instead of relying on their capacity to organize citizen voice.

In addition to the imperatives of organizational reproduction, advo-cacy-averse donors and state actors more interested in expert knowledge than in input by larger publics compound the incentives to choose insti-tutional over public advocacy. Legal obstacles to advocacy and in some cases just the mere lack of knowledge of what are the legal limits add to an organizational focus on service, program building, and technical expertise. Why then should NGOs build public accountability by engag-ing with an often fickle, uninformed, politics-fatigued citizenry? Indeed, the NGO respondents in the Harwood study, cited in Chapter 3, could not identify incentives to engage with publics. It seemed only rational to have constituents stay away from public advocacy work except for occasionally signing a petition or e-mailing their legislators.

Disincentives to public advocacy find an echo in perceptions that advocacy is not a part of democracy, but rather a part of democracy's problems and that mobilized citizens are a threat to liberal democra-cies. Samuel Huntington assessed the explosion of advocacy in the 1960s as dangerous to democracy and looked toward "some measure of apa-thy" to sustain "the effective operation of a democratic political system" (Huntington 1982: 115). The overloading of the political process with political advocacy, Mancur Olson argued, results in civic distrust, ineffi-cient cartelization, and loss of authority of elected officials (Olson 1982). On the other side of this debate, a substantial body of literature points to the importance of civic engagement for sustaining democratic legiti-macy and connections of trust to institutional politics (Berry 1999; Put-nam 2001; Skocpol 2003). What remains controversial is how citizens' engagement in and with their societies has actually changed. Whether civic engagement has declined (Putnam 2001), altered its form from a membership-based civic culture to more fluid issue networks anchored in lifestyle politics (Bennett 1998), turned into mere "checkbook" advocacy (Zald and McCarthy 1987), or shows signs of all of the above – what manifests itself in changing individual engagement practices also shapes organizational development.

Statistical evidence that the number of advocacy groups is growing does not tell us much about the actual state of democratic public voice. Some of this perceived growth is due to highly professionalized but overall "disembodied" advocacy in the beltways of power in Washington, DC, Brussels, or London. These professional advocacy NGOs emulate

the organizational logic of the corporate sector, in which economies of scale and the efficiencies available through contracting out have shaped the kinds of organizational structures observed. Most movement activities, from recruitment and fund raising to lobbying legislators, can be contracted out, and thus a "movement organization" may be little more than a part-time staffer with a fax machine. (Davis et al. 2005: xvi)

This organization model results in outsourcing advocacy into specialized lobbying practices that only leave a small public footprint (Geller and Salamon 2007: 5) or handing it over to PR agencies with little interest in actually engaging citizens.

Moreover, if NGO advocacy is turning into a formulaic commodity, then it is not surprising that the corporate sector begins to clone similar kinds of operations, further adding to confusion about the democratic basis of public interests. Large businesses have long discovered the value of branding themselves not just as money-making but also as public interest corporations. Wal-Mart has its Families for Wal-Mart nonprofit; Monsanto has its Monsanto Fund. Other businesses choose more circuitous means to build alliances with nonprofits, forming what have been dubbed Astroturf NGOs.[1] In spring 2010, the New York Times profiled Richard B. Berman, director of the Center for Consumer Freedom, a Washington, DC, nonprofit that primarily protects the food-producing industry against animal rights advocates. Berman, a former lobbyist on Capitol Hill, is not only director of the Center for Consumer Freedom; he also founded and is on the board of five other NGOs, among them the American Beverage Institute, which devotes itself to fighting against Mothers Against Drunk Driving and other organizations that promote the lowering of legal blood alcohol limits for drivers; the Employment Freedom Action Committee that engages in anti-unionization issues; and the Employment Policy Institute dedicated to abolishing the minimum wage. Yet directing or being on the board of these nonprofits is not his

---

[1] Astroturf NGOs' names tend to invoke a mission that obscures their real purpose, such as the Forest Protection Society, funded by the logging industry, or Mothers Against Pollution, funded by the Association of Liquid Paperboard Carton Manufacturers to combat the use of glass milk bottles (Wilson 2006).

main job: His main job is directing Berman and Company, a for-profit communications firm that gets as much as 70 percent of its revenues from these six nonprofits.[2] Berman simply exchanged the title of "lobbyist" for "public interest advocate." Which interests he represents remains relatively unknown to the general public.

Thus, Astroturf NGOs very deliberately evoke publicness in their name, while in their operations they shut the public out to advance special interests. For example, the National Smoker Alliance, which campaigned fiercely in the United States to end the ban on smoking in bars in California, turned out to be created and financed by the Phillip Morris tobacco giant. Consumers for Cable Choice, supposedly an NGO with more than a million members, was actually an Astroturf NGO funded by the telecommunications industry in 2006 to support deregulation of the telecommunication market (Dahan and Leca 2008: 13).

Yet Astroturf NGOs are not limited to business. They can also be found in the political realm, building their reputation on grassroots support that in effect turns out to be rather anemic. Libertycentral.org, created by Virginia Thomas, the wife of Supreme Court Judge Clarence Thomas, promotes itself as "America's Public Square" and as an NGO for "citizen activists." Yet the only thing a citizen activist is able to do on its website is to donate, post information, or press the "shop now" button to acquire a mug or a T-shirt. Astroturf NGOs thus wrap themselves in a cloak of public engagement. They calibrate their image as to suggest a strong base and grassroots support, while in fact they avoid transparency and limit public input.

The proliferation of Astroturf NGOs and its byproduct, the hijacking of the public interest, make it all the more imperative for the nongovernmental sector to acquire legitimacy via engaging broader publics. These trends have compelled large organizations to invest more in public outreach. To combat the claims of the Australian Forest Protection Society (funded by the logging industry), environmental groups such as the Wilderness Society have simply *had* to launch massive public campaigns. Civic challenges increasingly are being framed as "who do you speak for?" and thus force NGOs to address their publicness. NGOs that stand for civic principles and practice public outreach have a more compelling answer to that question than Astroturf NGOs that are mere fronts

---

[2] Stephanie Strom (2010). "Nonprofit Advocate Carves out an Unusual For-Profit Niche," *New York Times*, June 18, 2010, p. 1.

for private business interests. The degree to which institutionalized and special interests can dominate information and advocacy in a democracy determines the extent of integration and coherence of its publics (Bimber 2003: 246). Leaving public advocacy to a few large players, in particular to well-funded private interests posing as organized voices of publics, hollows out the very foundations of civil society.

Establishing stronger public accountability of the NGO sector thus provides an answer to the potentially negative fallout from NGOization. It means balancing the inherent pulls to professionalize, institutionalize, and bureaucratize with an emphasis on practicing public outreach and on not just gauging but also activating publics. By contrast, an accountability debate that solely focuses on issues of inner-organizational accountability, on donors having the right to inspect the books, or on avoiding mission drift fails to address the core problems of NGOization.

TURNING TOWARD PUBLIC ADVOCACY

This book has provided evidence that NGOs tend to increase engagement with, and mobilization of, publics under two conditions: (1) when they face a critical juncture because access to political institutions is blocked or endangered by challenges to their legitimacy and (2) when governments actively encourage, promote, and fund NGO public outreach. The first condition – persistent marginalization and exclusion – has been previously identified as among the forces leading to mobilization. Without trying to diminish the insights from the "contentious politics" approach, this book has added the second, often neglected dimension of an actively enabling governance culture as a possibility for democratizing civil society. Neither condition is mutually exclusive; in fact, closed governance arenas and resulting NGO voice might lead to governance reform that enables and steadies that voice.

Of course, there are variations in these conditions, as when organizations marginalize themselves from the policy process in their own areas of interest, taking the role of relief or charity agents without much advocacy at all. However, even these organizations can encounter critical junctures, brought on by declining donations or other external challenges that endanger their mission. An instructive example is the development of modern era food banks in the United States, which have often avoided policy work only to discover that hunger problems were beyond their capacity to address. When Bread for the World, a leading Christian anti-hunger

NGO, put out its fourth Report on the State of World Hunger in 1994, it pleaded with its members to consider practicing more advocacy:

Food banks and other direct service agencies can draw upon a wealth of resources to turn toward advocacy. They have powerful community leaders on their boards, mailing lists of concerned people, and relatively large budgets. Even 5 percent of those budgets devoted to education and 5 percent to advocacy would make a major difference. Charitable organizations have, by and large, earned the respect of the public. That respect forms a reservoir of good will that can be gently tapped to draw more people from service to citizenship. (Bread for the World 1994, quoted in Poppendieck 1998: 271)

Of the 72 food banks that Bread for the World surveyed before making this plea, two-thirds had no budget for advocacy or lobbying, and only four had set aside two percent or more of their budget for these tasks. The report went on to identify those who shied away from becoming advocates against hunger. They were the very community leaders who had a reputation for strong public voice: "Many do not have boards that currently support this type of activity." Food banks were also reluctant to be seen as political or partisan. One staff member put it succinctly, "some of our board people are very conservative business folk, very prominent Republicans in our state. They would find it uncomfortable if we were identified a little too closely with Democrats and Democratic thought." Food banks seemed to be generally content with branding themselves as a "band aid," because, as another food bank director put it, feeding the hungry conveys a gentle and benign image: "Advocates for the hungry are not viewed as change agents that should be feared. We are not engaged in class struggle, we are just feeding people, and this is something that should be supported" (quoted in Poppendieck 1998: 276).

If we fast forward 15 years from 1994, we discover that donations shrank in the midst of the global economic and financial crisis. Food banks in the United States were ailing, with estimates of reductions in donations of between 20 and 40 percent. In this uncharted territory, the largest American food bank network, America's Second Harvest, which included more than 200 food banks, changed its name to the more provocative Feeding America; the explicit goal of this name change was to "elevate hunger-relief programs for greater visibility and involvement. . . . Our new identity invites the public to understand and commit to fighting hunger."[3] This is a carefully calibrated turn from the image of the farm providing

---

[3] Philanthropy Newsdigest 9/9/08, at http://foundationcenter.org/pnd/news/story.jhtml?
id=226800017 (accessed June 1, 2010).

plentiful harvest to the acknowledgment of poverty and the fact that America or many Americans need to be fed.

Other food banks have formed statewide associations to organize more effective advocacy, albeit carefully stretching and bending their interpretation of advocacy so as not to threaten their charity status.[4] Even though some food banks still exclusively use the term "hunger," others have adopted the public language of poverty reduction and are committed to mobilizing their constituencies to fight poverty. The crisis in donations thus altered the "band-aid" approach of food banks and brought about stronger advocacy-oriented voice and strategies. Organizing publics to address poverty, moreover, relies on different public accountability measurements than donations to food banks. Constituencies will judge the NGO by their attempts to politicize poverty and not just by how effective they are in alleviating immediate hardships. At critical junctures, NGOs thus can turn from organizations of survival into organizations of public advocacy and resistance (Reitzes 1995).

The second set of conditions that promote NGO voice is less researched. We have established that government can incentivize NGOs to become more committed public actors by making it easier for them to practice advocacy and enabling the organization of civil society, not just along associational dimensions but also as publics. Such an approach entails, for example, loosening restrictions on political action for the nongovernmental sector and demanding stronger engagement with publics when committing funds to NGOs. Empirical evidence for this argument was provided in Chapters 4 and 5. Local governments in Seattle and Bremen incentivized networked public spheres that enabled NGOs to feel the pulse of their constituencies, find organized ways to channel their input, and transmit knowledge and grassroots policy goals to the institutionalized realms of politics. We found that the ability of NGOs to foster public accountability depends on whether networked, managed, or restricted communication processes form the basis for governance. We come back to the role of governance at the end of this chapter.

We have identified two broad sets of conditions – critical junctures and enabling governance – in which NGO voice might become stronger. However, critical junctures are often not welcome, and changes in governance

---

[4] The association of New York State food banks, for example, only uses the term "advocacy" when it refers to "advocacy on behalf of the food banks at the local, state, and federal levels of government," thus carefully avoiding any appearance of public mobilization. Food Bank Association New York State, at http://www.foodbankassocnys.org/about.cfm (accessed January 22, 2010).

conditions are not easy to initiate. Looking beyond these conditions, there might be other tangible changes in civil society that might prove to be advantageous for strengthening organizational publics. In particular, bringing in new communication technologies and forming transnational alliances for NGO action are considered to be promising forces for mobilization of early 21st-century publics. I address each in turn and then conclude with a final reflection on the role of government in turning NGOs from proxy publics into catalysts for public voice.

THE ROLE OF NEW MEDIA

The turn toward stronger public accountability of NGOs might well be facilitated by new information and communication technologies (ICTs). In the first phase of the Internet, NGOs employed web 1.0 technology primarily for informational purposes and to enhance their public images. They contributed to and made use of the "information abundance" (Bimber 2003: 229ff.) that the web came to host, allowing NGOs to find outlets for expression apart from traditional media and monthly mailed newsletters. With the arrival of web 2.0 technology, the communicative means of the NGO sector have been all but revolutionized. Research has provided convincing evidence of ICTs' potential to enhance civil society's capacity for voice, advocacy, and mobilization (i.e., Bimber 2003; Chadwick and Howard 2008; Bennett 2009). New ICTs substantially alter the way that NGOs communicate internally, in their alliances, and with broader constituencies. On the most basic level, they have lowered the costs for participation and organizing (Earl and Kimport 2011: 39), allowing in particular resource-poor NGOs to expand their public presence, distribute information widely, and organize more decentrally. ICTs provide NGOs with a wide array of means to connect with members and supporters and enable the emergence of new organizational forms that are less structured and more openly networked and fluid than traditional member organizations. ICTs also facilitate "large and flexible coalitions exhibiting the 'strengths of thin ties'" (Bennett 2004: 125) by dispersing power in networks and helping equalize the playing field between large professionalized NGOs and smaller, less organized groups. As Bruce Bimber has observed, "The traditional boundaries, resources, and structures of organizations have less influence over who has facility with political information and communication and who does not" (Bimber 2003: 229). ICTs provide the nongovernmental sector with an expanding tableau of external communication strategies, ranging from viral campaigns to spontaneous swarm action or flash mobs. Overall, ICTs offer low-cost means to connect an organization with its supporters and mobilize citizens for public action via the web. Globally anchored public events and campaigns like the Seattle WTO protests of 1999 or the worldwide antiwar protests of 2003, as well as small, locally organized public meetings, now operate with the power of web technology.

Yet the fact that technology is available and increasingly used does not mean that the NGO sector has optimized it as a resource for practicing public advocacy and organizing publics. This is why the research for this book is not based on exceptional moments of NGO-driven mobilization, but instead has tried to capture snapshots of everyday organizational practices. Chapter 6 pointed to systematic underutilization of interactive web 2.0 technology among European women's NGO networks. When in 2004, Stephen Ross from Columbia's School of Journalism published a report on the role of media in 54 humanitarian relief NGOs in the United States and Europe, one of its central findings was that those NGOs had barely begun to tap the potential of the web (Ross 2004: 19). At the time, most sites included only basic information, few humanitarian relief NGOs had internal search engines, and technologies such as streaming video or blogs were virtually ignored. Meanwhile, as many NGOs are still trying to figure out how to best use web 2.0 technology, and they find themselves with competition: Professional communication intermediaries such as moveon.org and clearinghouses such as Kiva, Avaaz or Change act as transmission belts between individual citizens and social justice causes, providing direct ways for concerned citizens to make their voice heard and make a difference while bypassing issue-specific organizations altogether. Kiva is an entrepreneurial NGO that connects microlenders directly with recipients in the global South. Avaaz is a virtual campaign platform that provides the technology for launching campaigns and has been the electronic conduit for 13 million members and more than 50 million actions since 2007.[5] Change is a so-called 'B Corp', a corporation certified by a nonprofit to meet higher standards of transparency and accountability that acts as a conduit for individually started campaigns. All are innovative in their approach to public engagement. They provide site visitors with a set of communication tools to articulate support for a cause or organize a campaign themselves. In many ways, they make participating in public affairs easier. The Avaaz website allows visitors to "shop" campaigns and easily click from "saving Syrian lives" to

[5] Avaaz Facts at http://www.avaaz.org/en/pressfaq.php (accessed February 2, 2012).

"Stay Strong – Save the Amazon" or "Clean Out Corruption in India."
It is constructed to be in constant "high alert" mode, with the numbers
of supporters for a given campaign moving across a bar and individual
voices of supporters rolling across the screen.

It is too early to assess to what degree such people-powered web
movements directly compete with NGOs for attention. Although they are
high-powered engines for users to express their opinion and to raise the
visibility of causes, it remains to be seen whether the "donate and click"
engagement mode they provide translates into more consistent mobilization for specific issues. NGOs that have had long-term engagements
with some of the issues that Avaaz campaigns for, however, are concerned about this new mode of engagement. Dennis Searle, an independent communications consultant who helped *Oxfam* devise a web-based
communication strategy, asks, "How long will it be before . . . NGOs see
their supporter base eroded by digital native organizations such as Kiva
and Avaaz, plus numerous national and local advocacy and development
groups that can apparently provide digital native audiences with direct,
tangible ways of making a difference?" (Searle 2009).

Bimber and colleagues correctly claim that the Internet facilitates organizing without organization (Bimber, Flanagin, and Stohl 2009: 79; see
also Flanagin et al. 2006). Internet-based organizing, they argue, incorporates two dimensions of experience: the *mode of interaction* and the
mode of engagement (Flanagin et al. 2006: 29). In both these modes,
organization, as we tend to understand it, has lost its centrality. Both
ICT-mediated interaction and engagement can happen outside of a given
organizational context; for example, on a Facebook page, in a Twitter
swarm, or in engagement in a flash mob. Such actions might represent a
one-time and spontaneous expression of voice – individualized acts that
take place apart from the organized context of the nongovernmental sector. I agree with the authors that web 2.0 technology has indeed taken
organization out of organizing, but I contend that effects of these new
modes are uncharted in two respects. First, spontaneous organizing might
lower the bar for engagement, but will it also foster the individual commitment that it takes to sustain public advocacy over longer periods around
complex issues that remain unresolved? It is certainly too early to make
predictions, but I suggest that it will take the organized contexts of NGOs
to bring spontaneous organizing together with viable long-term commitments to a cause. Two, what remains unresolved on the technology path
from organization to organizing is how constituent voice will be transmitted to and sustained in the institutional realm of politics. If specific
goals are to remain at the center of mobilization efforts to change politics

or policies, a campaign might need to be frequently retooled or retuned to adapt its messages and strategies to changing political environments. Retooling and retuning of campaigns to keep up pressure on institutional actors over longer periods of time will almost certainly require NGO expertise. In sum, although the Internet has the promise of decoupling organization from conventional organizing and public membership management, it is too early to know whether that promise actually helps or hinders stronger public NGO advocacy. NGOs could be sidelined by new online intermediaries that connect citizens directly to causes. Or NGOs might increasingly seize these technological repertoires to enlarge their public profile and engage in organizing efforts based on web 2.0 technology. The competition with online intermediaries might actually turn into a win-win arrangement that would allow NGOs to expand their public accountability, foster issue alliances among NGOs for specific campaigns, and allow citizens to support NGO causes in globally visible campaigns, while stabilizing the web-based campaigns of intermediaries like Avaaz with the expertise and longer term perspectives of NGOs.

TRANSNATIONALIZATION

The second development that will affect NGOs' public engagement practices is that the issues they tackle increasingly resonate transnationally and thus need transnational organizing (i.e., Vedder 2007; Wessler et al. 2008; Steffek and Hahn 2010). Civil society theories of the pre-1989 era insisted on a national demos as an essential prerequisite for mobilizing citizens for public advocacy. By contrast, 21st-century publics will be considerably less bound by nation states. As issues travel and coalesce across borders, NGOs need to adapt to new politics of scale in their organization and engagement strategies.[6] Some new transnational networks are temporary and highly differentiated, organized around a specific purpose or event by loose alliances or "advocacy coalitions" (Keck and Sikkink 1998). In such networks, NGOs might operate alongside state agencies, movements actors, and academics, and stay mostly independent in their choice of strategies for public outreach. Other contexts in which NGOs engage transnationally are provided by international organizations such as the UN, the EU, or the ILO, where parameters of formal incorporation

---

[6] This is not just an issue for large NGOs that engage with global industries or global problems such as climate change. Transnationalization is just as relevant for the local Slovenian women's NGO joining with an Austrian NGO in responding to an EU-wide call for action for equal pay.

of NGOs are more clearly set and the effect on NGOs engaging publics tends to be negative.

Whereas it is obvious that transnationalization alters the public advocacy and outreach practices of NGOs, its long-term reverberations are much less clear. Will it overall increase spaces in which publics can form? Or will it actually accelerate the professionalization, bureaucratization, and institutionalization of NGOs while further undermining their public accountability? On the upside, transnationally operating NGOs and their networks might have more capacity to pool resources, launch large-scale campaigns, and thus generate public attention. Having to navigate different communication styles and to bridge cultural cleavages, NGOs might increase their awareness of discursive hierarchies (Doerr 2008)[7] and of the need to adapt outreach strategies to multiple and dispersed constituencies. On the downside, establishing public accountability seems more daunting on the transnational level than in smaller contexts. Even a minimum of organizational transparency might be more difficult to achieve for an NGO operating on the transnational level than in smaller arenas. First, most of the time NGOs in transnational governance arenas do not get what they want to the fullest extent that they want it. Being perceived as compromising on core goals might not strike NGO leaders as a good idea and thus might limit transparency, as well as debate with and engagement of constituencies. Second, semi-institutionalized venues of international organizations have become comfort zones for many large NGOs, which are by now well integrated into the circuits of institutional politics. Kerstin Martens, in her study on Amnesty International within the UN system, observes that "the UN has gradually integrated NGOs into many of its processes and procedures. Today, NGOs regularly collaborate with the UN in agenda-setting activities and advise its commissions and committees. Moreover, they also assist UN institutions during drafting processes and provide them with information on issues of their concern. NGOs even work in co-operation with operational UN agencies and implement projects together" (Martens 2006: 371). She calls this the "institutionalization" of NGOs within the UN system. Granting consultative status in a specific area of expertise to an NGO gives the UN access to that NGO's expertise. Martens traces Amnesty International's path at the UN "from campaigning for human rights standards to drafting them" and from being outsiders employing

---

7 Nicole Doerr, in her exploration of the European Social Forum as a "Europeanist Movement Institution," shows the development of a form of open public debate in which activist translators enhance the voice of marginalized groups (Doerr 2008).

occasional contestation to being insiders with professional staff (Martens 2006: 379). NGOs in transnational governance arenas thus might be just as susceptible to the lures of institutional advocacy and to validation by established political actors as NGOs in national or local governance contexts. Institutional advocacy does not always have to come at the expense of public accountability, but it does make outreach to constituencies and generating publics for NGO agendas more susceptible to institutional sanctions.

Recall the opening quote in Chapter 1 from Kofi Annan hailing the NGO sector as the central democratizing force of the 21st century. In the absence of transnational *demoi*, organized NGOs have been anointed as proxies; they legitimize international organizations by serving as stand-ins for civil society. However, if they are to be "transmission belts" (Steffek and Nanz 2008: 8) between international organizations and citizens, then the question is whether this belt has a reverse function or operates only in one direction. Steffek and colleagues elaborate that NGOs operating as a transmission belt might be able to "bypass the bottleneck of interest aggregation and representation through the hierarchical structures of the state" and place their demands squarely into the centers of global governance (Steffek et al. 2010: 101). To what degree they will maintain ties with their constituents in the process is much less clear.

One dynamic that we observe to be in play is transnational configurations of power that might produce new levels of resistance against conflating institutional advocacy with civil society participation. These power configurations are particularly palpable in the different approaches of southern and northern NGOs to advocacy. Southern NGOs have for some time adopted NGOized strategies and advocacy repertoires from the North, yet often with a bad fit (Hudock 1999). Even in transnational campaigns, northern NGOs tend to keep the upper hand when it comes to goal definition, strategies, and tools to achieve certain goals (i.e., Hertel 2006). As a consequence, some southern NGOs start to reject northern frames and strategies and replace them with their own stronger public-oriented mobilizations. This trend has led globalization scholars such as Sonia Alvarez to explore whether in fact a movement "beyond NGOization" is in the making, drawing from the experience that NGOized civil societies "revealed limits for actually implementing hard-won policy gains, which requires public pressure, secured through changes in public opinion, not just through policy monitoring" (Alvarez 2009: 178). Alvarez sees the source of NGOs' movement toward more public engagement and movement building in the frustrations with having been a dutiful insider citizen on the stages of international organizations. Many NGOs started to realize that the path to substantive social change was blocked by the dominant neoliberal agenda of international organizations and northern donors, including their responsibility for a "dramatic rolling back of the State . . . and the concomitant erosion of citizenship and social policies" during the 1990s. According to Alvarez, there is movement by NGOs, in Latin America in particular, to abandon "project centered logics" in favor of "process-oriented logics" (179).

Although I share Alvarez's insistence on identifying alternative modes and spaces for NGO advocacy, I maintain that the forces that have NGOized civil societies, and in the process dampened public accountability of NGOs, remain strong. From an institutional perspective, if indeed we see a global move to ameliorate the negative fallout from NGOization in decades to come, it will have to be accompanied by structural adjustments in the way state and nonstate actors relate. Governments, which are experiencing growing voter apathy and thus a legitimacy crisis institutionally, might grow increasingly wary of the thin democratic inclusion premise on which today's culture of citizenship practices is based. If governments and international organizations attribute higher value to thicker notions of citizenship, they will seek out the nongovernmental sector to provide more substance to the bridging function between institutional politics and civil society. NGOs thus would gain incentives to become stronger transmission belts between citizens and organized politics and to rely on public accountability for legitimacy.

THE PATH AHEAD: GOVERNMENTS, DONORS, AND PUBLIC ACCOUNTABILITY OF NGOS

The current predicament of the nongovernmental sector evokes the "glass half- full" or "glass half-empty" expression. NGOs are neither the Davids of our times, nor have they and will they become the democratic Goliaths of the future. NGOs tend to act in and respond to an environment that steers political action into institutionally channeled forms, while, in the process, limiting public discussion and alternative action repertoires. A case in point is the pervasive demobilization around poverty issues in the United States, which has been recently challenged by the Occupy movement. Anna Marie Smith, in her analysis of U.S. welfare reform, has documented for example how women's NGOs are complicit in state withdrawal from redistributive policies and have become willing collaborators in the moral policing of the so-called welfare queens (Smith 2007: 4).

Paul Amar extends this line of thinking by arguing that "the participation of women's NGOs in this project is essential for the ideological construction of this process as a vehicle for the delivery of therapeutic interventions, when they would otherwise be read as deploying punitive and disempowering mechanisms" (Amar 2011: 311; also quoted in Smith 2007: 4). Yet, complicity in projects that disempower constituents is not an inevitable effect of NGOization. This book has explored alternative governance processes that enable NGOs to become catalysts of publics. We have seen governments awarding funds supporting the self-organizing of city neighborhoods, thereby building capacity for advocacy by fostering stronger connections between NGOs and citizens. Neither Seattle nor Bremen represents a democratic utopia, and – as with the case of Seattle – progress is easily stalled when policy priorities shift before these enabling processes settle deeper in a city's civic DNA. Yet overall, governance-supported NGO outreach has generated more vibrant NGO-mediated publics in Seattle and Bremen than in comparable cities. Governance created the foundation for NGOs to increase their public accountability and, in the process, helped citizens generate public voice within a networked urban public sphere.

As traditional means by which governments generate political legitimacy erode, the NGO sector might actually see its power in civil society increase. Therefore, we might not enter an era of post–NGOization, but rather an era of altered NGOization, in which governments enable NGOs to tune more into and better aggregate their publics, thereby strengthening their own legitimacy.

Foundations and private donors, although not part of this investigation, are of course also implicated in enhancing NGO public accountability. In the United States, where public and private philanthropy provide a larger proportion of nonprofit funding than in Europe,[8] initiatives to establish stronger public accountability of NGOs require endorsement and promotion by foundations and private donors. Yet in the past they have been just as unlikely as governments to embrace the idea of stronger public accountability for two reasons. First, most of the capital of foundations and private donors is conceived of as an investment that

---

[8] We tend to, however, overestimate the role of the foundation sector. Hammack and Anheier state that in 2005, foundations provided about 1 percent of the income of charitable nonprofits in the United States; other private donors provided 12 percent. By contrast, government made grants equal to 9 percent of nonprofit income and contributed substantially more via non-grant-related service contracting (Hammack and Anheier 2010: 7, fn 8).

is supposed to show tangible results. Foundations, in particular, are at the forefront of the drive to strengthen NGO accountabilities via performance criteria that tend to be either management focused or tied into the "stakeholder" language, thereby reinforcing the "marketization of the nonprofit sector" (Eikenberry and Kluver 2004: 132). Second, foundations and private donors tend to be reluctant to sponsor grassroots mobilization, for political as well as management reasons. They want to avoid liberal bias, mission drift, and loss of control over donor-sponsored agendas. Debra Minkoff and Jon Agnone show, for example, that in the area of women's rights, foundations prefer Washington-based "professional advocates" and that those organizations that locate themselves and their efforts nationally, employ a paid staff, and limit their involvement in more disruptive forms of social protest reap substantial financial benefits" (Minkoff and Agnone 2010: 366). Only a few smaller and more progressive foundations in the United States have embraced the idea of "constituency-controlled funding" by handing over the power to make funding decisions to groups of constituents (Ostrander 2005: 44). Yet, by and large, foundation research struggles to identify the motives for resource-rich foundations, in particular, to sponsor public advocacy of NGOs and stronger commitment to citizen voice (Ostrander 2005: 35). Overall, foundations "favor professional advocacy over grassroots organizing" (36) and thus exacerbate the pull toward institutional advocacy at the expense of public outreach.

As argued earlier, public accountability of NGOs encompasses the four modes of transparency, debate, engagement, and activation. To strengthen their public accountability, NGOs would be asked and enabled to provide more transparency in terms of their operation and finances, as well as their mission and goals. Governance conditions would reflect a commitment to initiating debates that are open, inclusive, and allow for interactivity between organizations and constituencies. Funders would need to encourage NGOs to promote active engagement of constituents and interested citizens in NGO projects. Finally, the shared goal of government, other funders, and NGOs would be a greater activation of citizen voice, thus enabling NGOs to serve as catalysts for stronger publics.

    This is a challenging agenda. But the path ahead is marked with four obvious guideposts that provide direction: (1) *Let NGOs talk politics.* Governments would need to make sure that legal stipulations do not unduly stifle the sector's contributions to politics by producing cultures of intimidation around political voice. Politics is at the core of negotiating public interests, and organized citizen voice should not be contingent on having the financial means to hire lobbying organizations and lawyers. As outlined in Chapter 4, recent UK attempts to reform charity regulations might be a template for other countries as well. (2) *Make all contributions to organizations with charity status public.* Allowing NGOs to engage in political advocacy without mandating that the sources of contributions be public is detrimental to democracy. The current controversy in the United States about 501(c)(4) status charities emphasizes this need for financial transparency. As part of their operation, many Super-PACs[9] have created 501(c)(4)s that are not only tax-exempt but also do not have to disclose donors and can spend unlimited amounts on political advocacy. These donations might not dry up with different disclosure rules and thus transparency might not alter the inherent inequality in access to political advocacy, but at the very least an informed public would be better able to assess the interests behind specific charity operations. (3) *Require NGOs to reach out to constituencies.* Government programs and services that are administered by NGOs could have specific language attached that demand outreach beyond the occasional symbolic act. If governments and other funders want it, NGOs will have incentives to increase their public accountability. In the past, most governments have found advantages in having NGOs be their proxy publics, but public legitimacy challenges to both political institutions and NGOs may change this equation. (4) *Let NGOs talk failure.* Governments as well as private donors would need to find ways to *not* punish failure. Failure of programs and projects often is the result of a mismatch between program intention and constituency realities. If NGOs can admit to failures, they can put publics into the equation. If they are not allowed to admit failure, their constituencies are relegated to a residual factor, because the voice of authentic witnesses of specific program impact will be dampened for strategic reasons. Thus, allowing public debate about failed civil society projects would encourage NGO outreach and in the process give validation to the voice of constituencies. (5) *Empower NGOs to organize publics independently.* Governments can strengthen civil society autonomy. Oversight and accountability notwithstanding, establishing procedures by which communities are invited to

---

[9] Super-PACs are a new form of political action committee that are legally allowed to operate in the U.S. since 2010. They can raise unlimited amounts of donations from corporations, associations, and individuals that can be used to directly advocate for or against political candidates for office. Whereas Super-PACs have to disclose sources of donations at least every three months, they can avoid disclosure if they incorporate part of their operation as a 501(c)(4) nonprofit.

debate and have a say in the uses of resources and making these debates more than just occasional or merely symbolic listening exercises would raise the civic stakes in which NGOs operate. It would also discourage NGOs from trying to manage their publics instead of cultivating them, from targeting constituencies instead of actively engaging them. In sum, governance that would more boldly empower civil society would go a long way in helping NGOs evolve from proxy publics into organizational catalysts for public voice.

Yet there are clear obstacles to governments' enabling of NGOs: We have examined the tendency to individualize civic engagement, calling on individual citizens to perform social service through volunteer agencies or to participate on occasion in deliberative meeting contexts. There is also the more principled question of what interests specific state actors should have in strengthening collective civic voice. Political parties, in general, would rather have citizens join their organizations than have them express preferences through NGO advocacy. And in political systems where parties are essentially beholden to big donors, shielding charities from financial disclosure is in the parties' interest. Governments might hold on to the legitimacy chain, however porous, that elections provide. And NGOs and governments jointly might find compelling reasons to strengthen ties through institutional channels at the expense of enabling publics. Yet to the degree that political decision makers and NGOs are caught in this apparent win-win configuration, democracy might lose out.

These concerns will be debated and challenged in the coming years. Governments need lifelines into civil society that transcend the four-year election cycle, and NGOs are best positioned to be these lifelines. NGOs, in turn, need government encouragement to become what they are well positioned to be: catalysts for public advocacy and incubators of a more vibrant public sphere.

Appendix 1: Interviews for Chapter 5

A total of 60 semi-structured interviews were conducted between 2000 and 2007. In each of the six cities, I asked stakeholders in urban development from NGOs, government, and the media what they saw as the most important local conflicts in urban development at the time. Issues that they mentioned most often were selected to serve as empirical cases. I chose the interviewees through a snowball sampling procedure. Interviews were conducted in person during site visits; they were generally accompanied by participant observation of meetings and events. Interviews were recorded and transcribed, unless interviewees asked not to be recorded. The interviewees were granted anonymity.

OAKLAND

OAK-1-JB: Policy advocacy NGO
OAK-2-LL: Ethnic advocacy NGO
OAK-3-DG: Urban development NGO
OAK-4-HS: Ethnic advocacy NGO
OAK-5-GM: Urban development activist
OAK-6-GN/KK: Urban development activists
OAK-7-US: Policy advocacy NGO
OAK-8-WW: Urban development activist
OAK-9-GM: Mayor's office
OAK-10-NA: Local journalist

SAN DIEGO

SD-1-CB: Community development corporation
SD-2-RS: Local journalist

SD-3-KK: Urban development activist
SD-4-RS: City Redevelopment Agency
SD-5-CM: Community activist
SD-6-SM: Community activist
SD-7-ND: Urban development NGO
SD-8-JS: Community development corporation
SD-9-DC: Union urban development specialist
SD-10-BO: Local newspaper editor
SD-11-AF: Urban development activist

SEATTLE

SEA-1-BV: City Department of Neighborhoods
SEA-2-JF: Urban development coalition
SEA-3-DK: City Department of Technology
SEA-4-CM: City Council Member, chief of staff
SEA-5-TD: Urban development NGO
SEA-6-LL: Urban development NGO
SEA-7-CW: Urban development NGO
SEA-8-BC: Department of Neighborhoods
SEA-9-MM: Mayor's Office, urban development strategist
SEA-10-MU: Journalist

BERLIN

BER-1-RR: Urban development NGO
BER-2-MR: Urban development NGO
BER-3-MT: Urban development NGO
BER-4-TT: Urban development corporation
BER-5-SP: Civic engagement NGO
BER-6-SK: Senate Office for Urban Integration
BER-7-FW: Citizen foundation
BER-8-KH: Senate Agency for Urban Development

BREMEN

BRE-1-BF: Urban development NGO
BRE-2-FH: City Department of Civic Engagement
BRE-3-JB: Urban development NGO
BRE-4-HG: Urban development NGO
BRE-5-TJ: Senate Office for Urban Development Programs

BRE-6-KW: Urban development NGO
BRE-7-TK: Urban development professor
BRE-8-FH: City Department of Civic Engagement
BRE-9-MP: Policy advocacy NGO
BRE-10-BH: Citizen foundation
BRE-11-JH: Urban development NGO
BRE-12-OF: City Department for Technology

LEIPZIG

LEI-1-RK: Department of Citizen Engagement
LEI-2-IH: Urban development NGO
LEI-3-RK: Department of Citizen Engagement
LEI-4-AK: Urban development NGO
LEI-5-IH: Citizen advocacy NGO
LEI-6-FB: City Department of Technology
LEI-7-PF: Neighborhood NGO
LEI-8-RK: Department of Citizen Engagement
LEI-9-RK: Urban development NGO

Appendix 2: Interviews for Chapter 6

The interviews for Chapter 6 were conducted between 2005 and 2008 in Berlin, Brussels, London, Vienna, and Warsaw. I established contact with the headquarters and member organization offices of the networks via e-mail and followed up with phone calls. Interviews were semi-structured and between 45 minutes and 120 minutes in length; three were conducted by phone.

EWL (2005). Interview with spokeswoman from Executive Committee, (phone). 2/14/05.

EWL (2007a). Interview with former member of Executive Committee. Berlin. 7/16/07.

EWL (2007b). Interview with Head of Member Association. London. 7/24/07.

EWL (2007c). Interview with Project Manager. Brussels. 10/12/07.

KARAT (2005). Interview with Executive Director, (phone). 2/10/05.

KARAT (2008). Interview with Executive Director. Warsaw. 7/28/08.

KARAT (2008a). Interview with Director of Network Member Organization. Warsaw. 7/28/08.

WAVE (2005). Interview with spokeswoman from Executive Office. Vienna. 2/10/05.

WECF (2005). Interview with member of Steering Committee, (phone). 2/10/05.

WECF (2007). Interview with Director of Member Organizations. London. 7/24/07.

WIDE (2007a). Interview with network member. London. 7/24/07.

WIDE (2007b). Interview with spokeswoman from Executive office. Brussels. 10/12/07.

Appendix 3: Website Analysis for Chapter 6

The website analysis for Chapter 6 used a modified and adapted version of the coding matrix established by Bennett, Foot, and Xenos (2011).

The coders assessed informational and activating content of the web pages as well as the targets of web-based mobilization. They assigned random reliability coding, and where coding differed, the coders worked in pairs to discuss and decide the coding for those cases. The coded levels refer to (1) the initial website of the main URL, (2) all sites that are clickable from the initial URL, and (3) all sites that are clickable from this second set of sites. We assumed that the importance of an issue is reflected by its posting on these first three levels of a site as opposed to deeper within the websphere of a TAN. Coding took place during November 2005 and October 2006. It should be noted that the results reflect snapshots during these two months and therefore cannot be generalized. Interview data (see Appendix 2) were used to validate the results of the website analysis.

Appendix 4: Issue Crawler Maps for Chapter 6

The web crawls for Chapter 6 were compiled with a tool provided by sociologist Richard Rogers from the University of Amsterdam. The Issue Crawler constructs networks of URLs by identifying and documenting linkages from, to, and between different starting points. We assumed that linking is intentional, and therefore linkage among TAN members or between TANs is indicative of shared concerns and agendas. In-links that a TAN receives indicate recognition from other TANs or TAN members (see also Bennett, Lang, and Segerberg 2013). I sampled the starting points as an original list of between two and five URLs. The resulting maps visualize the amount of co-linking that Issue Crawler detects in a network. The Issue Crawler "mines" the websites according to instructions that are documented in the legends to the respective maps. Iterations were chosen to be two or three levels out, and the crawls to be two or three levels in depth. Figure 6.2 illustrates the co-linking process. The size of the nodes indicates player strength in the network, based on the number of in- and out-links received by and sent to others in the network. Details for usage are provided at http://www.govcom.org/Issuecrawler_instructions.htm.

References

Adloff, Frank 2005. *Zivilgesellschaft. Theorie und politische Praxis.* Frankfurt a.M.: Campus Verlag.

Adorno, Theodor W. 1964 (2011). "Opinion Research and Publicness," in Andrew J. Perrin and Jeffrey K. Olick (eds.), *Friedrich Pollock, Theodor W. Adorno and Colleagues: Group Experiment and Other Writings. The Frankfurt School on Public Opinion in Postwar Germany.* Cambridge, MA: Harvard University Press, pp. 179–84.

Agence France-Press 2002. "US Does Missile Deal with Greenpeace USA for Five Years." http://www.spacedaily.com/news/bmdo-02b.htmlAFP (accessed January 9, 2002).

Aigner, Heidrun 2007. *Die Europäische Beschäftigungsstrategie. Gleichstellungspolitische Konzeptionen und Einbindung ost – westeuropäischer Frauennetzwerke.* M.A. thesis. University of Vienna.

Aksartova, Sada 2005. "NGO Diffusion as Production of Coercive Isomorphism." Presented at the Japan Society for the Promotion of Science, January 13.

_____ 2009. "Promoting Civil Society or Diffusing NGOs? U.S. Donors in the Former Soviet Union," in David C. Hammack and Steven Heydemann (eds.), *Globalization, Philanthropy, and Civil Society: Projecting Institutional Logics Abroad.* Bloomington: Indiana University Press, pp. 160–91.

Alexander, Jeffrey 2006. *The Civil Sphere.* Oxford: Oxford University Press.

Alexander, Jennifer, Jeffrey L. Brudney, and Kaifeng Yang 2010. "Introduction to the Symposium: Accountability and Performance Measurement: The Evolving Role of Nonprofits in the Hollow State." *Nonprofit and Voluntary Sector Quarterly* 39 (4): 565–70.

Allahwala, Ahmed and Roger Keil 2005. "Introduction to a Debate on the World Social Forum." *International Journal of Urban and Regional Research* 29 (2): 409–16.

Alvarez, Sonia E. 1999. "Advocating Feminism: The Latin American Feminist NGO 'Boom.'" *International Feminist Journal of Politics* 1 (2): 181–209.

_____ 2009. "Beyond NGO-ization? Reflections From Latin America." *Development* 52 (2): 175–84.

Amar, Paul 2011. "Turning the Gendered Politics of the Security State inside Out?" *International Feminist Journal of Politics* 13 (3): 299–328.

American Enterprise Institute 2003a. "We're Not from the Government – But We're Here to Help You. NGOs – The Growing Power of an Unelected Few." *AEI Conference Announcement 6/11/2003.* http://www.aei.org (accessed May 12, 2009).

_____ 2003b. "Nongovernmental Organizations: The Growing Power of an Unelected Few." Presented at AEI Conference, Washington DC. http://www.aei.org/event/329 (accessed November 23, 2010).

Ancelovici, Marcos 2002. "Organizing against Globalization: The Case of ATTAC in France." *Politics and Society* 30 (3): 427–63.

Anderson, Kenneth 2003. "International NGOs: A Law unto Themselves?" Presented at American Enterprise Institute Conference. http://www.aei.org (accessed April 7, 2010).

Andrews, Kenneth T., Matthew Baggetta, Chaeyoon Lim, Marshall Ganz, and Hahrie Han 2010. "Leadership, Membership, and Voice: Civic Associations at Work." *American Journal of Sociology* 115 (4): 1191–242.

Andrews, Kenneth T. and Bob Edwards 2005. "The Organizational Structure of Local Environmentalism." *Mobilization* 10 (2): 213–34.

Anheier, Helmut K. 2004. *Civil Society: Measurement, Evaluation, Policy.* London: Earthscan.

_____ 2009. "What Kind of Nonprofit Sector, What Kind of Society? Comparative Policy Reflections." *American Behavioral Scientist* 52: 1082–94.

Anheier, Helmut K., Marlies Glasius, and Mary Kaldor (eds.) 2004. *Global Civil Society 2004/5.* London: Sage.

Anheier, Helmut K. and Lester M. Salamon 2006. "The Nonprofit Sector in Comparative Perspective," in Walter W. Powell and Richard Steinberg (eds.), *The Non Profit Sector: A Research Handbook.* New Haven: Yale University Press, pp. 89–116.

Anheier, Helmut K. and Wolfgang Seibel 2001. *The Nonprofit Sector in Germany.* Manchester: Manchester University Press.

Anheier, Helmut K. and Stefan Toepler 2003. *Bürgerschaftliches Engagement zur Stärkung der Zivilgesellschaft im internationalen Vergleich.* Gutachten für die Enquête – Kommission Zukunft des Bürgerschaftlichen Engagements. KD Number 14/153. Opladen: Leske+Budrich, pp. 13–55.

Annan, Kofi 1998. "Emerging Power of Civil Society." Statement to the Parliamentary Group Parlatino in Sao Paulo, Brazil. July 14. Press release SG/SM/6638. http://www.un.org/News/Press/docs/1998/19980714.sgsm6638.html (accessed February 12, 2009).

_____ 2006. "Opening Address to the Fifty-Third Annual DPI/NGO Conference." New York. http://www.un.org/dpi/ngosection/annualconfs/53/sg-address.html (accessed October 22, 2010).

Arato, Andrew 1990. "Revolution, Civil Society and Democracy," *Praxis International* 10 (1–2): 24–38.

Arendt, Hannah 1958. *The Human Condition.* Chicago: University of Chicago Press.

Armony, Ariel C. 2004. *The Dubious Link: Civic Engagement and Democratization.* Stanford: Stanford University Press.

Asen, Robert and Daniel C. Brouwer (eds.) 2001. *Counterpublics and the State.* Albany: State University of New York.

Atkinson, Jeff 2007. *International NGOs and Southern Advocacy: Case Studies of Two Oxfam Campaigns in South Asia.* London: University of London.

Attafuah, Ken A. 2007. *The Contributions of Civil Society Organizations to Democratic Development in Ghana's Fourth Republic.* RAO Convention. At www.g-rap.org/docs/2007%20rao%20convention%20report.pdf (accessed June 12, 2012).

Australian Bureau of Statistics 2002. *Non-Profit Institutions Satellite Account.* Baltimore: Johns Hopkins University Center for Civil Society Studies. http://www.ccss.jhu.edu/index.php?section=content&view=16&sub=91& tri=93 (accessed May 13, 2009).

Axelrod, Toby 2012. "German Fund Pulls NGO Cash." *Jewish Chronicle.* February 2. http://www.ngo-monitor.org/article/german_fund_pulls_ngo_cash (accessed February 13, 2012).

Bachrach, Peter and Aryeh Botwinick 1992. *Power and Empowerment: A Radical Theory of Participatory Democracy.* Philadelphia: Temple University Press.

Bagić, Aida 2006. "Women's Organizing in Post–Yugoslav Counties: Talking about Donors," in Myra Marx Ferree and Aili Mari Tripp (eds.), *Global Feminism. Transnational Women's Activism, Organizing and Human Rights.* New York: New York University Press, pp. 141–65.

Banaszak, Lee Ann 2010. *The Women's Movement inside and outside the State.* New York: Cambridge University Press.

Barber, Benjamin 1984. *Strong Democracy: Participatory Politics of a New Age.* Berkeley: University of California Press.

Barker, Hannah and Simon Burrows (eds.) 2002. *Press, Politics and the Public Sphere in Europe and North America, 1760–1820.* Cambridge: Cambridge University Press.

Bartlett, Scott 2000. "Discursive Democracy and a Democratic Way of Life," in Lewis Edwin Hahn (ed.), *Perspectives on Habermas.* London: Open Court Publishing, pp. 367–86.

Barzilai, Gad 2003. *Communities and Law: Politics and Cultures of Legal Identities.* Ann Arbor: University of Michigan Press.

Bass, Gary D., David F. Arons, Kay Guinane, and Matthew F. Carter 2007. *Seen but not Heard: Strengthening Nonprofit Advocacy.* Washington, DC: Aspen Institute.

BAW Institut für regionale Wirtschaftsförderung 2005. *Europaregion Nordwest de. Bremen.* http://www.ihk-oldenburg.de/.../europaregion-nordwest_studie .pdf (accessed November 13, 2010).

Beck, Ulrich 1996. "World Risk Society as Cosmopolitan Society? Ecological Questions in a Framework of Manufactured Uncertainties." *Theory, Culture & Society* 13 (4): 1–32.

———— 2007. *World at Risk.* Cambridge: Polity Press.

Behning, Ute and Birgit Sauer (eds.) 2005. *Was bewirkt Gender Mainstreaming? Evaluierung durch Policy-Analysen.* Frankfurt a.M.: Campus.

Bellah, Robert 1985. *Habits of the Heart.* Berkeley: University of California Press.

Bendell, Jem and Phyllida Cox 2006. "The Donor Accountability Agenda," in Lisa Jordan and Peter Van Tuijl (eds.), *NGO Accountability. Politics, Principles and Innovations.* London: Earthscan, pp. 109–26.

Benhabib, Seyla 1992. *Situating the Self: Gender, Community and Postmodernism in Contemporary Ethics.* London: Routledge.

Bennett, Lance W. 1990. "Towards a Theory of Press-State Relations in the United States." *Journal of Communication* 40 (2): 103–25.

———— 1998. "The UnCivic Culture: Communication, Identity, and the Rise of Lifestyle Politics." *PS: Political Science and Politics* 31 (4): 741–62.

———— 2002. "The Internet and Global Activism," in Nick Couldry and James Curran (eds.), *Contesting Media Power.* Lanham: Rowman & Littlefield, pp. 17–37.

———— 2004a. "Communicating Global Activism: Strengths and Vulnerabilities of Networked Politics," in Wim Vande Donk, Brian D. Loader, Paul G. Nihon, and Dieter Rucht (eds.), *Cyberprotest: New Media, Citizens and Social Movements.* London: Routledge, pp. 123–46.

———— 2004b. "Social Movements beyond Borders: Understanding Two Eras of Transnational Activism," in Donnatella Della Porta and Sidney Tarrow (eds.), *Transnational Protest and Global Activism.* Lanham: Rowman & Littlefield, pp. 203–26.

———— 2008. "Changing Citizenship in the Digital Age," in W. Lance Bennett (ed.), *Civic Life Online.* Cambridge, MA: MIT Press, pp. 1–24.

———— 2009. *Grounding the European Public Sphere: Looking beyond the Mass Media.* KFG Working Paper, Free University Berlin.

———— 2010. "The Press, Power and Public Accountability," in Stuart Allan (ed.), *The Routledge Companion to News and Journalism.* London: Routledge, pp. 105–15.

Bennett, Lance W., Kirsten Foot, and Mike Xenos 2011. "Narratives and Network Organization: A Comparison of Fair Trade Systems in Two Nations." *Journal of Communication* 61 (2): 219–45.

Bennett, Lance W., Sabine Lang, and Alex Segerberg 2013. "European Issue Publics Online: Citizen Engagement in EU vs. National Level Advocacy Networks," in Thomas Risse and Marianne van de Steeg (eds.), *The Europeanization of Public Spheres and the Diffusion of Ideas.* Cambridge: Cambridge University Press.

Bennett, Lance W., Victor Pickard, David Lozzi, Carl Schroeder, Taso Lagos, and Courtney Caswell Pickard 2004. "Managing the Public Sphere: Journalistic Construction of the Great Globalization Debate." *Journal of Communication* 54 (3): 437–55.

Berkovitch, Nitza and Neve Gordon 2008. "The Political Economy of Transnational Regimes: The Case of Human Rights." *International Studies Quarterly* 52 (4): 881–904.

Berman, Sheri 1997. "Civil Society and Political Institutionalization." *American Behavioral Scientist* 40 (5): 562–74.

_____ 2001. "Civil Society and Political Institutionalization," in Bob Edwards, Michael W. Foley, and Mario Diani (eds.), *Beyond Tocqueville: Civil Society and the Social Capital Debate in Comparative Perspective*. Boston: Tufts University Press, pp. 32–42.

Bermeo, Nancy and Phillip Nord (eds.) 2003. *Civil Society before Democracy: Lessons from Nineteenth-Century Europe*. Lanham: Rowman & Littlefield.

Berry, Jeffrey M. 1977. *Lobbying for the People*. Princeton, NJ: Princeton University Press.

_____ 1999. "The Rise of Citizen Groups," in Theda Skocpol and Morris P. Fiorina (eds.), *Civic Engagement in American Democracy*. Washington, DC: Brookings Institution Press, pp. 367–94.

_____ 2010. "Urban Interest Groups," in L. Sandy Maisel and Jeffrey M. Berry (eds.), *The Oxford Handbook of American Political Parties and Interest Groups*. New York: Oxford University Press, pp. 502–18.

Berry, Jeffrey M. and David F Arons 2003. *A Voice for Nonprofits*. Washington, DC: Brookings Institution Press.

Berry, Jeffrey M., Kent E. Portney, and Ken Thomson 1993. *The Rebirth of Urban Democracy*. Washington, DC: Brookings Institution Press.

Bertelsmann Foundation 2000. *Bürgerorientierte Kommunen in Deutschland – ein Wegweiser*, edited by Heidi Sinning and Ansgar Wimmer. Gütersloh: Bertelsmann Publishing.

Betsill, Michele M. and Elisabeth Corell. 2008. *NGO Diplomacy: The Influence of Nongovernmental Organizations in International Environmental Negotiations*. Cambridge, MA: MIT Press.

Bexell, Magdalena, Jonas Tallbert, and Anders Uhlin 2010. "Democracy in Global Governance: The Promises and Pitfalls of Transnational Actors." *Global Governance* 16: 81–101.

Bimber, Bruce 2003. *Information and American Democracy: Technology in the Evolution of Political Power*. Cambridge: Cambridge University Press.

Bimber, Bruce, Andrew J. Flanagin and Cynthia Stohl 2005. "Reconceptualizing Collective Action in the Contemporary Media Environment." *Communication Theory* 15 (4): 365–88.

_____ 2009. "Technological Change and the Shifting Nature of Political Organization," in Andrew Chadwick and Philip N. Howard (eds.), *Routledge Handbook of Internet Politics*. London: Routledge, pp. 72–85.

_____ 2012. *Collective Action in Organizations: Interaction and Engagement in an Era of Technological Change*. Cambridge: Cambridge University Press.

Bloodgood, Elisabeth 2011. "The Yearbook of International Organizations and Quantitative Non-State Actor Research," in Bob Reinalda (ed.), *The Ashgate Research Companion to Non-State Actors*. Farnham: Ashgate, pp. 19–34.

Blueprint Research and Development 2002. *The Industry of Philanthropy*. San Francisco.

Blumenthal, Julia 2005. "Governance – eine kritische Zwischenbilanz." *Zeitschrift für Politikwissenschaft* 15 (4): 1149–80.

Blumer, Herbert 1954. "What is Wrong with Social Theory?" *American Socio-logical Review* 1: 3–10.

Bob, Clifford 2005. *The Marketing of Rebellion: Insurgents, Media, and International Activism.* New York: Cambridge University Press.

Bode, Ingo 2007. "Organisationsentwicklung in der Zivilgesellschaft. Grenzen und Optionen in einem unerschlossenen Terrain." *Forschungsjournal Neue Soziale Bewegungen* 20 (2): 92–101.

Bohman, James 1996. *Public Deliberation: Pluralism, Complexity, and Democracy.* Cambridge, MA: MIT Press.

Borchgrevink, Axel 2006. *A Study of Civil Society in Nicaragua.* NORAD Paper # 699. Oslo: Norwegian Institute of International Affairs.

Boris, Elizabeth and Rachel Mosher-Williams 1998. "Nonprofit Advocacy Organizations." *Nonprofit and Voluntary Sector Quarterly* (27): 488–506.

Boris, Elizabeth T. and C. E. Steuerle (eds.) 2006. *Nonprofits and Government: Collaboration and Conflict*, 2nd ed. Washington, DC: Urban Institute.

Bourdieu, Pierre 1977. *Outline of a Theory of Practice.* Cambridge: Cambridge University Press.

Bourdieu 1984. *Distinction: A Social Critique of the Judgement of Taste.* Cambridge: Harvard University Press.

Bourdieu, Pierre and Luc Wacquant 1992. *An Invitation to Reflexive Sociology.* Chicago. University of Chicago Press.

Bourjaili, Natalia 2006. "Some Issues Related to Russia's New NGO Law." *International Journal of Not-for-Profit Law* 8 (3): 4–6.

Braithwaite, Mary 2000. "Mainstreaming Gender in the European Structural Funds." Paper presented to the Mainstreaming Gender in European Public Policy Workshop, University of Wisconsin-Madison, October 14.

Brandy, Joe and Jackie Smith (eds.) 2005. *Coalition across Borders: Transnational Protest and the Liberal Order.* Lanham, MD: Rowman & Littlefield.

Breen, Oonagh B. 2008. "EU Regulation of Charitable Organizations: The Politics of Legally Enabling Civil Society." *International Journal of Not-for-Profit Law* 10 (3): 50–78.

Brenner, Neil, Peter Marcuse, and Margit Mayer 2009. "Cities for People, not for Profit." *City* 13 (1):176–84.

Bretherton, Charlotte and Liz Sperling 1996. "Women's Networks and the European Union: Towards an Inclusive Approach?" *Journal of Common Market Studies* 34 (4): 487–508.

Brinkerhoff, Jennifer M. and Derick W. Brinkerhoff 2002. "Government-Nonprofit Relations in Comparative Perspective: Evolution, Themes and New Directions." *Public Administration and Development* 22: 3–18.

Broder, John M. 2005. "Letter from San Diego: Sun, Sand, and a Sea of Municipal Headaches." *New York Times.* http://www.nytimes.com/2005/01/02/national/02diego.html (accessed February 2, 2005).

Brodi, Evelyn 2006. "The Legal Framework for Nonprofit Organizations," in Walter W. Powell and Richard Steinberg (eds.), *The Non Profit Sector: A Research Handbook.* New Haven: Yale University Press, pp. 243–66.

Brooks, Ethel 2005. "Transnational Campaigns against Child Labor: The Garment Industry in Bangladesh," in Joe Brandy and Jackie Smith (eds.), *Coalition across Borders: Transnational Protest and the Liberal Order.* Lanham: Rowman & Littlefield, pp. 121–40.

Brown, David and Mark H. Moore (2001). "Accountability, Strategy, and International Nongovernmental Organizations." *Nonprofit and Voluntary Sector Quarterly* 30 (3): 569–87.

Brown, Michael and John May 1991. *The Greenpeace Story.* New York: Dorling Kindersley.

Browning, Robyn 2009. "So Many NGOs." *Notes from the Field in Tanzania.* University of Minnesota School of Public Health. http://blog.lib.umn.edu/enge/notes09/2009/07/so_many_ngos.html (accessed December 11, 2009).

Brunnengräber, Achim, Ansgar Klein, and Heike Walk (eds.). *NGOs im Prozess der Globalisierung.* Bonn: Bundeszentrale für politische Bildung.

Calhoun, Craig 1992. *Habermas and the Public Sphere.* Cambridge, MA: MIT Press.

_____ 1994. "Social Theory and the Politics of Identity," in Craig Calhoun (ed.), *Social Theory and the Politics of Identity.* Malden: Blackwell, pp. 9–36.

Cammaerts, Bart 2006. "The eConvention on the Future of Europe: Assessing the Participation of Civil Society and the Use of ICTs in European Decision-Making Processes." *Journal for European Integration* 28 (3): 225–45.

Campbell, John L. 2005. "Where Do We Stand? Common Mechanisms on Organizations and Social Movements Research," in Gerald F. Davis, Doug McAdam, Richard W. Scott, and Mayer N. Zald, (eds.), *Social Movements and Organization Theory.* New York: Cambridge University Press, pp. 41–68.

Canilglia, Beth S. and JoAnn Carmin 2005. "Scholarship on Social Movement Organizations: Classic Views and Emerging Trends." *Mobilization* 10 (2): 201–12.

Carothers, Thomas 2002a. "The End of the Transition Paradigm." *Journal of Democracy* 13 (1): 5–21.

_____ 2002b. "A Reply to My Critics." *Journal of Democracy* 13 (3): 33–8.

Cartmell, Matt 2008. "Oxfam Turns to WS to Update Image." *PR Week,* July 31. http://www.prweek.com/uk/news/835806/Oxfam–turns–WS–update–image/ (accessed June 14, 2012).

Castells, Manuel and Gustavo Cardoso (eds.) 2006. *The Network Society: From Knowledge to Policy.* Washington, DC: Johns Hopkins University Press.

Center on Philanthropy 2009. *Giving USA 2009.* Bloomington: Indiana University Press.

Ceraso, Karen. 1999. "Seattle Neighborhood Planning: Citizen Empowerment or Collective Daydreaming?" *Shelterforce* 108, November/December. http://www.nhi.org/online/issues/108/seattle.html (accessed July 25, 2010).

Chadwick, Andrew and Philip N. Howard (eds.) 2008. *Routledge Handbook of Internet Politics.* London: Routledge.

Chambers, Simone 2003. "A Critical Theory of Civil Society," in Will Kymlicka and Simone Chambers, *Alternative Conceptions of Civil Society.* Princeton, NJ: Princeton University Press, pp. 90–110.

Chandhoke, Neera 2003. *The Conceits of Civil Society.* New York: Oxford University Press.

Charnovitz, Steve 2005. *Accountability of Nongovernmental Organizations (NGOs) in Global Governance*. George Washington University Law School Public Law and Legal Theory Working Paper No. 145. http://ssrn.com/abstract=716381 (accessed September 30, 2010).

_____ 2009. "Recent Scholarship on NGOs." *American Society of International Law* 103 (4): 777–84.

Chaskin, Robert J. and Sunil Garg 1997. "The Issue of Governance in Neighborhood-Based Initiatives." *Urban Affairs Review* 32: 631–62.

Chaves, Mark, Laura Stephens, and Joseph Galaskiewicz 2004. "Does Government Funding Suppress Nonprofits Political Activity?" *American Sociological Review* 69 (2): 292–316.

Cichowski, Rachel 2002. "'No Discrimination Whatsoever': Women's Transnational Activism and the Evolution of EU Sex Equality Policy," in Nancy Naples and Manisha Desai (eds.), *Women's Activism and Globalization: Linking Local Struggles and Transnational Politics*. New York: Routledge, pp. 220–38.

_____ 2007. *The European Court and Civil Society: Litigation, Mobilization and Governance*. Cambridge: Cambridge University Press.

Clabby, Kathryn 2007. *Overcaution and Confusion: The Impact of Ambiguous IRS Regulation of Political Activities by Charities and the Potential for Change*. http://www.ombwatch.org/files/npadv/paci2rpt.pdf (accessed November 1, 2007).

Clark, Christopher 2006. *Iron Kingdom: The Rise and Downfall of Prussia 1600–1947*. Cambridge, MA: Harvard University Press.

Clark, Peter 2000. *British Clubs and Societies 1500–1800: The Origins of an Associational World*. New York: Oxford University Press.

Clavero, Sara, Mary Daly, and Mary Braithwaite 2004. "Gender-Sensitive and Women Friendly Public Policies: A Comparative Analysis of Their Progress and Impact." Research Program funded by the European Commission in the 5th Framework Program. http://www.equapol.gr/pdf/HPSE_CT_2002_00136_DEL5_Total.pdf (accessed June 1, 2008).

Clemens, Elisabeth S. 1997. *The People's Lobby: Organizational Innovation and the Rise of Interest Group Politics*. Chicago: University of Chicago Press.

_____ 2005. "Two Kinds of Stuff: The Current Encounter of Social Movements and Organizations," in Gerald F. Davis, Doug McAdam, W. Richard Scott, and Mayer N. Zald (eds.), *Social Movements and Organization Theory*. New York: Cambridge University Press, pp. 351–66.

_____ 2006. "The Constitution of Citizens. Political Theories of Nonprofit Organizations," in Walter W. Powell and Richard Steinberg (eds.), *The Non Profit Sector: A Research Handbook*. New Haven: Yale University Press, pp. 207–20.

Clemens, Elisabeth S. and Deborah C. Minkoff 2004. "Beyond the Iron Law: Rethinking the Place of Organizations in Social Movement Research," in David A. Snow, Sarah A. Soule, and Hanspeter Kriesi (eds.), *The Blackwell Companion of Social Movements*. Malden, MA: Blackwell, pp. 155–70.

Cloward, Richard A. and Frances Fox Piven 1984. "Disruption and Organization: A Rejoinder." *Theory and Society* 13: 587–99.

Coaffee, Jon and Patsy Healey 2003. "My Voice: My Place: Tracking Transformations in Urban Governance." *Urban Studies* 40 (10): 1979–99.

Cohen, Jean 1999. "American Civil Society Talk," in Robert K. Fullenwider (ed.), *Civil Society, Democracy, and Civic Renewal*. Lanham: Rowman & Littlefield, pp. 55–88.

Cohen, Jean and Andrew Arato 1992. *Civil Society and Political Theory*. Cambridge, MA: MIT Press.

Cohen, Samy 2006. *The Resilience of the State: Democracy and the Challenges of Globalization*. Boulder, CO: Lynne Rienner.

Coleman, James S. 1988. "Social Capital in the Creation of Human Capital." *American Journal of Sociology* 94: 95–120.

Cooper, Glenda 2009. "When Lines between NGO and News Organization Blur." Presented at Nieman Journalism Lab, Harvard University, November 16. http://www.niemanlab.org/ngo (accessed February 12, 2012).

Cottle, Simon and David Nolan 2009. "How the Media's Codes and Roles Influence the Ways NGOs Work." Presented at Nieman Journalism Lab, Harvard University, November 16. http://www.niemanlab.org/ngo (accessed February 12, 2012).

Council of Europe 1998. *Gender Mainstreaming: Conceptual Framework, Methodology and Presentation of Good Practices*. Final Report of Activities of the Group of Specialists on Mainstreaming. Strasbourg: Council of Europe.

Cravens, Jayne 2004. *Learning from the Not-So-Nice Volunteers*. http://www.merrillassociates.net/topic/2004/12/02/nice-and-not-so-nice-volunteers (accessed December 1, 2009).

Cronin, Karena and Helene Perold 2006. "Volunteering and Social Activism." *International Journal for Volunteer Administration* 26 (1). http://www.ijova.org/PastIssues/volume_xxvi_01.html.

Cullen, Pauline 2005. "Conflict and Cooperation within the Platform of European Social NGOs," in Joe Brandy and Jackie Smith (eds.), *Coalition across Borders: Transnational Protest and the Liberal Order*. Lanham, MD: Rowman & Littlefield, pp. 71–94.

Dahan, Nicolas M. and Bernard Leca 2008. "Engaging Activist Groups for Corporate Political Activity. An Exploration of Some of the Determinants." Presented at the Third Colloquium on Corporate Political Activity, Paris. http://www.villanova.edu/business/assets/documents/excellence/leadership/10.pdf (accessed April 12, 2011).

Dahl, Robert 1961. *Who Governs? Democracy and Power in an American City*. New Haven: Yale University Press.

———— 1967. "The City in the Future of Democracy." *The American Political Science Review* 61 (4): 953–70.

Dann, Otto, ed. 1984. *Vereinswesen und bürgerliche Gesellschaft*. Munich: Oldenbourg.

Darley, Julian 2000. "Making the Environment News on the Today Programme," in Joe Smith (ed.), *The Daily Globe: Environmental Change, the Public and the Media*. London: Earthscan, pp. 151–67.

Darnton, Robert and Daniel Roche (eds.) 1989. *Revolution in Print: The Press in France 1775–1800*. Berkeley: University of California Press.

Davis, Gerald F., Doug McAdam, Richard W. Scott, and Mayer N. Zald (eds.) 2005. *Social Movements and Organization Theory.* New York: Cambridge University Press.

Dechalert, Preecha 1999. *NGOs, Advocacy, and Popular Protest: A Case Study of Thailand.* International Working Paper No. 6. London School of Economics, Centre for Civil Society.

DeFilippis, James 2001. "The Myth of Social Capital in Community Development." *Housing Policy Debate* 12 (4): 781–806.

de Haart, Joep and Paul Dekker 2003. "A Tale of Two Cities: Local Patterns of Social Capital," in Marc Hooghe and Dietlind Stolle (eds.), *Generating Social Capital: Civil Society and Institutions in Comparative Perspective.* New York: Palgrave Macmillan, pp. 153–69.

Della Porta, Donnatella and Sidney Tarrow 2004a. "Multiple Belongings, Flexible Identities, and the Construction of 'Another Politics': Between the European Social Forum and Local Social Fora," in Donnatella Della Porta and Sidney Tarrow (eds.), *Transnational Protest and Global Activism.* Lanham: Rowman & Littlefield, pp. 175–202.

―――― 2004b. "Transnational Processes and Social Activism," in Donnatella Della Porta and Sidney Tarrow (eds.), *Transnational Protest and Global Activism.* Lanham: Rowman & Littlefield, pp. 1–21.

―――― (eds.) 2004c. *Transnational Protest and Global Activism.* Lanham: Rowman & Littlefield.

Delli Carpini, Michael X 2004. "Mediating Democratic Engagement: The Impact of Communications on Citizens' Involvement in Political and Civic Life," in Lynda Lee Kaid (ed.), *Handbook of Political Communication Research.* Mahwah, NJ: Erlbaum Publishing, pp. 395–434.

DeMars, William E. 2005. *NGOs and Transnational Networks: Wild Cards in World Politics.* London: Pluto Press.

Demirovic, Alex 1998. "NGOs and Social Movements: A Study in Contrasts." *Capital, Nature & Society* 8 (3): 83–92.

Desai, Manisha 2005. "Transnationalism: The Face of Feminist Politics Post–Beijing." *International Social Science Journal* 57 (184): 319–30.

Deutsche Gesellschaft für Verbandsmanagement (DGVM) 2007. *Verbändestatistik.* http://www.verbaende.com/8AF9F995EF0B47D09BFFD7ED8E7244C0 .htm (accessed March 1, 2009).

"Die Gleichmacher." 2007. *Der Spiegel* (1): 27.

Diers, Jim 2004. *Neighborhood Power: Building Community the Seattle Way.* Seattle: University of Washington Press.

Disney, Jennifer Leigh and Joyce Gelb 2001. "Feminist Organizational 'Success.'" *Women and Politics* 21 (4): 39–76.

Docherty, Ian, Robina Goodlad, and Ronan Paddison 2001. "Civic Culture, Community and Citizen Participation in Contrasting Neighbourhoods." *Urban Studies* 38 (12): 2225–50.

Doerr, Nicole 2008. "Deliberative Discussion, Language, and Efficiency in the WSF Process." *Mobilization* 13 (4): 395–410.

―――― 2009. "Multilingualism and the Case of the European Social Forum Process." *Social Movement Studies* 8 (2): 149–65.

Donges, Patrick and Otfried Jarren 1999. "Politische Öffentlichkeit durch Netz-kommuniation," in Klaus Kamps (ed.), *Eletronische Demokratie?* Opladen: Westdeutscher Verlag, pp. 85–108.

Donini, Antonio 2006. "The Bureaucracy and the Free Spirits: Stagnation and Innovation in the Relationship between the UN and NGOs," in T. G. Weiss and L. Gordenker (eds.), *NGOs, the UN, and Global Governance*. Boulder, CO: Lynne Rienner, pp. 83–101.

Downey, Dennis J. 2009. "Institutional Activism and Community Building: Human Relations Responses to 9/11 in Orange County, California." *American Behavioral Scientist* 53 (1): 99–113.

Dryzek, John 1996. "The Informal Logic of Institutional Design," in Robert E. Goodwin (ed.), *The Theory of Institutional Design*. Cambridge: Cambridge University Press, pp. 103–25.

Dubnick, Melvin J. and George Frederickson (eds.) 2011. *Accountable Governance: Problems and Promises*. Armonk: M. E. Sharpe.

Duncan, Pete and Sally Thomas 2000. *Neighbourhood Regeneration: Resourcing Community Involvement*. Bristol: Policy Press.

Dunn, Alison 2008. "Charities and Restrictions on Political Activities: Developments by the Charity Commission for England and Wales in Determining Regulatory Barriers." *International Journal of Not-for-Profit Law* 11 (1): 51–66.

Earl, Jennifer and Katrina Kimport 2011. *Digitally Enabled Social Change: Activism in the Internet Age*. Cambridge, MA: MIT Press.

Ebrahim, Alnoor 2009. "Placing the Normative Logics of Accountability in 'Thick' Perspective." *American Behavioral Scientist* 52: 885–904.

Ebbesson, John 2007. "Public Participation," in Daniel Bodansky, Jutta Brunner, and Ellen Hey (eds.), *The Oxford Handbook of International Environmental Law*. New York: Oxford University Press, pp. 681–703.

Economist 2000. "Sins of the Secular Missionaries." http://www.economist.com/node/276931 (accessed April 13, 2011).

Edelman Trust Barometer 2006. *Annual Trust Barometer 2006. The Seventh Global Opinion Leaders Study*. http://www.edelman.com/image/insights/content/FullSupplement.pdf.

———— 2012. "Global Results." http://www.trust.edelman.com, (accessed February 11, 2012).

Edgar, Gemma 2008. *Agreeing to Disagree: Maintaining Dissent in the NGO Sector*. Discussion Paper No. 100. Australia Institute.

Edwards, Bob, Michael W. Foley, and Mario Diani (eds.) 2001. *Beyond Tocqueville: Civil Society and the Social Capital Debate in Comparative Perspective*. Boston: University Press of New England.

Edwards, Michael 2004. *Civil Society*. London: Polity Press.

Edwards, Michael and David Hulme 1996. "Too Close For Comfort? The Impact of Official Aid on Nongovernmental Organizations." *World Development* 24: 961–73.

Eick, Volker 2003. "New Strategies of Policing the Poor." *Policing and Society* (4): 365–79.

———— 2005. "Neoliberaler Truppenaufmarsch? Nonprofits als Sicherheitsdienste in benachteiligten Quartieren," in Georg Glasze, Robert Puetz, and Manfred

Rolfes (eds.), _Diskurs – Stadt – Kriminalität_. Bielefeld: Transcript Publishing House, pp. 167–202.

Eikenberry, Angela M. and Jodie Drapal Kluver 2004. "The Marketization of the Nonprofit Sector: Civil Society at Risk?" _Public Administration Review_ 64 (2): 132–40.

Einhorn, Barbara 2006. "Gender Mainstreaming as a Key Issue in the Context of Political Transformation in Central and Eastern Europe," in Sirkku Hellsten, Anna Maria Holli, and Krassimira Daskalova (eds.) _Women's Citizenship and Political Rights_. Basingstoke: Palgrave MacMillan, pp. 67–85.

Eliasoph, Nina 1996. "Making a Fragile Public: A Talk-Centered Study of Citizenship and Power," _Sociological Theory_ 14 (3): 262–89.

——— 1998. _Avoiding Politics: How Americans Produce Apathy in Everyday Life_. Cambridge: Cambridge University Press.

Elshtain, Jean Bethke 1999. "A Call to Civil Society." _Society_ 36 (5): 11–19.

Enquête–Kommission Deutscher Bundestag 2002. "Zukunft des Bürgerschaftlichen Engagements," _Bürgerschaftliches Engagement: auf dem Weg in eine zukunftsfähige Bürgergesellschaft_. Bundestags–Drucksache 14/8900.

Entine, Jon 2003. "Capitalism's Trojan Horse: Social Investment and Anti-Free Market NGOs." Presented at the American Enterprise Institute Conference, "Nongovernmental Organizations: The Growing Power of an Unelected Few," Washington, DC. http://www.aei.org/event/329 (accessed November 23, 2010).

EQUAL European Thematic Group 4 2005. _EQUAL as a Driving Force for Gender Mainstreaming_. Summary Report. http://ec.europa.eu/employment_social/equal/data/document/ (accessed August 1, 2009).

EQUAL Policy Brief 2005. "Strengthening Gender Equality Bodies and NGOs." http://ec.europa.eu/employment_social/equal/data/document/0506_madrid_pb4eobodies_en.pdf (accessed June 5, 2008).

Eriksen, Erik O. 2007. "Conceptualizing European Public Spheres," in John Erik Fossum and Philip R. Schlesinger (eds.), _The European Union and the Public Sphere_. London: Routledge, pp. 23–43.

Eriksen, Erik O. and J. E. Fossum 2002. "Democracy through Strong Publics in the EU?" _Journal for Common Market Studies_ 40 (3): 401–24.

Ertmann, Thomas 2003. "Liberalization, Democratization, and the Origins of a "Pillarized" Civil Society in Nineteenth-Century Belgium and the Netherlands," in Nancy Bermeo and Phillip Nord (eds.), _Civil Society before Democracy: Lessons from Nineteenth-Century Europe_. Lanham: Rowman & Littlefield, pp. 155–80.

European Anti-Poverty Network 2007. _Implementing the New Round of the Structural Funds: What Has Happened to Social Inclusion and Non-Governmental Organizations?_ http://www.eapn.org/publications.htm (accessed June 8, 2008).

European Commission 2000. _The Commission and Non-Governmental Organizations: Building a Stronger Partnership_. Brussels: European Commission.

European Commission 2001. Fifth Community Action Programme on Equal Opportunities (2001-2006). Available at http://europa.eu/legislation_

summaries/employment_and_social_policy/equality_between_men_and_women/
c10904_en.htm (accessed June 22, 2012).

———. 2002a. *Communication from the Commission: Towards a Reinforced Culture of Consultation and Dialogue – General Principles and Minimum Standards for Consultation of Interested Parties by the Commission*. COM 2002, 704, December 11. Brussels: European Union.

———. 2002b. *Mainstreaming Equal Opportunities for Women and Men in Structural Fund Programmes and Projects: The New Programming Period 2002–2006*, Technical Papers 3. Brussels: European Commission.

———. 2006. *Not Alone: A Research on Successful Partnerships between Private Companies and Citizens' Organizations in Europe. Final Report.* http://cccdeutschland.org (accessed February 12, 2010).

———. 2008. *Document de Travail de la Commission accompagnant le Rapport d"évaluation final de la stratégie–cadre et du programme d'action communautaire concernant la stratégie communautaire en matière d'égalité entre les femmes et les hommes 2001–2006*, SEC 20082365. http://ec.europa.eu/employment_social/gender_equality/actions/index_en.html (accessed March 11, 2009).

European Council 2001. *Decision 2001/51/EC, 12/20/2000 Establishing a Programme Relating to the Community Framework Strategy on Gender Equality 2001–2005.* http://europa.eu/legislation_summaries/employment_and_social_policy/equality_between_men_and_women/c10904_en.htm (accessed November 4, 2011).

European Women's Lobby (EWL) 2002a. *Put Your Weight behind Equality in Europe: Petition to the Presidium of the Convention.* http://www.iiav.nl/epublications/2005/EWLInfoEuropeanConstitution.pdf (accessed June 14, 2008).

———. 2002b. *Gender Mainstreaming in the Structural Funds: Establishing Gender Justice in the Distribution of Financial Resources.* http://www.womenlobby.org/Document.asp?DocID=4728&tod=175424 (accessed May 3, 2006).

———. 2003. *Letter to Valéry Giscard d-Estaing Regarding the Draft Constitutional Treaty, June 3.* http://www.womenlobby.org (accessed June 14, 2008).

———. 2004. *Beijing + 10. 1995–2005 Review of the Implementation of the Beijing Platform for Action by the European Union.* http://www.womenlobby.org/pdf/beijing–en.pdf (accessed May 3, 2006).

———. 2005. *Briefing Document on the Treaty Establishing a Constitution for Europe.* http://www.womenlobby.org/site/module_cate.asp?docid=226&parentCat=18 (accessed June 14, 2008).

Evans, Peter 2004. "Development as Institutional Change: The Pitfalls of Monocropping and the Potentials of Deliberation." *Studies in Comparative Institutional Development* 38 (4): 30–52.

Evers, Adalbert 2009. "Gefährdung von Zivilität. Zum Verhältnis von Zivilgesellschaft und Drittem Sektor." *Forschungsjournal Neue Soziale Bewegungen* 1: 79–84.

Eyerman, Ron, and Andrew Jamison 1989. "Environmental Knowledge as an Organizational Weapon: The Case of Greenpeace." *Social Science Information* 28 (1): 99–119.

Farrow, Cherry 2000. "Communicating about Climate Change: An NGO View," in Joe Smith (ed.), *The Daily Globe: Environmental Change, the Public and the Media*. London: Earthscan, pp. 189–197.

Feldman, Shelley 1997. "NGOs and Civil Society: Unstated Contradictions." *Annals of the American Academy of Political and Social Science* 554: 46–65.

Fenton, Natalie 2009. "Has the Internet Changed How NGOs Work with Established Media?" Presented at the Nieman Journalism Lab, Harvard University, November 16. http://www.niemanlab.org/ngo (accessed February 12, 2012).

Fernando, Jude and Alan Heston 1996. "NGOs between States, Markets, and Civil Society." *Annals of the American Academy of Political and Social Sciences* 554: 8–20.

Ferree, Myra Marx, William Anthony Gamson, Jürgen Gerhards, and Dieter Rucht 2002. *Shaping Abortion Discourse: Democracy and the Public Sphere in Germany and the United States*. New York: Cambridge University Press.

Ferree, Myra Marx and Carol McClurg Mueller 2003. "Feminism and the Women's Movement: A Global Perspective," in David A. Snow, Sarah Anne Soule, and Hanspeter Kriesi (eds.), *The Blackwell Companion to Social Movements*. Oxford: Blackwell, pp. 576–608.

Ferree, Myra Marx and Aili Mari Tripp 2006. *Global Feminism: Transnational Women's Activism, Organizing, and Human Rights*. New York: New York University Press.

Fine, Robert and Shirin Rai (eds.) 1997. *Civil Society: Democratic Perspectives*. London: Frank Cass.

Fishkin, James S. 1997. *The Voice of the People: Public Opinion & Democracy*. New Haven: Yale University Press.

Flanagin, Andrew J., Cynthia Stoll, and Bruce Bimber 2006. "Modeling the Structure of Collective Action." *Communications Monographs* 73 (1): 29–54.

Foley, Michael W. and Robert Edwards 1996. "The Paradox of Civil Society." *Journal of Democracy* 7 (3): 38–52.

———— 1997. "Escape from Politics? Social Theory and the Social Capital Debate." *American Behavioral Scientist* 40 (5): 550–61.

Fossum, Jan E. and Philip Schlesinger 2007. *The European Union and the Public Sphere: A Communicative Space in the Making?* London: Routledge.

Foster, John W. 2005. "The Trinational Alliance against NAFTA: Sinews of Solidarity," in Joe Brandy and Jackie Smith (eds.), *Coalition across Borders: Transnational Protest and the Liberal Order*. Lanham: Rowman & Littlefield, pp. 209–30.

Frankel, Boris 1997. "Confronting Neoliberal Regimes: The Post-Marxist Embrace of Populism and Realpolitik." *New Left Review* 226: 57–92.

Frantz, Christine and Kerstin Martens 2006. *Nichtregierungsorganisationen*. Wiesbaden: VS Verlag.

Fraser, Nancy 1992. "Rethinking the Public Sphere: A Contribution to the Critique of Actually Existing Democracy," in Craig Calhoun (ed.), *Habermas and the Public Sphere*. Cambridge: Cambridge University Press, pp. 109–42.

Fritsche, Miriam 2003. *Neues Regieren im Quartier?* Unpublished M.A. Thesis, Berlin.

———— 2008. "Wohl und Weh von Quartiersbudgets: Einblicke in die lokale Umsetzung eines Verfahrens zur partizipativen Fördermittelvergabe," in Olaf Schnur (ed.), *Quartiersforschung zwischen Theorie und Praxis.* Wiesbaden: VS Verlag, pp. 147–68.

Fuchs, Gesine 2006. "Case Study: Polish Non-Governmental Women's Organizations and the EU," in Heiko Pleines (ed.), *Participation of Civil Society in New Modes of Governance: The Case of the New EU Member States.* Part 3. Bremen: Working Papers of the Research Center for East European Studies, pp. 54–65.

Funk, Nanette 2006. "Women's NGOs in Central and Eastern Europe: The Imperialist Criticism." *Femina politica* 15 (1): 68–84.

Gabriel, Oscar W. 2002. "'Bürgerbeteiligung in den Kommunen,' Deutscher Bundestag, Enquete–Kommission 'Zukunft des Bürgerschaftlichen Engagements,'" in *Bürgerschaftliches Engagement und Zivilgesellschaft.* Opladen: Westdeutscher Verlag, pp. 121–160.

Garsztecki, Stefan 2006. "Zivilgesellschaft in Polen." *Polen News.* http://www .polen–news.de/puw/puw-83–07.html (accessed January 3, 2009).

Gastil, John 2008. *Political Communication and Deliberation.* Los Angeles: Sage Publications.

Gazley, Beth 2010. "Linking Collaborative Capacity to Performance Measurement in Government-Nonprofit Partnerships." *Nonprofit and Voluntary Sector Quarterly* 39 (3): 653–73.

Geissel, Brigitte (2005). "*Zivilgesellschaft und* Local Governance: Good Fellows?" *Forschungsjournal Neue Soziale Bewegungen* 3: 19–28.

Geller, Stephanie L. and Lester M. Salamon 2007. *Nonprofit Advocacy: What Do We Know?* Working Paper Series No. 22. Baltimore: Johns Hopkins Center for Civil Society.

Geller Stephanie L. and Lester M. Salamon 2009. *Listening Post Project Roundtable on Nonprofit Advocacy and Lobbying.* Communique No. 13. Washington, D.C.

Gellner, Ernest 1994. *The Conditions of Liberty: Civil Society and Its Rivals.* London: Hamish Hamilton.

Gender Mainstreaming Experts International (GMEI) 2008. *Mission Statement.* http://www.gmei.de/ (accessed April 8, 2008).

Gensicke, Thomas and Sabine Geiss 2004. "Die Freiwilligensurveys 1999–2004," in European Volunteers Center (ed.), *Voluntary Action in Germany. Facts and Figures.* http://www.cev.be/66–cev_facts_e_figures_reports_–EN.html (accessed August 2, 2010).

German Federal Ministry of the Interior 1999. *Moderner Staat – moderne Verwaltung. Das Programm der Bundesregierung.* Berlin: German Federal Ministry.

Gesellschaft für Stadtentwicklung 2007. "Eperimenteller Wohnungs– und Städtebau." Forschungsfeld Stadtumbau West. Modellvorhaben Bremen Osterholz-Tenever. Abschlussbericht. Bremen. http://www.ote-wohnen.de/otg_website_archive.pdf (accessed March 13, 2011).

Ghodsee, Kristen 2004. "Feminism-by-Design: Emerging Capitalisms, Cultural Feminism, and Women's Nongovernmental Organizations in Postsocialist Eastern Europe." *Signs: Journal of Women in Culture and Society* 20 (3): 727–53.

Gibbons, Sheila 2005. "European News Media, AKA Bastion of Gender Bias." *Maynard Institute for Journalism Education News.* http://www.maynardije .org/columns/guests/050629_europe/ (accessed June 14, 2008).

Glazer, Nathan 1998. *The Limits of Social Policy.* Cambridge, MA: Harvard University Press.

Goffman, Ervin 1959. *The Presentation of Self in Everyday Life.* Garden City, NY: Doubleday.

Gosewinkel, Dieter, Dieter Rucht, Wolfgang van den Daele, and Jürgen Kocka (eds.) 2003. *Zivilgesellschaft – national und international.* WZB Jahrbuch. Berlin: Edition Sigma.

Government Advisory Group on Campaigning and the Voluntary Sector 2007. Report. London.

Grant, Wyn 2000. *Pressure Groups and British Politics.* London: Macmillan.

Gray, Richard T. and Sabine Wilke (eds.) 1996. *German Unification and its Discontents: Documents from the Peaceful Revolution.* Seattle: University of Washington Press.

Greven, Michael T. 2000. "Can the European Union Finally Become a Democracy?," in Michael T. Greven and Louis W. Pauly (eds.), *Democracy beyond the State? The European Dilemma and the Emerging Global Order.* Lanham: Rowman & Littlefield, pp. 35–62.

Grewal, Inderpal and Victoria Bernal 2013. *The NGO Form: Feminist Struggles, States and Neoliberalism.* Durham: Duke University Press.

Grunberg, Laura 2000. "NGOization of Feminism in Romania: The Failure of a Success." *Analyze: Journal of Feminist Studies* 7. http://www.ana.org.ro/ romaniacentrulana/editura/rev700/contents700.html (accessed July 30, 2009).

Guadagnini, Maria and Alessia Dona 2007. "Women's Policy Machinery in Italy between European Pressure and Domestic Constraints," in Joyce Outshoorn and Johanna Kantola (eds.), *Changing State Feminism.* Basingstoke: Palgrave Macmillan, pp. 164–81.

Gunter, Michael M. 2004. *Building the Next Arc: How NGOs Work to Protect Biodiversity.* Hanover, NH: Dartmouth College Press.

Gutmann, Amy and Dennis Thompson 1996. *Democracy and Disagreement.* Cambridge, MA: Harvard University Press.

Habermas, Jürgen 1962. *Strukturwandel der Öffentlichkeit. Untersuchungen zu einer Kategorie der bürgerlichen Gesellschaft.* Neuwied: Luchterhand.

―――― 1989 [1962]. *Structural Transformation of the Public Sphere.* Cambridge, MS: MIT Press.

―――― 1992. "Further Reflections on the Public Sphere," in Craig Calhoun (ed.), *Habermas and the Public Sphere.* Cambridge, MA: MIT Press, pp. 421–461.

―――― 1996. *Between Facts and Norms: Contributions to a Discourse Theory of Law and Democracy.* Cambridge, MA: MIT Press.

―――― 1998. "Does Europe Need a Constitution? A Response to Dieter Grimm" in Jürgen Habermas, *The Inclusion of the Other.* Cambridge: Polity Press, pp. 155–161.

———— 2006. "Political Communication in Media Society: Does Democracy Still Enjoy an Epistemic Dimension?" *Communication Theory* 16 (4): 411–26.

Hale, Matthew 2007. "Superficial Friends: A Content Analysis of Nonprofit and Philanthropy Coverage in Nine Major Newspapers," *Nonprofit and Voluntary Sector Quarterly* 36 (3), 465–86.

Hammack, David C. and Helmuth K. Anheier 2010. "American Foundations: Their Role and Contributions to Society," in Helmuth K. Anheier and David C. Hammack (eds.), *American Foundations: Roles and Contributions.* Washington, DC: Brookings Institution Press, pp. 3–27.

Harwood Institute for Public Innovation 2009. *The Organization – First Approach.* Bethesda, MD: Harwood Institute.

Haus, Michael 2005. "Zivilgesellschaft und soziales Kapital im städtischen Raum." *Aus Politik und Zeitgeschichte* 3: 25–31.

Haus, Michael and Hubert Heinelt (eds.) 2002. *Bürgergesellschaft, soziales Kapital und lokale Politik.* Opladen: Leske+Budrich.

Haus, Michael, Heinelt, Hubert, and Murray Stewart (eds.) 2005. *Urban Governance and Democracy: Leadership and Community Involvement.* London: Routledge.

Hauser, Gerard A. 2001. "Prisoners of Conscience and the Counterpublic Sphere of Prison Writing," in Robert Asen and Daniel C. Brouwer (eds.), *Counterpublics and the State.* Albany: State University of New York Press, pp. 35–58.

Havel, Václav 1985. "The Power of the Powerless," in Václav Havel (ed.), *The Power of the Powerless: Citizens against the State in Central-Eastern Europe.* Armonk, NY: M. E. Sharpe.

Heins, Volker 2008. *Nongovernmental Organizations in International Society: Struggles over Recognition.* New York: Palgrave MacMillan.

Helfferich, Barbara and Felix Kolb 2001. "Multilevel Action Coordination in European Contentious Politics," in Douglas R. Imig and Sidney Tarrow (eds.), *Contentious Europeans. Protest and Politics in an Emerging Polity.* Lanham: Rowman & Littlefield, pp. 143–62.

Hellmuth, Eckhart 1990. *The Transformation of Political Culture: England and Germany in the Late 18th Century.* London: Oxford University Press.

Hemment, Julie 2004. "The Riddle of the Third Sector: Civil Society, International Aid, and NGOs in Russia." *Anthropological Quarterly* 77 (2): 215–41.

———— 2007. *Empowering Women in Russia: Activism, Aid, and NGOs.* Bloomington: Indiana University Press.

Henderson, Sarah L. 2003. *Building Democracy in Contemporary Russia: Western Support for Grassroots Organizations.* Ithaca: Cornell University Press.

Herbst, Susan 1996. "Public Expression outside the Mainstream." *Annals of the American Academy of Political and Social Science* 546: 120–31.

Hertel, Shareen 2006. *Unexpected Power. Conflict and Change among Transnational Activists.* Ithaca: Cornell University Press.

Herzog, Hanna 2008. "Re/visioning the Women's Movement in Israel." *Citizenship Studies* 12 (3): 265–82.

Hill, Toni 2004. "Three Generations of UN-Civil Society Relations." *UN Non-Governmental Liaison Service.* http://www.globalpolicy.org/component/content/article/177/31824.html (accessed February 2, 2010).

Hirsch, Joachim 2001. "Des Staates neue Kleider. NGOs im Prozess der Internationalisierung des Staates," in Ulrich Brand, Alex Demirovic, and Christoph Görg (eds.), *Nichtregierungsorganisationen in der Transformation des Staates.* Münster: Westfälisches Dampfboot, pp. 13–42.

Hirschman, Albert O. 1970. *Exit, Voice, and Loyalty: Responses to Decline in Firms, Organizations, and States.* Cambridge, MA: Harvard University Press.

Holli, Anne Maria and Johanna Kantola 2007. "State Feminism Finnish Style: Strong Policies Clash with Implementation," in Joyce Outshoorn and Johanna Kantola (eds.), *Changing State Feminism.* Basingstoke: Palgrave Macmillan, pp. 82–101.

Hölscher, Lucian 1979. *Öffentlichkeit und Geheimnis. Eine begriffsgeschichtliche Untersuchung zur Entstehung der Öffentlichkeit in der frühen Neuzeit.* Stuttgart: Klett-Cotta.

Hooghe, Marc and Dietlind Stolle 2003. *Generating Social Capital: Civil Society and Institutions in Comparative Perspective.* New York: Palgrave Macmillan.

Hopgood, Stephen 2006. *Keepers of the Flame: Understanding Amnesty International.* Ithaca: Cornell University Press.

Hoskyns, Catherine 1996. *Integrating Gender, Women, Law and Politics in the European Union.* London: Verso.

Howell, Jude 2007. "Gender and Civil Society: Time for Cross-Border Dialogue." *Social Politics* 14 (4): 415–36.

Hudock, Ann C. 1999. *NGOs and Civil Society: Democracy by Proxy?* Cambridge: Polity Press.

Hudson, Allan 2002. "Advocacy by UK-Based Development NGOs." *Nonprofit and Voluntary Sector Quarterly* 13: 402–18.

Hulme, David and Michael Edwards (eds.) 1997. *NGOs, States, and Donors: Too Close for Comfort?* New York: St. Martin's Press.

Huntington, Samuel 1982. *American Politics.* Cambridge, MA: Harvard University Press.

Imig, Douglas and Sidney Tarrow (eds.) 2001. *Contentious Europeans: Protest and Politics in an Emerging Polity.* Lanham: Rowman & Littlefield.

Incite 2007. *The Revolution Will Not Be Funded: Beyond the Non-Profit Industrial Complex.* Cambridge: South End Press.

Inglehart, Ronald 1977. *The Silent Revolution: Changing Values and Political Styles among Western Publics.* Princeton, NJ: Princeton University Press.

International Center for Not-for-Profit Law 2009. "Global Trends in NGO Law." *Review* 1 (1): 1–13.

International Center for Not-for-Profit Law 2009. "Political Activities of NGOs: International Law and Best Practice." *International Journal of Not-for-Profit Law* 12 (1). http://www.icnl.org/knowledge/ijnl/vol12iss1/index.htm (accessed June 24, 2011).

Jacobs, Ronald N. and Daniel J. Glass 2002. "Media Publicity and the Voluntary Sector: The Case of Nonprofit Organizations in New York City." *Volunteers:*

International Journal of Voluntary and Nonprofit Organizations 13 (3): 235–52.

Jaeger, Hans-Martin 2007. "'Global Civil Society' and Political Depoliticization." *International Political Sociology* 1 (3): 257–77.

Jenkins, Craig J. 1983. "Resource Mobilization Theory and the Study of Social Movements." *Annual Review of Sociology* 18: 161–85.

———. 2006. "Nonprofit Organizations and Political Advocacy," in Walter W. Powell and Richard Steinberg (eds.), *The Non Profit Sector: A Research Handbook*. New Haven: Yale University Press, pp. 307–32.

Jenkins, Craig J. and Craig M. Eckert 1986. "Channeling Black Insurgency: Elite Patronage and Professional Social Movement Organizations in the Development of the Black Movement." *American Sociological Review* 51: 812–29.

Jenson, Jane 2008. "Writing Women out, Folding Gender in: The European Union 'Modernises' Social Policy." *Social Politics* 15 (2): 131–53.

Joachim, Jutta 2007. *Agenda Setting: The UN, and NGOs*. Washington, DC: Georgetown University Press.

Johns, Gary 2003. *The NGO Challenge: Whose Democracy Is It Anyway? Non-Governmental Organisations: The Growing Power of the Unelected Few*. Presented at an American Enterprise Institute Conference, Washington, DC.

Johns Hopkins Comparative Non-Profit Project 2000. *2000 National Survey of Giving, Volunteering and Participating*. Baltimore: Johns Hopkins.

Jönsson, Christer and Jonas Tallberg (eds.) 2010. *Transnational Actors in Global Governance: Patterns, Explanations, and Implications*. Basingstoke: Palgrave.

Jordan, Lisa and Peter van Tuijl (eds.) 2006. *NGO Accountability: Politics, Principles and Innovations*. London: Earthscan.

Kaldor, Mary 2003a. *Global Civil Society: An Answer to War*. London: Polity Press.

———. 2003b. "The Idea of a Global Civil Society." *International Affairs* 79: 583–93.

Kant, Immanuel 1996 [1795]. *Practical Philosophy*, edited by Mary J. Gregor. Cambridge: Cambridge University Press.

Kantola, Johanna 2008. "Domesticated Actors: Institutionalizing Gender Policy in the European Union." Unpublished paper for ECPR Joint Sessions, Rennes.

Kantola, Johanna and Joyce Outshoorn (eds.) 2007. *Changing State Feminism*. London: Palgrave Macmillan 2007.

Kantor, Paul and H. V. Savitch 2005. "How to Study Comparative Urban Development Politics: A Research Note." *International Journal of Urban and Regional Research* 29 (1): 135–51.

Katzenstein, Mary Feinsod 1998. "Stepsisters: Feminist Movement Activism in Different Institutional Spaces," in David S. Meyer and Sidney G. Tarrow (eds.), *The Social Movement Society: Contentious Politics for a New Century*. Lanham: Rowman & Littlefield, pp. 195–216.

———. 2010. "Protest Movements inside Institutions," in Mona Lena Krook and Sarah Childs (eds.), *Women, Gender, and Politics: A Reader*. New York: Oxford University Press, pp. 47–54.

Keane, John 1988. *Democracy and Civil Society*. London: Verso.

———— 2003. *Global Civil Society*. Cambridge: Cambridge University Press.

Keck, Margaret and Kathryn Sikkink 1998. *Activists beyond Borders: Advocacy Networks in International Politics*. Ithaca: Cornell University Press.

Kennedy, Baroness Helena, Brian Lamb, Francesca Quint, and Greg Clark 2007. "Campaigning: How Far Can You Go down the Political Route?" *Third Sector*, November 21. http://www.thirdsector.co.uk/news/Article/767936/campaigning-far-go-down-political-route (accessed October 13, 2011).

Keystone 2010. *Keystone Accountability 2004–2009: Public Report*. http://www.keystoneaccountability.org/node/365 (accessed April 1, 2008).

Khagram, Sanjeev, James Riker, and Kathryn Sikkink (eds.) 2002. *Restructuring World Politics. Transnational Social Movements, Networks, and Norms*. Minneapolis: University of Minnesota Press.

Kirkpatrick, Owen L. 2007. "The Two 'Logics' of Community Development: Neighborhoods, Markets, and Community Development Corporations." *Politics & Society* 35 (2): 329–59.

Klas, Gerhard 2005. "Kein Geld mehr für kritische NGOs." *Heise Online News Dienst*, December 9. http://www.heise.de/tp/artikel/21/21524/html (accessed March 4, 2010).

Klausen, Jan Erling and David Sweeting 2005. "Legitimacy and Community Involvement in Local Governance," in Michael Haus, Hubert Heinelt, and Murray Stewart (eds.), *Urban Governance and Democracy: Leadership and Community Involvement*. London: Routledge, pp. 214–33.

Klein, Ansgar, Heike Walk, and Achim Brunnengräber 2005. "Mobile Herausforderer und alternative Eliten. NGOs als Hoffnungstraeger einer demokratischen Globalisierung," in Achim Brunnengräber, Ansgar Klein, and Heike Walk (eds.), *NGOs im Prozess der Globalisierung*. Bonn: Bundeszentrale für politische Bildung, pp. 10–77.

Klein, Naomi 1999. *No Logo: Taking Aim at the Brand Bullies*. New York: Picador.

Klitsounova, Elena 2008. *Promoting Human Rights in Russia by Supporting NGOs: How to Improve EU Strategies*. CEPS Working Document (287). http://www.ceps.eu 4/2009 (accessed April 1, 2008).

Knutsen, Wenjue Lu and Ralph S. Brower 2010. "Managing Expressive and Instrumental Accountabilities in Nonprofit and Voluntary Organizations: A Qualitative Investigation." *Nonprofit and Voluntary Sector Quarterly* 39 (4): 588–610.

Koch-Mehrin, Silvana 2005. "Open Letter to the Members of the European Parliament." http://www.koch-mehrin.de (accessed March 17, 2010).

Kocka, Jürgen 2006. "Civil Society in Historical Perspective," in John Keane (ed.), *Civil Society: Berlin Perspectives*. New York: Berghahn Publishers.

Koehler, Bettina and Markus Wissen 2003. "Glocalizing Protest: Urban Conflicts and the Global Social Movements." *International Journal of Urban and Regional Research* 27 (4): 942–51.

Kohler-Koch, Beate 1996. "Catching up with Change: The Transformation of Governance in the European Union." *Journal of European Politics* 3 (3): 359–80.

———— 1998. "European Networks and Ideas: Changing National Policies?" *European Integration* 6 (6). http://ssrn.com/abstract=307519 (accessed May 13, 2011).

Kohler-Koch, Beate and Vanessa Buth 2011. "Der Spagat der europäischen Zivilgesellschaft – zwischen Professionalität und Bürgernähe," in Beate Kohler-Koch and Christine Quittkat (eds.), *Die Entzauberung partizipativer Demokratie. Zur Rolle der Zivilgesellschaft bei der Demokratisierung von EU-Governance.* Frankfurt a.M.: Campus, pp. 167–210.

Kohler-Koch, Beate and Christine Quittkat (eds.) 2011. *Die Entzauberung partizipativer Demokratie. Zur Rolle der Zivilgesellschaft bei der Demokratisierung von EU-Governance.* Frankfurt a.M.: Campus.

Koopmans, Ruud 1993. "The Dynamics of Protest Waves: West Germany, 1965 to 1989." *American Sociological Review* 585: 637–58.

Koopmans, Ruud and Paul Statham (eds.) 2010. *The Making of a European Public Sphere.* Cambridge: Cambridge University Press.

Koslowski, Rey and Antje Wiener 2002. "Practicing Democracy Transnationally," in Yale H. Ferguson and Barry R. J. Jones (eds.), *Political Space: Frontiers of Change and Governance in a Globalizing World.* Albany: State University of New York Press, pp. 281–96.

Krehely, Jeff 2001. "Assessing the Current Data on 501(c)(3) Advocacy: What IRS Form 990 Can Tell Us," in Elizabeth J. Reid and Maria D. Montilla (eds.), *Exploring Organizations and Advocacy.* Washington, DC: Urban Institute. http://www.urban.org/pdfs/org_advocacy.pdf (accessed July 10, 2009).

Kriesi, Hanspeter 1996. "The Organizational Structure of New Social Movements in a Political Context," in Doug McAdam, John D. McCarthy, and Mayer N. Zald (eds.), *Comparative Perspectives on Social Movements.* New York: Cambridge University Press, pp. 152–84.

Krizsan, Andrea and Violetta Zentai 2006. "Gender Equality Policy or Gender Mainstreaming: The Case of Hungary." *Policy Studies* 27 (2): 135–51.

Kuhl, Mara 2003. *Gender Mainstreaming and the Women's Movement.* Presented at "Gender and Power in the New Europe," Lund, August 20–23.

Landes, Joan B. 1998. "The Public and the Private Sphere: A Feminist Reconsideration," in Joan B. Landes (ed.), *Feminism, the Public and the Private.* New York: Oxford University Press, pp. 135–63.

Lane, Jan-Erik 2008. *Globalization – The Juggernaut of the 21st Century.* Aldershot: Ashgate Publishing.

Lang, Sabine 1997. "The NGOization of Feminism," in Joan W. Scott, Cora Kaplan, and Deborah Keates (eds.), *Transitions, Environments, Translations: Feminisms in International Politics.* London: Routledge, pp. 101–20.

———— 1999. NGOs and Local Government Communication – Data from Four European Countries. Unpublished manuscript.

———— 2000. "The NGOization of Feminism: Institutionalization and Institution Building within the German Women's Movements," in Bonnie G. Smith (ed.), *Global Feminisms since 1945.* New York: Routledge, pp. 290–304.

———— 2001. *Politische Öffentlichkeit im modernen Staat.* Baden-Baden: Nomos.

———— 2003. "Local Political Communication and Citizen Participation," in Philippe Maarek and Gadi Wolfsfeld (eds.), *Political Communication in a New Era – A Cross-National Perspective*. London: Routledge, pp. 171–92.

———— 2004. "The State of Local Publics – Media and Communication in the Age of Globalization," in Wolfram Esser and Barbara Pfetsch (eds.), *Comparing Political Communication: Theories, Cases, and Challenges*. New York: Cambridge University Press, pp. 151–83.

———— 2007. "Gender in Post-Unification Germany: Between Institutionalization, Deregulation, and Privatization," in Joyce Outshoorn and Johanna Kantola (eds.), *Changing State Feminism*. Basingstoke: Palgrave Macmillan, pp. 124–43.

———— 2009a. "Gendering a European Public Sphere? Transnational Women's Advocacy Networks in the European Union," in Inaki Blanco and Bart Cammaerts (eds.), *Media Agoras: Democracy, Diversity and Communication*. London: Routledge, pp. 198–219.

———— 2009b. "Assessing Advocacy: European Transnational Women's Networks and Gender Mainstreaming." *Social Politics* 16 (3): 327–57.

———— 2009c. Coverage of NGOs in the Fields of Urban Development and Women's Issues in National Newspapers. Unpubl.

———— 2013. "Women's Advocacy Networks: The European Union, Women's NGOs, and the Velvet Triangle," in Inderpal Grewal and Victoria Bernal (eds.), *The NGO Form: Feminist Struggles, States and Neoliberalism*. Durham: Duke University Press (forthcoming).

Levy, Jonah D. 1999. *Tocqueville's Revenge: State, Society, and Economy in Contemporary France*. Cambridge, MA: Harvard University Press.

Lewis, Stephen 2006a. "Speech at Harvard Law School," February 26. Unpublished manuscript.

———— 2006b. "Remarks to a High Level Panel on UN Reform," Geneva. http://www.sarpn.org/documents/d0002065/index.php (accessed June 12, 2008).

Liebert, Ulrike 2002. "Europeanizing Gender Mainstreaming. Constraints and Opportunities in the Multi-Level Euro-Polity." *Feminist Legal Studies* 10: 241–56.

Lippmann, Walter 1925 [1993]. *The Phantom Public*. New Brunswick: Transaction Publishers.

Lipschutz, Ronnie D. (ed.) 2006. *Civil Societies and Social Movements. Domestic, Transnational, Global*. Aldershot: Ashgate.

Lipschutz, Ronnie D. and James K. Rowe 2005. *Globalization, Governmentality and Global Politics: Regulation for the Rest of Us?* London: Routledge.

Lofland, John 1996. *Social Movement Organizations: Guide to Research on Insurgent Realities*. New Brunswick: Aldine Transaction.

Lombardo, Emanuela 2005. "Integrating or Setting the Agenda? Gender Mainstreaming in the European Constitution-Making Process." *Social Politics* 12 (3): 412–32.

Lombardo, Emanuela and Petra Meier 2008. "Framing Gender Equality in the European Union Political Discourse." *Social Politics* 15 (1): 101–29.

Lowndes, Valerie, Garry Stroker, and Louis Pratchett, 1998. *Enhancing Participation in Local Government.* London: Department of the Environment, Transport and the Regions.

MacDonald, Laura 2005. "Gendering Transnational Social Movement Analysis: Women's Groups Contest Free Trade in the Americas," in Joe Brandy and Jackie Smith (eds.), *Coalition across Borders: Transnational Protest and the Liberal Order.* Lanham: Rowman & Littlefield, pp. 21–42.

MacPherson, Crawford B. 1971. *Democratic Theory. Essays in Retrieval.* Oxford: Clarendon Press.

Maloney, William A., Graham Smith, and Gerry Stroker 2000. "Social Capital and Associational Life," in Stephen Baron, John Field, and Tom Schuller (eds.), *Social Capital: Critical Perspectives.* Oxford: Oxford University Press, pp. 212–25.

Mansbridge, Jane J. 1983. *Beyond Adversary Democracy.* Chicago: University of Chicago Press.

Marksova-Tominova, M. 2006. "Die Koalition KARAT: Ein Zusammenschluss von Frauenorganisatonen der ehemaligen sozialistischen Länder." *Femina politica* 15 (1): 115–17.

Marschall, Miklos 2002. "Legitimacy and Effectiveness: Civil Society Organizations." Presented at "Contribution to Poverty Reduction Strategies Forum," Baden, Austria, October 29–November 1. http://www.info.worldbank.org/etools/docs/.../3pl_marchel_speeech_eng.doc (accessed December 19, 2011).

Martens, Kerstin 2005. *NGOs and the United Nations: Institutionalization, Professionalization, and Adaptation.* New York: Palgrave.

———— 2006. "Institutionalizing Societal Activism within Global Governance Structures: Amnesty International and the United Nations System." *Journal of International Relations and Development* 9: 371–95.

Martin, Deborah G. 2004. "Nonprofit Foundations and Grassroots Organizing: Reshaping Urban Governance." *Professional Geographer* 56 (3): 394–405.

Mathews, Jessica T. 1997. "Power Shift." *Foreign Affairs* 76 (1): 50–66.

Mattson, Kevin 1998. *Creating a Democratic Public: The Struggle for Urban Participatory Democracy during the Progressive Era.* University Park: Pennsylvania State University Press.

Maxwell, Michael P. 2006. "NGOs in Russia: Is the Recent Russian NGO Legislation the End of Civil Society in Russia?" *Tulane Journal of International and Comparative Law* 15 (10): 235–63.

Mayer, Lloyd H. 2011. *Charities and Lobbying: Institutional Rights in the Wake of Citizen United.* Notre Dame Law School Legal Studies Research Paper No. 10–39. Notre Dame University.

Mayer, Margit 2003. "The Onward Sweep of Social Capital: Causes and Consequences for Understanding Cities, Communities and Urban Movements." *International Journal of Urban and Regional Research* 27 (1): 110–32.

Mayntz, Renate 1998. "New Challenges to Governance Theory," in Renate Mayntz, *Über Governance. Institutionen und Prozesse politischer Regelung.* Frankfurt, a. M.: Campus, pp. 13–28.

Mazey, Sonia 1998. "The European Union and Women's Rights. From the Europeanization of National Agendas to the Nationalization of a European Agenda?" *Journal of European Public Policy* 5 (1): 131–52.

——— 2002. "Gender Mainstreaming Strategies in the E.U.: Delivering on an Agenda?" *Feminist Legal Studies* 10: 227–40.

McAdam, Doug and Richard W. Scott 2005. "Organizations and Movements," in Gerald F. Davis, Doug McAdam, Richard W. Scott, and Mayer N. Zald (eds.), *Social Movements and Organization Theory*. New York: Cambridge University Press, pp. 4–40.

McAdam, Doug, Sidney Tarrow, and Charles Tilly 2001. *Dynamics of Contention*. Cambridge: Cambridge University Press.

McCann, Michael 1994. *Rights at Work*. Chicago: University of Chicago Press.

McDonald, John W. 2004. "A View from Another World – The Policymaker's Perspective," in Mari Fitzduff and Cheyanne Church (eds.), *NGOs at the Table: Strategies for Influencing Policies in Areas of Conflict*. Lanham: Rowman & Littlefied, pp. xi–xvii.

McFalls, Lawrence 2007. *A Matter of Life and Death: Iatrogenic Violence and the Formal Logic of International Intervention*. Center for the Study of Global Politics, Working Paper. Ontario: Trent University.

Media Matters for America 2009. "CBS, Fox Reports on Town Hall Disruptions Ignore Conservative Strategy," August 5. http://mediamatters.org/research/200908050017 (accessed November 9, 2011).

Meier, Petra 2006. "Implementing Gender Equality: Gender Mainstreaming or the Gap between Theory and Practice," in Sirkku Hellsten, Anne Maria Holli, and Krassimira Daskalova (eds.), *Women's Citizenship and Political Rights*. New York: Palgrave Macmillan, pp. 179–98.

Mendelson, Sarah E. and John K. Glenn (eds.) 2002. *The Power and Limits of NGOs*. New York: Columbia University Press.

Meyer, John W. and Brian Rowan 1977. "Institutionalized Organizations: Formal Structure as Myth and Ceremony." *American Journal of Sociology* 83 (2): 340–63.

Meyer, Marshall and Craig M. Brown 1977. "The Process of Bureaucratization." *American Journal of Sociology* 83 (2): 364–85.

Migdal, Joel 2001. *State in Society*. New York: Cambridge University Press.

Mill, John Stuart 1998 [1861]. "Considerations on Representative Government," in John Stuart Mill, *On Liberty and Other Essays*. Oxford: Oxford University Press, pp. 203–467.

Millns, Susan 2007. "Gender Equality, Citizenship, and the EU's Constitutional Future." *European Law Journal* 13 (2): 218–37.

Mills, C. Wright 1959. *The Sociological Imagination*. New York: Oxford University Press.

Minkoff, Deborah 1997. "Sequencing of Social Movements." *American Sociological Review*, 62: 779–99.

——— 2001. "Producing Social Capital. National Social Movements and Civil Society," in Bob Edwards, Michael W. Foley and Mario Diani (eds.), *Beyond Tocqueville: Civil Society and the Social Capital Debate in Comparative Perspective*. Boston: University Press of New England, pp. 183–93.

Minkoff, Deborah and Jon Agnone 2010. "Consolidating Social Change: The Consequences of Foundation Funding for Developing Social Movement Infrastructure," in Helmuth K. Anheier and David C. Hammack (eds.), *American Foundations: Roles and Contributions*. Washington: Brookings Institution Press, pp. 347–67.

Minkoff, Deborah and John D. McCarthy 2005. "Reinvigorating the Study of Organizational Processes in Social Movements." *Mobilization* 10 (2): 289–308.

Minkoff, Deborah and Walter W. Powell 2006. "Nonprofit Mission: Constancy, Responsiveness, or Deflection?" in Walter W. Powell and Richard Steinberg (eds.), *The Non Profit Sector: A Research Handbook*. New Haven: Yale University Press, pp. 591–611.

Minnix, Chris 2007. "Global Humanitarianism: NGOs and the Crafting of Community." *Rhetoric & Public Affairs*, 10 (1): 157–9.

Mitra, Aditi 2009. "Feminist Organizing in India: A Study of Women in NGOs." *Women's Studies International Forum* 34: 66–75.

Moghadam, Valentine M. 2000. "Transnational Feminist Networks: Collective Action in an Era of Globalization." *International Sociology* 15: 57–85.

_____ 2005. *Globalizing Women: Transnational Feminist Networks*. Baltimore: Johns Hopkins University Press.

Montoya, Celeste 2008. "The European Union, Capacity Building, and Transnational Networks: Combating Violence against Women through the Daphne Program." *International Organizations* 62 (2): 359–72.

Moore, David, Katerina Hadzi-Miceva, and Nilda Bullain 2008. "A Comparative Overview of Public Benefit Status in Europe." *International Journal of Not-for-Profit Law* 11 (1): 5–35.

Morena, Edouard 2006. "Funding and the Future of the Global Justice Movement." *Development* 49 (2): 29–33.

Morris, Trevor and Simon Goldsworthy 2008. *PR: A Persuasive Industry*. Houndmills: Palgrave Macmillan.

Morrison, J. Bart and Paul Salipante 2007. "Governance for Broadened Accountability: Blending Deliberate and Emergent Strategizing." *Nonprofit and Voluntary Sector Quarterly* 36 (2): 195–217.

Mouffe, Chantal 2005. *On the Political: Thinking in Action*. London: Verso.

Mumford, Lewis 1961. *The City in History: Its Origins, Its Transformations, and Its Prospects*. San Diego: Harcourt Brace and Company.

Mutz, Diana 2006. *Hearing the Other Side: Deliberative versus Participatory Democracy*. New York: Cambridge University Press.

Nanz, Patricia 2006. *Europolis: Constitutional Patriotism beyond the Nation-State*. Manchester: Manchester University Press.

Nanz, Patricia and Jens Steffek 2004. "Global Governance, Participation and the Public Sphere." *Government and Opposition* 29 (2): 314–343.

"National Briefing. West California: Missile Protesters Plead Guilty." 2002. *New York Times*, January 10.

Norman Lear Center 2009. "The Effectiveness and Value of Celebrity Diplomacy." Panel Discussion at the USC Annenberg School for Communication, April 21. http://www.learcenter.org/pdf/celebritydiplomacy.pdf (accessed December 4, 2011).

North, Douglass C. 1990. *Institutions, Institutional Change and Economic Performance*. New York: Cambridge University Press.

Norwegian Agency for Development Cooperation (NORAD) 2004. *Study of the Impact of the Work of Save the Children in Ethiopia: Building Civil Society*. Evaluation Report Prepared by the Chr. Michelsen Institute. http://www.norad.no/default.asp?V_ITEM_ID=2860 (accessed October 10, 2008).

Nyamugasira, Warren 1998. "NGOs and advocacy: how well are the poor represented?" *Development in Practice* 8 (3): 197–308.

O'Connell, Brian 1999. *Civil Society: The Underpinnings of American Democracy*. Hanover: University Press of New England.

O'Kelly, Ciaran 2011. "Accountability and a Theory of Representation," in Melvin J. Dubnick and George Frederickson (eds.), *Accountable Governance: Problems and Promises*. Armonk: M. E. Sharpe, pp. 255–68.

Olson, Mancur 1982. *The Rise and Decline of Nations*. New Haven: Yale University Press.

OMB Watch 2007. *Overcaution and Confusion: The Impact of Ambiguous Regulation of Political Activities by Charities and the Potential for Change*. Washington, DC: OMB Watch Reports.

Ostrander, Susan A. 2005. "Legacy and Promise for Social Justice Funding: Charitable Foundations and Progressive Social Movements, Past and Present," in Daniel R. Faber and Deborah McCarthy (eds.), *Foundations for Social Change: Critical Perspectives on Philanthropy and Popular Movements*. Lanham: Rowman & Littlefield, pp. 33–60.

Outshoorn, Joyce and Jantine Oldersma 2007. "New Politics, New Opportunities: The Women's Policy Agency in the Netherlands in the Last Decade," in Joyce Outshoorn and Johanna Kantola (eds.), *Changing State Feminism*. Basingstoke: Palgrave Macmillan, pp. 182–200.

Page, Clarence 2012. "Where Did Haiti's Aid Go?" *Chicago Tribune*, January 29. http://articles.chicagotribune.com/2012-01-29/news/ct-oped-0129-page-20120129_1_aid-agencies-organizations-camps (accessed February 13, 2012).

Painter, Genevieve 2004. *Gender Mainstreaming in Development and Trade Policy and Practice: Learning from Austria, Belgium, and the UK*. http://www.eurosur.org/wide/GM/gm–painter.htm (accessed June 12, 2010).

Pallotta, Dan 2008. *Uncharitable*. Boston: Tufts University Press.

Parliament of the Commonwealth of Australia, House of Representatives Standing Committee on Community Affairs 1991. *"You Have Your Moments": A Report on Funding of Peak Health and Community Organisations*. Canberra: Commonwealth of Australia.

Parmentier, Ramy 1999. "Greenpeace and the Dumping of Waste at Sea: A Case of Non-State Actors' Intervention in International Affairs." *International Negotiation* 4: 433–55.

Parry, Geraint, George Moyser, and Neil Day 1992. *Political Participation and Democracy in Britain*. Cambridge: Cambridge University Press.

Paterson, Lindsay 2000. "Civil Society and Democratic Renewal," in Stephen Baron, John Field, and Tom Schuller (eds.), *Social Capital: Critical Perspectives*. Oxford: Oxford University Press, pp. 39–55.

Pekkanen, Robert 2006. *Japan's Dual Civil Society: Members without Advocates.* Stanford: Stanford University Press.

Peratis, Kathleen 2006. "Diversionary Strike on a Rights Group." *Washington Post*, August 31.

Peruzzotti, Enrique 2006. "Civil Society, Representation and Accountability: Restating Current Debates on the Representativeness and Accountability of Civic Associations," in Lisa Jordan and Peter Van Tuijl (eds.), *NGO Accountability, Politics, Principles and Innovations*. London: Earthscan, pp. 43–59.

Peters, P. Guy and Jon Pierre 2004. "Multi-Level Governance and Democracy: A Faustian Bargain?," in Ian Bache and Matthew Flinders (eds.), *Multi-Level Governance*. Oxford: Oxford University Press, pp. 75–91.

Peterson, Mark A. 1992. "Interest Mobilization and the Presidency," in Mark P. Petracca (ed.), *The Politics of Interests*. Boulder: Westview Press, pp. 221–42.

Petrikova, Ivica 2007. "Too Many Bad Cooks Spoiling the Broth? Effectiveness of NGOs in Addressing Child Labor in El Salvador." *Colby College Digital Commons*. http://digitalcommons.colby.edu/honorstheses/281 (accessed March 11, 2010).

Petriwskyj, Andrea M. 2007. "Citizen Participation as Volunteering? Opportunities and Challenges for an Inclusive Definition." *Australian Journal on Volunteering* 12 (2): 82–8.

Petriwskyj, Andrea M. and Jeni Warburton 2007. "Redefining Volunteering for the Global Context: A Measurement Matrix for Researchers." *Australian Journal on Volunteering* 12 (1): 7–13.

Pettigrew, Andrew M. 1990. "Is Corporate Culture Manageable?," in David C. Wilson and Robert H. Rosenfeld (eds.), *Managing Organizations*. London: McGraw-Hill, pp. 267–72.

Phillips, Anne 1996. "Why Does Local Democracy Matter?," in Lawrence Pratchett and David Wilson (eds.), *Local Democracy and Local Government*. New York: St. Martin's Press, pp. 20–37.

Pierson, Paul 2000. "Increasing Returns, Path Dependence, and the Study of Politics." *American Political Science Review* 94 (2): 251–67.

Pitkin, Hannah 1981. "Justice: On Relating Public and Private." *Political Theory* 9 (3): 327–52.

Poletta, Francesca 2006. *It Was Like a Fever: Storytelling in Protest and Politics.* Chicago: University of Chicago Press.

Pollack, Mark A. and Emilie Hafner-Burton 2000. *Mainstreaming Gender in the European Union*. http://www.jeanmonnetprogram.org/papers/00/000201.html (accessed August 22, 2007).

Poppendieck, Janet 1998. *Sweet Charity? Emergency Food and the End of Entitlement.* New York: Penguin.

Powell, Walter W. and Richard Steinberg 2006. *The Non Profit Sector: A Research Handbook*. New Haven: Yale University Press.

Prakash, Aseem and Mary Gugerty (eds.) 2009. *Rethinking Advocacy Organizations: A Collective Action Perspective.* New York: Cambridge University Press.

Pratchett, Lawrence and David Wilson 1996. "Local Government under Siege," in Lawrence Pratchett and David Wilson (eds.), *Local Democracy and Local Government*. New York: St. Martin's Press, pp. 1–19.

Progress 2007. *Decision No. 1672/2006/EC of the European Parliament and of the Council of 10/24/2006 establishing a Community Programme for Employment and Social Solidarity – PROGRESS*. Brussels.

Pudrovska, Tetyana and Myra Marx Ferree 2004. "Global Activism in 'Virtual Space': The European Women's Lobby in the Network of Transnational Women's NGOs on the Web." *Social Politics* 11 (1): 117–43.

Putnam, Linda L., Nelson Phillips, and Pamela Chapman 2006. "Metaphors of Communication and Organization," in Stuart R. Clegg, Cynthia Hardy, and Walter R. Nord (eds.), *Handbook of Organization Studies*. London: Sage, pp. 375–408.

Putnam, Robert 1995. "Bowling Alone: America's Declining Social Capital. *The Journal of Democracy* 6 (1): 65–78.

_____ 2001. *Bowling Alone: The Collapse and Revival of American Community*. New York: Simon and Schuster.

_____ 2002. *Social Capital Community Benchmark Survey*. http://www.hks. harvard.edu/saguaro/measurement.htm (accessed September 23, 2009).

Rabkin, Jeremy 2003. "Why the Left Dominates NGO Advocacy Networks." Presented at American Enterprise Institute Conference, "Nongovernmental Organizations: The Growing Power of an Unelected Few," Washington, DC. http://www.aei.org/event/329 (accessed November 23, 2010).

Rai, Shirin 2004. "Gendering Global Governance." *International Feminist Journal of Politics* 6(4): 579–601.

Rasche, Andreas and Daniel E. Escher 2006. "From Stakeholder Management to Stakeholder Accountability: Applying Habermasian Discourse Ethics to Accountability Research." *Journal of Business Ethics* 65 (3): 251–67.

Rawls, John 1993. *Political Liberalism*. New York: Columbia University Press.

Rees, Teresa 1999. "Mainstreaming Equality," in Sophie Watson and Lesley Doyal (eds.), *Engendering Social Policy*. Buckingham: Open University Press, pp. 165–83.

_____ 2005. "Reflections on the Uneven Development of Gender Mainstreaming in Europe." *International Feminist Journal of Politics* 7 (4): 555–74.

Reid, Elizabeth J. 1999. "Nonprofit Advocacy and Political Participation," in Elizabeth T. Boris and C. E. Steuerle (eds.), *Nonprofits and Government: Collaboration and Conflict*, 2nd ed. Washington, DC: Urban Institute, pp. 291–327.

Reimann, Kim D. 2006. "A View from the Top: International Politics, Norms and the Worldwide Growth of NGOs." *International Studies Quarterly* 50 (1): 45–67.

Reimer, Sabine 2005. *Civil Society – A New Solution between State and Market?* CIVICUS Civil Society Index Report for Germany. Berlin: Maecenata Institute.

Reitzes, Maxine 1995. "How Should Civil Society Formations Relate to the Structures of Representative Government?," in Richard Humphries (ed.), *Civil*

Society after Apartheid: Proceedings of a Conference Convened by the Centre for Apartheid South Africa. Doornfontein, South Africa: Centre for Policy Studies.

Risse, Thomas 2001. "Transnational Actors and World Politics," in Walter Carlsnäs, Thomas Risse, and Beth Simmons (eds.), *Handbook of International Relations*. London: Sage, pp. 255–74.

———— 2004. "Global Governance and Communicative Action." *Government and Opposition* 39 (2): 288–313.

———— 2010. *A Community of Europeans? Transnational Identities and Public Spheres*. Ithaca: Cornell University Press.

Rogers, Richard 2004. *Information Politics on the Web*. Cambridge, MA: MIT Press.

Rolandsen Agustín, Lise 2008. "Civil Society Participation in EU Gender Policy-Making: Framing Strategies and Institutional Constraints." *Parliamentary Affairs* 61 (3): 419–25.

Rosanvallon, Pierre 2007. *The Demands of Liberty: Civil Society in France since the Revolution*. Cambridge, MA: Harvard University Press.

Ross, Steven S. 2004. *Towards New Understandings: Journalists and Humanitarian Relief Coverage*. Report for the Fritz Institute. New York: Columbia University.

Roth, Roland 1994. *Demokratie von unten. Neue soziale Bewegungen auf dem Wege zur politischen Institution*. Köln: Bund-Verlag.

———— 2005. "Transnationale Demokratie. Beiträge, Möglichkeiten und Grenzen von NGOs," in Achim Brunnengräber, Ansgar Klein, and Heike Walk (eds.), *NGOs im Prozess der Globalisierung*. Bonn: Bundeszentrale für politische Bildung, pp. 80–128.

Rothschild, Joyce and Allen J. Whitt, 1986. *The Cooperative Workplace*. Cambridge: Cambridge University Press.

Rucht, Dieter 2001. "Lobbying or Protest? Strategies to Influence EU Environmental Policies," in Douglas Imig and Sidney Tarrow (eds.), *Contentious Europeans: Protest and Politics in an Emerging Polity*. Lanham: Rowman & Littlefield, pp. 125–42.

Ryan, Mary 1992. "Gender and Public Access: Women's Politics in Nineteenth-Century America," in Craig Calhoun (ed.), *Habermas and the Public Sphere*. Cambridge, MA: MIT Press, pp. 259–88.

Salamon, Lester A. 1993. *The Global Associational Revolution*. Baltimore: Johns Hopkins University Press.

———— 1995. *Partners in Service: Government-Nonprofit Relations in the Modern Welfare State*. Baltimore: Johns Hopkins University Press.

———— 1999. *Global Civil Society: Dimensions of the Nonprofit Sector*. Baltimore: Johns Hopkins Institute for Policy Studies.

Salamon, Lester A., Helmut K. Anheier, and Regina List 1999. "Civil Society in a Comparative Perspective," in Lester M. Salamon, Helmut K. Anheier, Regina List, Stefan Toepler, S. Wojciech Sokolowski, and Associates, *Global Civil Society, Dimensions of the Nonprofit Sector*. Baltimore: Johns Hopkins Comparative Nonprofit Sector Project, pp. 3–39.

Salamon, Lester A. and Stephanie Lessans Gellner 2008. *Nonprofit America: A Force for Democracy?* Communique No. 9, July 30. Baltimore: Johns Hopkins University Center for Civil Society Studies.

Santoro, Wayne A. and Gail M. McGuire, 1997. "Social Movement Insiders: The Impact of Institutional Activists on Affirmative Action and Comparable Worth Policies." *Social Problems* 44 (4): 502–19.

Sauer, Birgit 2007. "What Happened to the Model Student? Austrian State Feminism since the Mid-1990s," in Joyce Outshoorn and Johanna Kantola (eds.), *Changing State Feminism*. Basingstoke: Palgrave Macmillan, pp. 41–61.

Sawer, Marian 2002. "Governing of the Mainstream: Implications for Community Representation." *Australian Journal of Public Administration* 61 (1): 39–49.

Scambler, Graham (ed.) 2001. *Habermas, Critical Theory, and Health*. London: Routledge.

Schmitter, Phillippe 1969. "Three Neofunctional Hypotheses about International Integration." *International Organization* 23 (1): 61–6.

Schnur, Olaf (ed.) 2008. *Quartiersforschung zwischen Theorie und Praxis*. Wiesbaden: VS Verlag.

Schudson, Michael 1998. *The Good Citizen: A History of American Civic Life*. Cambridge, MA: Harvard University Press.

Scott, Joan W. 1988. *Gender and the Politics of History*. New York: Columbia University Press.

Searle, Denise 2009. "Blogging or Flocking? Why NGOs Face Challenges in Embracing the Internet's Potential." *NGOs and the News*. Harvard University Nieman Journalism Lab Special Report. http://www.nieman.harvard.edu (accessed March 3, 2010).

Sell, Susan K. and Aseem Prakash 2004. "Using Ideas Strategically: The Contest between Business and NGO Networks in Intellectual Property Rights." *International Studies Quarterly* 48:143–75.

Sellers, Jeffery M. 2002. *Governing from Below: Urban Regions and the Global Economy*. New York: Cambridge University Press.

Sending, Ole Jacob and Iver B. Neumann 2006. "Governance to Governmentality: Analyzing NGOs, States, and Power." *International Studies Quarterly* 50 (3): 651–72.

Sholkwer, Nikita 2009. "Andreas Schockenhoff: Es ist Zeit, mit den russischen NGO auf Augenhöhe zu reden." *Deutsche Welle*, Russian Version, May 5.

Silliman, Jael 1999. "Expanding Civil Society: Shrinking Political Spaces – The Case of Women's Nongovernmental Organizations." *Social Politics* 1: 23–53.

Sirianni, Carmen and Lewis Friedland 2001. *Civic Innovation in America*. Berkeley: University of California Press.

Skocpol, Theda 1996. "What Tocqueville Missed: Government Made All That 'Volunteerism' Possible." *Slate Magazine Online*, November 15. http://www.slate.com/id/2081 (accessed October 24, 2008).

———— 1999a. "Advocates without Members: The Recent Transformation of American Civic Life," in Theda Skocpol and Morris P. Fiorina (eds.), *Civic*

Engagement in American Democracy. Washington, DC: Brookings Institution Press and Russell Sage Foundation, pp. 461–509.

———— 1999b. "Associations without Members." *American Prospect.* http://www.prospect.org/cs/articles?article=associations_without_members access (accessed August 16, 2009).

———— 1999c. "How Americans Became Civic," in Theda Skocpol and Morris P. Fiorina (eds.), *Civic Engagement in American Democracy.* Washington, DC: Brookings Institution Press and Russell Sage Foundation, pp. 27–80.

———— 2003. *Diminished Democracy.* Norman: University of Oklahoma Press.

Skrentny, John David 2003. *The Minority Rights Revolution.* Cambridge, MA: Harvard University Press.

Skvortsova, Anna 2007. *NGOs in Russia.* Information and Analyses Center for Social and Health NGOs. http://www.hse.fi/NR/rdonlyres/D40BF349--2AE2--4CF1--B75F-0B5898755AE5/6104/PresentationAS2_102 007Skvortsova.pdf (accessed February 1, 2009).

Smismans, Stijn 2006a. "Civil Society and European Governance: From Concepts To Research Agenda," in Stijn Smismans (ed.), *Civil Society and Legitimate European Governance.* Cheltenham: Elgar Publishing, pp. 3–22.

———— 2006b. *New Modes of Governance and the Participatory Myth.* Eurogov European Governance Papers No N-06-01. http://www.connex-network.org/eurogov/pdf/egp-newgov-N-06-01.pdf (accessed April 14, 2009).

Smith, Andrea 2007. "The NGOization of Palestine," in Incite (ed.), *The Revolution Will Not Be Funded: Beyond the Non-Profit Industrial Complex.* Cambridge: South End Press, pp. 165–184.

Smith, Anna Marie 2007. *Welfare Reform and Sexual Regulation.* Cambridge: Cambridge University Press.

Smith, Steven Rathgeb 1999. "Government Financing of Nonprofit Activity," in Elizabeth T. Boris and C. E. Steuerle (eds.), *Nonprofits and Government: Collaboration and Conflict,* 2nd ed. Washington, DC: Urban Institute, pp. 177–211.

Smith, Steven Rathgeb and Kirsten A. Gronbjerg 2006. "Scope and Theory of Government-Nonprofit Relations," in Walter W. Powell and Richard Steinberg (eds.), *The Non Profit Sector: A Research Handbook.* New Haven: Yale University Press, pp. 221–42.

Smith, Steven Rathgeb and Michael Lipsky 1993. *Nonprofits for Hire: The Welfare State in the Age of Contracting.* Cambridge, MA: Harvard University Press.

Somers, Margret 1995. "Narrating and Naturalizing Civil Society and Citizenship Theory: The Place of Political Culture and the Public Sphere." *Sociological Theory* 13 (3): 229–74.

Sooryamoorthy, R. and K. D. Gangrade 2001. *NGOs in India: A Cross Sectional Study.* Westport: Greenwood Press.

Spiro, Peter J. 2007. "Non-Governmental Organizations and Civil Society," in Daniel Bodansky, Jutta Brunner and Ellen Hey (eds.), *Oxford Handbook of International Environmental Law.* New York: Oxford University Press, pp. 770–90.

Splichal, Slavko 2002. *Principles of Publicity and Press Freedom.* Lanham: Rowman & Littlefield.

Squires, Judith 2005. "Is Mainstreaming Transformative? Theorizing Mainstreaming in the Context of Diversity and Deliberation." *Social Politics* 12 (3): 366–88.

―――― 2007. *The New Politics of Gender Equality.* Basingstoke: Palgrave Macmillan.

Stadt Leipzig 2005. *Statusreport zur Lokalen Demokratiebilanz.* Leipzig.

Staggenborg, Suzanne 1988. "The Consequences of Professionalization and Formalization in the Pro-Choice Movement." *American Sociological Review* 53 (4): 585–606.

Staples, Joan 2008. "What Future for the NGO Sector?" *Dissent* 25: 15–18.

―――― 2007. *NGOs out in the Cold: Howard Government Policy towards NGOs.* University of South Wales Faculty of Law Research Series; Democratic Audit of Australia, Discussion Paper No. 19/06. http://papers.ssrn.com/sol3/papers/cfm?abstract_id=959533 (accessed August 13, 2011).

Statistics Canada 2005. *Cornerstones of Community: Highlights of the National Survey of Nonprofit and Voluntary Organizations, Ottawa.* http://www.ccss.jhu.edu/index.php?section=content&view=16&sub=91&tri=93 (accessed March 5, 2009).

Steinberg, Gerald 2009. "Human Rights NGOs Need a Monitor." *Forward*, December 30. http://forward.com/articles/122209/human-rights-ngos-need-a-monitor (accessed January 4, 2012).

Steffek, Jens 2010. "Public Accountability and the Public Sphere of International Governance." *Ethics and International Affairs* 24 (10): 45–68.

Steffek, Jens, Ralf Bendrath, Simon Dalferth, Kristina Hahn, Martina Piewitt, and Meike Rodekamp 2010. "Assessing the Democratic Legitimacy of Transnational CSOs: Five Criteria," in Jens Steffek and Kristina Hahn (eds.), *Evaluating Transnational NGOs. Legitimacy, Accountability, Representation.* London, New York: Routledge, pp. 100–25.

Steffek, Jens and Kristina Hahn (eds.) 2011. *Evaluating Transnational NGOs: Legitimacy, Accountability, Representation.* London, New York: Routledge.

Steffek, Jens and Patricia Nanz 2008. "Emergent Patterns of Civil Society Participation in Global and European Governance" In Jens Steffek, Claudia Kissling, and Patricia Nanz (eds.) *Civil Society Participation in European and Global Governance. A Cure for the Democratic Deficit?* Houndmills: Palgrave Macmillan, pp. 1–29.

Stifterverband für die deutsche Wissenschaft *et al.* 2011. *Zivilgesellschaft in Zahlen. Abschlussbericht Modul 1.* http://www.stifterverband.org/statistik_und_analysen/dritter_sektor/projektstruktur/modul_1/index.html (accessed January 28, 2012).

Stoker, Gary 1998. "Governance in Theory: Five Propositions." *International Social Science Journal* 155: 17–28.

Stolle, Dietlind and Marc Hooghe (eds.) 2003. *Generating Social Capital. Civil Society and Institutions in Comparative Perspective.* Houndmills: Palgrave.

Stolle, Dietlind and Thomas R. Rochon 1998. "Are All Associations Alike? Member Diversity, Associational Type, Capital." *American Behavioral Scientist* 4: 47–65.

Stubbs, Paul 2007. "Community Development in Contemporary Croatia: Globalisation, Neoliberalisation and NGO-isation," in Lena Dominelli (ed.), *Revitalizing Communities in a Globalising World*. Burlington: Ashgate, pp. 161–74.

SustainAbility 2003. *The 21st Century NGO: In the Market for Change*. London: SustainAbility.

Take, Ingo 1999. *NGOs as Strategic Actor in International Politics*. World Society Research Group, Working Paper No. 10. Darmstadt: Technical University Darmstadt.

Tallberg, Jonas and Christer Jönsson 2010. "Transnational Actor Participation in International Institutions: Where, Why, and with What Consequences?," in Christer Jönsson and Jonas Tallberg (eds.), *Transnational Actors in Global Governance: Patterns, Explanations, and Implications*. Basingstoke: Palgrave, pp. 1–21.

Tarrow, Sidney 1998. *Power in Movement: Social Movements and Contentious Politics*. Cambridge: Cambridge University Press.

_____ 2005. *The New Transnational Activism*. Cambridge: Cambridge University Press.

Taylor, Charles 1998. "The Dangers of Soft Despotism," in Amitai Etzioni (ed.), *The Essential Communitarian Reader*. Lanham: Rowman & Littlefield, pp. 47–54.

Tilly, Charles 1984. "Observations of Social Processes and their Formal Representations." *Sociological Theory* 22 (4): 595–602.

_____ 2007. *Democracy*. Cambridge: Cambridge University Press.

Thomson, Dale E. 2010. "Exploring the Role of Funders' Performance Reporting Mandates in Nonprofit Performance Measurement." *Nonprofit and Voluntary Sector Quarterly* 39 (4): 611–29.

Tocqueville, Alexis de 1945 [1835]. *Democracy in America*. New York: Vintage Books.

Trenz, Hans Joerg 2002. *Zur Konstitution politischer Öffentlichkeit in der EU*. Baden Baden: Nomos.

_____ 2004. "Media Coverage on European Governance: Exploring the European Public Sphere in National Quality Newspapers." *European Journal of Communication* 19 (3): 291–319.

True, Jacqui and Michael Mintrom 2001. "Transnational Networks and Policy Diffusion: The Case of Gender Mainstreaming." *International Studies Quarterly* 45: 27–57.

Union of International Organizations 2005/6. *Statistics on International Organizations 2004* http://www.uia.org/statistics/organizations/types–2004.pdf (accessed January 9, 2009).

United Nations. 1992. *Agenda 21 Charter*. http://www.un.org/esa/dsd/agenda21 (accessed June 7, 2011).

United Nations Department of Economic and Social Affairs 2010. *UN/DESA Civil Society Participation in 2009*. http://www.un–ngls.org/spip.php?article1746 (access February 24, 2010).

United Nations ECOSOC 2009a. *Accredited NGOs.* http://www.un.org/esa/coordination/ngo (accessed May 24, 2009).

United Nations ECOSOC 2009b. *Consultative Status with ECOSOC.* http://www.un.org/esa/coordination/ngo (accessed May 24, 2009).

United States Department of State 1995–2003. *US Government Assistance to and Cooperative Activities with Eurasia, Fiscal Years 1994–2002.* Washington, DC: Bureau of European and Eurasian Affairs.

Urban Institute National Center for Charitable Statistics 2006. *Number of Nonprofit Organizations in the US, 1996–2006.* http://nccsdataweb.urban.org/PubApps/profile1.php?state=US (accessed March 1, 2009).

Vedder, Anton (ed.) 2007. *NGO Involvement in International Governance and Policy. Sources of Legitimacy.* Leiden: Martinus Nijhoff.

Verba, Sidney, Kay Lehman Schlozman, and Henry E Brady 1995. *Voice and Equality: Civic Voluntarism in American Politics.* Cambridge, MA: Harvard University Press.

Vereinsstatistik 2008. *Survey of the Research Institute of Sociology at Cologne University in Cooperation with V&M Service.* http://www.registeronline.de/vereinsstatistik/2008/ (accessed March 1, 2009).

Verloo, Mieke 2001. *Another Velvet Revolution? Gender Mainstreaming and the Politics of Implementation.* IWM Working Papers, No. 4. Vienna: IWM.

———— 2005. "Displacement and Empowerment. Reflections on the Concept and Practice of the Council of Europe Approach to Gender Mainstreaming and Gender Equality." *Social Politics* 12 (3): 344–65.

———— 2007. *Multiple Meanings of Gender Equality: A Critical Frame Analysis of Gender Policies in Europe.* Budapest: CEU Press.

Vernon, Rebecca B. 2009. "Closing the Door on Aid." *International Journal on Not-for-Profit Law* 11 (4): 5–29.

Wacquant, Loic J. D. 1992. "The Structure and Logic of Bourdieu's Sociology," in Pierre Bourdieu and Loic J. D. Wacquant (eds.), *An Invitation to Reflexive Sociology.* Cambridge: Polity Press, pp. 2–59.

Walby, Sylvia 2002. "Feminism in a Global Era." *Economy and Society* 31: 533–57.

Walker, Edward T. 2009. "Privatizing Participation: Civic Change and the Organizational Dynamics of Grassroots Lobbying Firms." *American Sociological Review* 74 (1): 83–105.

Walker, Edward T. and John D. McCarthy 2010. "Legitimacy, Strategy, and Resources in the Survival of Community-Based Organizations." *Social Problems* 57 (3): 315–40.

Walker, Jack 1991. *Mobilizing Interest Groups in America: Patrons, Professions, and Social Movements.* Ann Arbor: University of Michigan.

Walzer, Michael 1995. "The Concept of Civil Society," in Michael Walzer (ed.), *Toward a Global Civil Society.* Providence: Berghahn Publishers, pp. 7–28.

Wampler, Brian and Leonardo Avritzer 2004. "Participatory Publics: Civil Society and New Institutions in Democratic Brazil." *Comparative Politics* 36 (3): 291–312.

Wapner, Paul 2007. "The State or Else! Statism's Resilience in NGO Studies." *International Studies Review* 9: 85–89.

Warkentin, Craig 2001. *Reshaping World Politics: NGOs, the Internet, and Global Civil Society*. Lanham: Rowman & Littlefield.

Warleigh, Alex 2001. "Europeanizing Civil Society: NGOs as Agents of Political Socialization." *Journal of Common Market Studies* 394: 619–39.

Weber, Max 1947. "Bureaucracy," in H. Gerth and C. Wright Mills (eds.), *From Max Weber: Essays in Sociology*. New York: Oxford University Press, pp. 196–244.

––––––– 1968. *Gesammelte Aufsätze zur Wissenschaftslehre*. Tübingen: Mohr.

Wessler, Hartmut, Bernhard Peters, Michael Brüggemann, Katharina Kleinen-von Königslöw, and Stefanie Sifft 2008. *Transnationalization of Public Spheres*. Houndmills: Palgrave Macmillan.

Willetts, Peter (ed.) 1996. *"The Conscience of the World": The Influence of Non-Governmental Organizations in the UN System*. Washington, DC: Brookings Institution Press.

––––––– 2000. "From 'Consultative Arrangements' to 'Partnership': The Changing Status of NGOs in Diplomacy at the UN." *Global Governance* 6 (20): 191–212.

––––––– 2002. "What is a Non-Governmental Organization?" *UNESCO Encyclopedia* EOLSS, Article 1.44.3.7. http://www.staff.city.ac.uk/p.willetts/ CS–NTWKS/NGO–ART.HTM (accessed May 12, 2009).

Wilson, Katherine 2006. "Grassroots vs. Astroturf – Discrediting Democracy." *Spinwatch*, June 18. http://www.spinwatch.org.uk/component/content/ article/50-dirty-tricks/264-grassroots-versus-astroturf-discrediting-democracy (accessed January 4, 2012).

Wing, Kenneth T., Thomas Pollak, and Amy Blackwood 2008. *The Nonprofit Almanac 2008*. Washington, DC: Urban Institute Press.

Wolfe, Alan 1989. *Whose Keeper? Social Science and Moral Obligation*. Berkeley: University of California Press.

Women in Development Europe (WIDE) 2005. *Gender Mainstreaming in Development and Trade Policy and Practice: Learning from Austria, Belgium, and the UK*. http://web.igtn.org (accessed March 13, 2011).

Woodward, Alison 2004. "Building Velvet Triangles: Gender and Informal Governance," in Thomas Christiansen and Simona A. Piattoni (eds.), *Informal Governance in the European Union*. Cheltenham: Elgar Publishing, pp. 76–93.

Woodward, Alison and Agnes Hubert 2007. "Reconfiguring State Feminism in the European Union: Changes from 1995–2006." Paper presented at the European Studies Association Tenth Biennial International Conference, Montreal, Canada.

Young, Iris Marion 2000. *Inclusion and Democracy*. New York: Oxford University Press.

––––––– 2001. "Activist Challenges to Deliberative Democracy." *Political Theory* 29 (5): 670–90.

Zald, Mayer N. and John D. McCarthy 1987. *Social Movements in an Organizational Society*. New Brunswick: Transaction Publishers.

Zaret, David 2000. *Origins of Democratic Culture. Printing, Petitions, and the Public Sphere in Early-Modern England*. Princeton: Princeton University Press.

Zimmer, Annette, Anja Appel, Claudia Dittrich, Chris Lange, Birgit Sitermann, Freia Stallmann, and Jeremy Kendall 2005. *The Third Sector and the Policy Process in Germany.* Third Sector European Policy Working Paper, No. 9. Münster. http://www.stiftungsverbund-westfalen.de/download/Zimmer_ThirdSector_PolicyProcess.pdf (accessed December 12, 2010).

Zippel, Kathrin S. 2004. "Transnational Advocacy Networks and Policy Cycles in the EU: The Case of Sexual Harassment." *Social Politics* 11 (1): 57–85.

———. 2006. *The Politics of Sexual Harassment: A Comparative Study of the United States, the European Union, and Germany.* New York: Cambridge University Press.

Zukin, Cliff, Scott Keeter, Molly Adonina, Krista Jenkins, and Michael X. Delli Carpini 2006. *A New Engagement? Political Participation, Civic Life, and the Changing American Citizen.* New York: Oxford University Press.

Zwingel, Susanne 2005. "How Do International Women's Rights Norms Become Effective in Domestic Contexts? An Analysis of CEDAW." Ph.D. Dissertation, Bochum.

Index

CPSIA information can be obtained
at www.ICGtesting.com
Printed in the USA
FFOW04n1640120315
11792FF